National Manhood and the Creation of Modern Quebec

National Manhood and the Creation of Modern Quebec

Jeffery Vacante

UBCPress · Vancouver · Toronto

26 25 24 23 22 21 20 19 18 17 5 4 3 2 1

Printed in Canada on FSC-certified ancient-forest-free paper (100% post-consumer recycled) that is processed chlorine- and acid-free.

ISBN 978-0-7748-3463-6 (hardcover)
ISBN 978-0-7748-3464-3 (pbk.)
ISBN 978-0-7748-3465-0 (pdf)
ISBN 978-0-7748-3466-7 (epub)
ISBN 978-0-7748-3467-4 (mobi)

Cataloguing-in-publication data for this book is available from Library and Archives Canada.

Canada

UBC Press gratefully acknowledges the financial support for our publishing program of the Government of Canada (through the Canada Book Fund), the Canada Council for the Arts, and the British Columbia Arts Council.

The author acknowledges the assistance of the J.B. Smallman Publication Fund and the Faculty of Social Science, University of Western Ontario.

Printed and bound in Canada by Friesens
Set in Minion and Helvetica by Marquis Interscript
Copy editor: Robert Lewis
Indexer: Judy Dunlop
Cover designer: George Kirkpatrick
Cover image: Jean Paul Lemieux, *Le soleil se lève, le soleil s'en va*. Reproduction rights kindly granted by Gestion A.S.L. inc.; image courtesy of Musée national des beaux-arts du Québec

UBC Press
The University of British Columbia
2029 West Mall
Vancouver, BC V6T 1Z2
www.ubcpress.ca

Contents

Acknowledgments

My academic home for the past number of years has been the department of history at the University of Western Ontario. I am fortunate to be a member of such a collegial department and grateful that it has provided me with the opportunity as well as the means to pursue my research. Within the department, Jonathan F. Vance was an enthusiastic early supporter of this project, and he has helped to guide it from the beginning. He recognized early on that I had something to say about Quebec history, and he encouraged me to find my own way of saying it. I am grateful for his support and his guidance over the years as well as for the example that he has set as a scholar and as a person. I am also grateful to a number of colleagues in the department who have in one way or another supported and encouraged my work throughout the years, including Roger Emerson, Keith Fleming, Margaret Kellow, and Ian K. Steele. In recent years, Peter Neary and Sam Clark have shown great interest in this project and become important sources of support for me.

Much of the research for this book took place at the D.B. Weldon Library at Western, the old Annexe Aegidius-Fauteux of the Bibliothèque nationale du Québec, the Archives de la Ville de Montréal, the Archives de l'Université de Montréal, and the old Centre de Recherche Lionel Groulx. I am grateful to the librarians and staff at each of these places for their kindness, helpfulness, and patience. I am also grateful to Nathalie Thibault, at the Musée national des beaux-arts du Québec, for her help finding a print of the Jean Paul Lemieux painting that is on the cover of this book.

To work with UBC Press is to find out just how well one can be treated by a university press in this country. The people who work there are professional, efficient, and genuinely interested in working with authors to help them produce works that they believe will be of interest to the scholarly community. In particular, I thank Darcy Cullen for taking on this project and for championing my work throughout the process and Ann Macklem for guiding it to publication. I also thank the UBC Press First-Time Author's Fund for providing support.

To live in Montreal in the 1980s and 1990s was to live against the backdrop of a perpetual and at times tense conversation about Quebec's place in Canada. Growing up in the city in the 1980s, I remember the tensions arising from the passage of Bill 178, the collapse of the Meech Lake Accord, the Oka Crisis, the failure of the Charlottetown Accord, and the 1995 referendum. It was a time when the news was dominated by great debates about the meaning of Quebec nationalism, the language of commercial signs, and the purpose of constitutional amendments. I was first exposed to this world by listening to my mother and my now late father as they engaged in ongoing discussions about those great issues of the day and in the process transformed our dinner table into nightly seminars on the meaning of Quebec nationalism and the finer points of the constitutional amending formula. They provided a home that was filled with books and newspapers and created an intellectually stimulating world that taught me that ideas, including my own, mattered. This book is in some ways a continuation of those conversations. It represents an attempt to understand the historical roots of some of the issues that I first encountered in those years. It is also an expression of gratitude to my parents, who have provided me with so much.

I now have two children of my own – Ryan and Ashley – and would like to provide them with a home that also encourages them to think for themselves and to engage meaningfully with the world around them. As I was completing this book, I found myself hoping that they might get to know the Montreal that I grew up knowing and that they might also come to understand how it came to look the way that it did when they came along. As they pursue their own paths in this world, I hope that one day they might pick up this book and discover the world that I knew and that also helped to shape their lives.

Finally, I wish to thank my wife and best friend, Tammy. We met in graduate school, and it seems like we have been engaged ever since in one long conversation about the great issues of our own time. Through her own work and by her example, Tammy has contributed to this book and to the world around her in more ways than she knows.

National Manhood and the Creation of Modern Quebec

Introduction

This book is an exploration of manhood in Quebec during the late nineteenth and early twentieth centuries. It looks at a number of French Canadians who sought to reconcile an agrarian model of manhood, which was tied to the land and the family and characterized by self-restraint and piety, with the urban model taking shape at this time, which was defined by greater materialism and individual autonomy.[1] It covers a period when the province of Quebec was making its final transition from a primarily agrarian and rural economy to one that was largely urban and industrial. Although French Canadians generally welcomed the development of large-scale industrialism, few were willing to embrace the type of manhood that went along with it because of a sense that this manhood was incompatible with their desire for cultural survival. Thus French Canadians came to articulate a model of manhood that permitted them to embrace industrial modernity without having to succumb to the cultural values with which this modernity was associated. This manhood was disentangled from the workplace, the family, and the land as well as distinct from emerging expectations about what it meant to be a man in English-speaking Canada. French Canadians embraced a model of manhood that was tied, instead, to a person's national identity. This national manhood permitted French Canadian men to define their gendered identity outside of the militarist and imperialist values that were emerging at this time as features of increasingly aggressive English Canadian expressions of manhood. And it served as an anchor for those men who were feeling displaced in the new industrial landscape. National manhood emerged during these years as an important part of the struggle for cultural survival as well as an expression of French Canadian modernity.

The embrace of national manhood was one part of a broader effort to modernize the province's institutions in a manner that would permit French Canadians to meet the challenges of the new industrial economy. French Canadians navigated the transition to industrial capitalism by employing a nationalist discourse that permitted them to negotiate a place for themselves in the modern world as men. National manhood permitted men to remain loyal to their community, Catholic faith, and culture while living in an urban and industrial setting. It also stood in marked contrast to a version of English Canadian industrial capitalism that many French Canadians came to describe as irrational, overly materialistic, and effeminate. French Canadians turned to nationalism as part of an effort to produce a new model of manhood that would in turn permit them to come to terms with industrial modernity. Nationalism was thus both a reaction to modernity as well as a product of that modernity.

The men putting forward these ideas about manhood, nationalism, and modernity – the men I have placed at the centre of this study – were mostly members of the French-speaking elite in Montreal. These men were important Catholic leaders, like Abbé Lionel Groulx, who was perhaps the most influential priest and public intellectual in French Canada during the interwar years. But they were also members of the lay Catholic leadership, members of the Catholic Action Movement in the 1920s and 1930s who were looking for ways to transform the Catholic Church into a more responsive and relevant institution for the masses. They were also journalists and novelists, like Jules-Paul Tardivel, whose writing is key to understanding the emergence of what I call national manhood. It is difficult, of course, to determine the extent to which such individuals shaped the popular mind. My intention in this study is not to establish the representativeness of these views or even to determine the degree to which these views came to dominate in the public mind. Rather, it is to suggest that a discussion about industrialism, modernity, survival, and manhood was taking place at this time on the basis of the terms being set by these thinkers. These ideas were embraced, altered, distorted, or rejected, or they simply remained unnoticed by a public that probably spent less time thinking about these matters, and certainly less time writing about them, than did these intellectuals. My intention is to suggest that this small and disparate group of intellectuals was thinking about the challenges associated with modernity in ways that would serve as the basis of a more popular and widely embraced nationalist movement in the first half of the twentieth century.

THE MATTER OF QUEBEC'S transition to modernity has preoccupied historians for some time. The province had been understood by historians, until recently, to have modernized more slowly than the rest of the country. This assumption was based on the belief that the province remained less urbanized than the rest of North America and that it lacked the political and institutional infrastructure regarded as necessary for the effective governance of a modern industrial state. It was reinforced by the rhetoric of influential figures in Quebec, which appeared to suggest that there existed within the province a widespread distrust of urbanization, industrialization, and the expansion of the state. And it encouraged English-speaking Canadians to discriminate against

French Canadians, who were perceived at the time to be resistant to modernity and to be less than interested in participating in the new industrial order.

Historians initially disagreed over what exactly had kept Quebec from progressing at the same rate as the rest of the country. For some historians, the roots of Quebec's economic inferiority could be traced to the British Conquest of New France in 1760, when French-speaking Canadians fell under British control and thereafter lived as a conquered people. The Conquest put an end to the colony's natural evolution toward statehood, some historians suggested, and instilled in French-speaking Canadians feelings of inferiority that discouraged them from competing with English-speaking Canadians for positions of leadership.[2] Other historians pointed to the religious elite within the province, who promoted an ideology that, these historians suggested, deprived French Canadians of the tools required to compete in the modern world.[3] If historians could not agree on the reason for French Canada's apparent failure to modernize, they did agree that French Canadians had failed to modernize at the same rate as other Canadians. By the middle of the twentieth century, then, we were left with a somewhat unflattering portrait of the province as an autocratic and backward place. Writing in the 1950s, the historian Michel Brunet lamented that the three dominant themes of French Canadian thought were "agriculturalism, anti-statism, and messianism."[4]

The level of French Canadian resistance to industrialism and to the growth of the state, it has now become evident, was overstated. In the 1970s a new generation of historians began to look past the religious discourses of the period and, employing the tools of the new social history of the time, uncovered evidence suggesting that Quebec had a dynamic business class and showing that the rates of industrialization and urbanization in the province were not all that different from the rates found in English-speaking Canada. This work emphasized those aspects of Quebec's past that made it appear more like the other provinces. By focusing on trends such as rates of urbanization and industrialization, rather than on traditional issues like linguistic and religious conflict, these historians made the province appear more urban and industrial than had previously been assumed.[5] Historians were quick to embrace this new narrative because it highlighted a part of the Quebec experience that had been until that time hidden.[6]

This new narrative served an important purpose in a society that was eager to erase the increasingly awkward perception that Quebec was somehow less well developed than the rest of the continent. "Coming of age in a Quebec where everyone was talking about modernization, living in an urban-industrial society," according to Paul-André Linteau, one of the leading proponents of this new approach to the past, "it was natural that we would want to understand the roots of contemporary Quebec." Linteau, therefore, along with his cohort of historians, "set off to explore the various factors that led to the emergence of an industrial, capitalist society in Quebec by the middle of the nineteenth century."[7] This new narrative, which tended to emphasize those aspects of Quebec's past that made it appear modern, also ended up downplaying the attention paid to those institutions that reminded people of Quebec's supposed backwardness, including the church.[8] More recently, historians have also attempted to integrate the church into this modernization thesis. Michael Gauvreau, for example, has looked at more progressive elements within the church, especially the Catholic Action Movements that emerged during the first decades of the twentieth century, and has demonstrated how Catholic organizations played an important role in modernizing the province and in paving the way for the Quiet Revolution.[9] This work has challenged the assumption that the modernization of the province necessarily occurred as part of a larger process of secularization.

Much of this work serves to remind us that French Canadians had a much more nuanced attitude toward the state than has been suggested. To be sure, many French Canadians during these years exhibited considerable distrust of their political leaders, an attitude that some said was due to the population's limited exposure to democratic institutions. This suggestion, of course, rests upon an assumption that English Canadians had a much more robust democratic experience. Such an assumption was reinforced by observers like Francis Parkman, the nineteenth-century American historian and perhaps the most influential interpreter of New France for an English-speaking audience until the middle decades of the twentieth century, who framed the Battle of the Plains of Abraham as a struggle of "the past against the future; of the old against the new; of moral and intellectual torpor against moral and intellectual life; of barren absolutism against a liberty, crude, incoherent, and chaotic, yet full of prolific vitality."[10]

But it is not necessarily the case that English Canadians had a more robust democratic tradition than French-speaking Canadians. Those English-speaking people who had arrived from Britain following the Conquest, as well as those who arrived from the American colonies following the revolution there, may have had greater exposure to democratic institutions, but they did not necessarily experience these institutions as full participants. Once they arrived in Canada, moreover, they also understood and experienced these institutions as colonists because significant constraints were imposed on the elected assemblies created in 1791.[11] If English-speaking Canadians in Lower Canada believed that they enjoyed a certain degree of influence in these institutions, this was simply a perception arising from their presumed proximity to the centre of imperial power. This assumption developed out of the fact that the governed shared a language and perhaps cultural traditions with those who governed them. But sharing a language with those individuals in positions of power did not necessarily translate into tangible political influence for the vast majority of English-speaking Canadians. In the end, Canadians, whether they were English or French speakers, were *colonists*. And although certain English-speaking Canadians may have enjoyed a privileged place in this democratic order by virtue of the fact that they shared a language with those who wielded political authority, the democratic experience of the vast majority of English-speaking Canadians remained circumscribed and thus resembled the experience of most French-speaking Canadians.

It must nonetheless be acknowledged that many French Canadians exhibited a heightened degree of wariness when it came to the state, and it could even be said that this wariness was one of the legacies of the Conquest. If the British Conquest of New France did not fundamentally transform the daily lives of most French-speaking Canadians, it nonetheless influenced the manner in which power was understood in the colony.[12] No matter how French-speaking Canadians may have been treated by their conquerors, the events following the Battle of the Plains of Abraham nonetheless ensured that the state appeared as a remote and somewhat foreign entity. Even with the arrival of representative institutions in the colony with the passage of the Constitutional Act in 1791, which created an elected assembly, the French Canadian voice (as well as English Canadian voices in the assembly, it must be said) could be ignored very easily by the unelected and English-dominated Legislative Council, which reinforced the perception that power was exercised for the benefit of English-speaking colonists.[13]

Many French Canadians remained suspicious of the state in the decades following the passage of the British North America Act in 1867, which restored to the Province of Quebec the assembly that it had lost with the Act of Union in 1840. Although the province regained considerable autonomy with this new assembly, suspicion of the state persisted because ultimate legislative authority remained at the federal centre, in Ottawa, which retained the right to disallow provincial legislation. Even though this right to disallow legislation eventually fell into disuse, a series of political decisions taken in Ottawa and in some of the other Canadian provinces, including the hanging of Louis Riel as well as the passage of regulations limiting access to French-language instruction at school, served to remind French Canadians that they were a minority with only limited influence in their new country. Thus, although many French Canadians, like Sir George-Étienne Cartier and Sir Wilfrid Laurier, served in powerful positions in Ottawa, that city continued to be seen by many French Canadians as the capital of an English-speaking country.

A more important reason for this suspicion of state power, however, was that provincial institutions, and the province's elected leaders, appeared to be doing little to protect French Canada's interests. There was little reason during the first half of the twentieth century for French Canadians to place much faith in the political process or in the men who sought to hold public office. The provincial Liberal Party, under the business-friendly leaders Lomer Gouin and then Louis-Alexandre Taschereau, dominated the political scene from 1905 until 1936, when Maurice Duplessis and the Union Nationale took over and went on to lead the province, except for an interruption during the Second World War, until 1959. The reactionary and autocratic Duplessis adopted the Liberals' pro-business approach to economic development as his own and allied himself with the conservative Catholic Church, whose institutional network, he hoped, would ensure public support for his policies. Although the province was industrializing rapidly, critics complained that the Liberals and then the Union Nationale were corrupt and that their programs for economic growth appeared to consist primarily of selling the province's natural resources to foreign bidders and of ensuring that French Canadians remained a compliant and cheap source of labour for English-speaking capitalists. It is little wonder, then, that some of the most prominent figures in Quebec during the interwar years expressed serious misgivings about the whole democratic process. Frustrated by the seeming inability of the province's democratic institutions and leaders to safeguard the interests of the population, the influential critic and editor Arthur Laurendeau suggested that democracy was preventing Quebec from moving forward and described those who were elected to public office as "disputatious babblers, vain and sterile."[14]

Such statements only reinforced the perception outside the province that Quebec was less democratic than the rest of the country and also less interested in using the power of the state to pursue the reforms needed to sustain a modern economy. The implicit assumption here is that English-speaking Canadians were much more open to the use of state power and thus more progressive than French-speaking Canadians. Indeed, such rhetoric as Laurendeau's had often been upheld as evidence of the province's backwardness and of its suspicion of democracy. This assumption persisted well into the middle decades of the twentieth century and was summed up neatly in 1958 by Pierre Elliott Trudeau, who wrote, "historically, French Canadians have not really believed in democracy for themselves; and English Canadians have not really wanted it for others."[15]

But French Canadian attitudes about the state were not all that different from English Canadian views. If many French Canadians remained suspicious of the idea of expanding state power during the interwar years, so too did many other Canadians. Led by the cautious William Lyon Mackenzie King for much of this period, the Canadian government took only limited steps prior to the Second World War to expand the size of government, and R.B. Bennett, who served as prime minister from 1930 to 1935, resisted until the very end of his time in office before significantly enlarging the government's role to deal with the crisis of the Great Depression. It is true that King would preside over the beginnings of the welfare state, but he would do so reluctantly and only as a result of the political pressure developing from the rise of leftist movements such as the Progressive Party and the Cooperative Commonwealth Federation.[16]

And it has also become increasingly clear in recent decades that the growing power of the state, which was viewed as an effective and progressive means of redistributing part of society's wealth to the disadvantaged and as a means of attenuating the excesses of the capitalist system, was not always achieved in the name of liberty or progressive ends. The idea of a more powerful state may have been a hallmark of modernity, but the manner in which the state used that power could also be regarded as anything but progressive. Some of the individuals most associated with progressive ends in Canada were also adherents to what we would consider regressive ends, including the strict control of immigrants and the sterilization of those thought to be mentally or physically unfit. The desire for social control led to abuses that reveal the dark undercurrents of the reform movement. The government's purported resistance to expanding state power on behalf of the poor and indigent was taking place at the same time as the state was embracing eugenics and becoming much more interested in limiting the freedoms of minority communities, controlling morality, and regulating sexuality.[17]

If French Canadians were not opposed to industrialism or to the exercise of state power any more than other Canadians, there were also plenty of French Canadians who called for greater state involvement in the economy. English Canadians tended to view French Canadians as very attached to an agrarian way of life, largely because of the prominence of those French Canadian leaders who spoke about the virtues of rural life. But alongside these voices were the voices of others, like Étienne Parent, who spoke in the middle years of the nineteenth century of embracing industry, and Victor Barbeau, who called during the interwar years for educational reform and modernization. For his part, Henri Bourassa, the nationalist leader and founder of *Le Devoir,* called on the state to use its power to ensure that French Canadians could acquire the skills necessary to compete in the new industrial economy, as well as to regulate business in a way that would ensure minimal abuses within the market economy and more equitably distribute society's wealth. Bourassa's call for a more activist government was perfectly consistent with calls from the Vatican for social justice, even if it appeared to contradict the church's teachings in Quebec, which remained much more protective of its political influence.[18]

The Catholic Church in Quebec, to be sure, played an important role in discouraging the expansion of state power. It had long opposed, for example, greater state interference in areas such as the delivery of social services or education. But the church resisted calls for greater state involvement in the economy less out of any deeply held antipathy to the exercise of state power and more out of the belief that the expansion of state power would disrupt a social order that it felt rested upon the autonomy of the family as well as undermine its own authority. The church had a long history of turning to the state in order to ensure its own power. In the years following the Conquest, the British leadership overcame any anti-Catholic sentiments it might have had and recognized that the church could play an important role in maintaining social order and thus in easing the colony's integration into the empire. And the church, for its part, realized that its very survival as an institution depended upon the benevolence of the state. It also recognized that as the constituted authority, the British state became crucial to the maintenance of social order in the colony. Over the next century, the church proved to be a dependable ally to the British, securing French Canadian loyalty, including during the Rebellions of 1837.

The church was not opposed to state power; indeed, it had long allied with political leaders as a means of using its institutional authority to prop up its own authority. Rather, it opposed particular issues that it believed undermined its own authority or challenged the social order that it wished to uphold. For this reason, the church objected to female suffrage, which many reformers had come to view as a potentially useful tool for cleaning up society, and was instrumental in delaying the vote for women in Quebec until 1940. It also resisted the implementation of family allowance programs in the 1940s, which were to be paid to mothers, and spoke out against mandatory education for children, arguing that all such reforms would undermine a man's authority within the home. The church rejected, in other words, any change that would threaten the autonomy of the patriarchal household or undermine its own power over the province's institutional network.[19] But it had never opposed the idea of state power. Thus, when the state stepped up its efforts to monitor and regulate sexual behaviour and effectively criminalized homosexuality, the church went along.

The church was also not so much opposed to industrialism as it was opposed to the disorder that industrialism was said to produce.[20] The primary question thus became not whether the province should embrace industrialism but just how its benefits could be distributed more equitably. The church, for example, was very concerned about French Canadians' place in the new economy. Notably, the priest and historian Lionel Groulx, one of the most influential public intellectuals following the Great War and sometimes described as the spiritual father of modern Quebec nationalism, warned that French Canadians were being "proletarianized" in this new economy.[21] The church was not prepared to surrender its authority to the state. Nor was it convinced that it was to blame for Quebec's difficulties. But neither was the church intent upon turning the clock back to create an idyllic agrarian world. And it did not criticize industrialism as much as it attacked the disorder that industrialism was thought to create. Instead, the church turned to nationalism, rather than the expansion of the state, as a means for French Canadians to defend their rights while also embracing the modern world. This nationalism was not a reactionary or old-fashioned nationalism. It was forward-looking and part of a larger attempt to come to terms with modernity.

Much of this debate was framed by a pervasive sense that manhood in Quebec was in a state of decline. Lionel Groulx was, it might be said, preoccupied with manhood, and he devoted much of his time to writing about ways of improving it.[22] He regularly criticized French Canadian men for being weak, describing them once as a "race de nouilles,"[23] and challenged teachers to do a better job of turning the province's school-age boys into strong and productive men.[24] Others, like Father Louis Lalande, complained about the state of manhood in the province, suggesting that French Canadian men had been "reduced to a state of pallid womanhood,"[25] and the conservative Catholic priest Georges Courchesne attacked schools for providing an "education for hermaphrodites" that failed to produce strong men ready to lead the province.[26] For his part, Henri Bourassa directed much of his anger at feminists, whom he described as "monsters, in every sense of the word," for attempting to destroy French Canadian manhood with their supposed efforts to undermine the gender boundaries that he argued were essential to the maintenance of patriarchal order.[27] This concern about the state of manhood was not restricted to conservative-minded individuals. The liberal journalist and novelist Jean-Charles Harvey, for one, blamed church-run schools for what he described as French Canada's slide into "effeminacy" and called on the state to exercise greater control over the province's schools so as to ensure that boys developed into "des simples hommes normaux."[28] By the 1930s younger activists like the journalist André Laurendeau had rejected the "sterile" nationalism of the past in favour of one that would more effectively turn French Canadians into "masters in our own house."[29] This new generation of men, in fact, sought primarily to infuse nationalism with greater vitality so as to rehabilitate French Canadian self-confidence and pride – that is, manhood.[30] Although these thinkers fundamentally disagreed on a number of issues, including on the meaning and uses of nationalism, they shared a concern about the state of manhood in the province and had come to believe that any effort to address Quebec's cultural, social, and economic problems had to include an attempt to shore up French Canadian manhood.

THE STUDY OF MANHOOD has not been without controversy. After all, the idea that *more* attention needs to be paid to men might appear absurd to those observers who can point out that the entire historical project has been preoccupied with men for quite some time. Although this observation is undoubtedly true, it is also true that few works have until recently treated men as gendered beings.[31] Early work on manhood grew out of the feminist movement as well as the male-liberation movement of the 1960s and the 1970s.[32] By the 1980s a number of self-described enlightened men had made common cause with feminist activists to challenge the barriers that women encountered in a male-dominated society. These activists also came to believe that true equality between the sexes would occur only when traditional assumptions about the gendered behaviour of both women and men were challenged.[33] True liberation would take place, in other words, only when men were released from the burdens placed upon them by an oppressive and patriarchal culture.[34]

The study of manhood was also influenced by the growth of women's history in the 1960s, which meant that it tended to follow the outline set out by women's historians for their own work, including its early focus on the separate-spheres paradigm. Early academic work on manhood thus explored various fraternal groups, male friendships, and male spaces.[35] Such work went a long way in revealing the ways that men understood their roles as men, and it examined the manner in which men carved out gendered spaces in the same way that women were shown to have created female spaces of their own. Yet much of this work on manhood appeared somewhat dated almost as soon as it appeared because it had adopted the separate-spheres paradigm as a conceptual framework at the very moment when many women's historians were beginning to turn away from it.[36] The result was that much of this early work tended to describe men's separate worlds, appearing more interested in uncovering men's previously unexamined male identities and in exploring the ways that men struggled to live up to society's expectations of them than in exploring the gendered dimension of power.[37]

The study of manhood was also shaped by the emergence of gender studies in the 1980s as well as by a larger shift away from social history within the historical profession. By the 1980s the profession had been shaken by a shift away from the materialist priorities of social historians of the 1960s and toward the study of discourse. In 1986 Joan Wallach Scott wrote an influential article that described gender as "a constitutive element of social relationships based on perceived differences between the sexes" and also as "a primary way of signifying relationships of power."[38] By calling on historians to explore the manner in which men and women had been represented in discourse and also how gender had been used to prop up male power, Scott called on historians to examine how attitudes about gender and how the language used to prop up gender differences were being used to preserve unequal relationships of power.

Although such a call raised the possibility that a whole new set of conceptual paths might be opened, some historians pointed out that works focusing on discourses would simply have the effect of resurrecting the old way of doing history by privileging the voices of the literate and thus unrepresentative elite from the past, while ignoring the real lives of most others. There was also a concern that this new history would sidestep the real experiences of men and women in favour of representations of those experiences, raising fears that such a shift in focus would downplay the material realities of women's oppression.[39] The historian Joy Parr observed that "feminists have worried that post-structuralism might perform 'a vanishing trick on questions of agency and responsibility' in sexual politics, so fragmenting masculine power that it becomes elusive to strategy and apparently politically benign."[40] Joan Sangster, too, warned, "There is a danger that historical work on masculinity will repeat one stream of the contemporary men's movement, which urges men to 'reclaim their tears' but ignores men's power and women's oppression." By focusing on the "nicer side of masculinity," she wrote, the study of manhood risked sidestepping "the unpleasant questions of power, domination and patriarchy."[41]

Those who study manhood must balance the activist roots of the field with the theoretical insights of gender history. Both strands certainly have the potential to recentre men in the historical narrative and thus to further marginalize women in society. Indeed, one of the major challenges confronting the historian of manhood is to reconcile suggestions about the contingent nature of male identity with the very real power that men have possessed and exercised. One such observer has warned that scholars are in danger of creating "a disciplinary field in which all genders and sexualities are equally constructed, even if they do not share equal political and social power."[42] But efforts to illustrate the contingent nature of manhood need not detract from the ongoing feminist historical project. One of the primary objectives of those who study manhood is to remove manhood from its presumed biological mooring by exposing it as a historically contingent and constructed identity. It is the invisibility of male power, after all, and the assumed naturalness of men's privileged position within society's patriarchal structure that have reinforced men's power over women for so long.

The study of manhood encountered a particular set of challenges in Quebec. The shift in the 1980s away from the material realities of the past in the larger historical profession was at odds with the dominant trend in Quebec historical writing at the time. The desire to integrate Quebec history into the larger narrative of North American economic and social development had depended very heavily upon empirical research intended to demonstrate in some tangible fashion that French Canadians had progressed at the same pace as other Western societies. Quebec historians deployed statistical evidence to point to a declining birthrate in the province, for example, in order to challenge the perception that French Canadians had continued to have large families well into the twentieth century, and they uncovered evidence that French Canadians had participated in commerce and business in much the same ways as English Canadians had. Their aim was to challenge a perception that Quebec was backward or had failed to progress along with the rest of the country.[43] Any work that shifted the emphasis away from quantifiable data and toward the discourses of a particular era threatened to once again highlight Quebec's distinctiveness and, in the process, to unravel a generation of social scientists' efforts to rewrite Quebec history as a narrative of progress toward a modern and secular – that is, normal – state.[44] The study of manhood, then, which was part of the drift within the historical profession away from the material past and toward the study of discourse, threatened to shine a light on those very discourses that marked Quebec society as different.

Literary critics have not felt these same pressures and have been looking at the gendered nature of Quebec's nationalist discourses for some time. In the process, these critics have produced a gendered reading of French Canadian nationalism that has done much to historicize manhood in ways that historians have not. Many of these critics place the Quiet Revolution at the centre of their work, viewing it as a key moment in the evolution of Quebec manhood because they suggest that it fulfilled many men's long-held desire to overthrow the power of mothers, wives, and the Catholic Church, which they had long blamed for French Canadian men's supposed emasculation.[45] Robert Schwartzwald, for example, reminds us that the church had been historically "represented as 'wedded' to the Anglo-Canadian bourgeoisie in a marriage where it takes care of all womanly vocations, while at the same time effeminizing its own sons." The discourses of decolonization that proliferated during the 1950s and 1960s, he argues, reflected a desire to break up this supposed alliance and were infused with "homophobic tropes," whereby "those found to be traitors or sell-outs to the cause of national revolution are gendered as passive/seductive men."[46] Schwartzwald suggests that French Canadian nationalists have defined their own heterosexual virility according to their ability to lead the province out of its figurative state of homosexual weakness and dependence within Canadian federalism.[47] Katherine A. Roberts agrees, reminding us that the "model of liberation" adopted by many nationalists during the 1950s incorporated a "pre-existing hierarchy of sexual relations," which was embedded in the period's decolonization discourses and intended to further their own ambitions for masculine and national liberation.[48] Because many nationalists associated the colonized man with a state of femininity, Roberts suggests that "the movement towards decolonization involves the desire for full masculinity and the concomitant destruction of one's femininity."[49] Or as Mary Jean Green has put it, "the image of the newly decolonized subject [w]as a virile, heterosexual man."[50] For this reason, according to Patricia Smart, "the revolutionary project is that of a son rebelling against the mother and seeking a 'virility' seemingly achievable only at women's expense."[51] Both man and nation would reclaim heterosexual virility only when the nation emerged from its figurative state of homosexual weakness and dependence. The Quiet Revolution, then, becomes an exclusively masculine project of personal and political empowerment because it represents the means through which the feminized, emasculated, and homosexualized man/nation can reassert his/its heterosexuality.

Historians in Quebec have become more interested in manhood in recent years.[52] Louise Bienvenue and Christine Hudon are leading the way with their studies of boys and the institutions that shape them.[53] Other historians have also begun to examine fatherhood in ways that shed light on the construction of manhood in the province.[54] These historians display little interest in the older preoccupation with progress and are less concerned that highlighting the particularities of the Quebec experience will necessarily cast Quebec's past as less modern than that of the rest of Canada. It turns out, in fact, that gender history has had the effect of emphasizing the ways that English and French Canadians resembled one another in more ways than they imagined. The types of discourses that were pointed to in the past as evidence of Quebec's backwardness have been shown to have characterized English Canadian life as well, so neither community can lay special claim to being in any real sense more advanced or modern than the other. By focusing on the discourses of the past, one finds that Quebec was engaged in a process of modernization that was no more difficult than the process undergone in English-speaking Canada. This book thus fits into the older normalizing narrative that continues to hold sway among some social historians, but it also fits into a new cultural history in the province that investigates Quebec's distinctiveness without the old concern that doing so will make Quebec appear backward.

THIS STUDY BUILDS UPON the insights of these literary critics and historians to suggest that a link between manhood and nationalism developed in response to the challenges associated with industrial changes in the late nineteenth and early twentieth centuries. It was during these years that a model of manhood based on agrarian values gave way to one that was inextricably tied to national identity. Since French Canadians could no longer depend on a fading agrarian ideal of manhood, and because they found themselves becoming increasingly marginalized within an industrial landscape that appeared to be more favourable to English-speaking Canadians, they came to define manhood beyond the farm, the shop floor, and the world of commerce. Manhood came to be linked much more closely to the fate of the French Canadian nation and ultimately to the fate of the provincial state, which were much more within the control of French Canadians themselves.

The present study begins in the late nineteenth century, at a time when a number of French Canadians were beginning to think about ways of reconciling agrarian models of manhood with the reality of industrial modernity. Chapter 1 explores some of the ways that some French Canadian leaders were beginning to move away from the idea of promoting an agrarian model of manhood and toward the idea of manhood becoming linked to a sense of national belonging. Chapter 2 looks at the ways that heterosexuality became much more explicitly affirmed as central to manhood in Quebec. This chapter focuses on urban reformers, medical professionals, and a number of Catholic priests who were growing increasingly concerned about the fate of manhood in the industrial city, where overcrowding, poverty, disease, and pollution appeared to be compromising men's physical health, which in turn was endangering these men's ability to participate fully in the new industrial arena and placing the future of the French Canadian race at risk. As part of their campaign to clean up the city and to improve men's physical and moral health, these reformers came to promote the city as a heterosexual space. Concern about young men's activities in the city beyond the watchful eye of the heterosexual family prompted reformers to pay greater attention to men's sexuality. To ensure the morality of the urban environment as well as the health of the race, reformers became more explicit in their identification of heterosexuality as one of the primary markers of modern French Canadian manhood.

Concern about dissolute manhood during these years also prompted a rethinking of the meaning of racial identity. At the same time that the formerly semi-private matters of personal hygiene and sexuality were emerging as issues of greater public interest, a growing number of observers came to downplay the biological assumptions about racial identity. Until the early twentieth century, many French Canadians had assumed that they were members of a distinct biological race and that their cultural characteristics had been transmitted to them through their blood. Although this interpretation had bolstered their claims of cultural distinctiveness, it had also conferred upon women, who physically reproduced the race, considerable influence. As French Canadian men's economic and political fortunes appeared to decline with the new century, however, and as the province's birthrate fell, some men began to question the wisdom of tying their fate to women's willingness to perpetuate the race. Those men who had come to depend on an ever-growing population in order to ensure their own political and economic ambitions came to resent the idea that their characteristics and abilities as men had in some way been transmitted to them through their mothers. Chapter 3 looks at men's attempts to dilute the biological dimension of racial identity in ways that might reduce their dependence on women's bodies. By curbing women's role in the perpetuation of the race, men emerged as the sole arbiters of racial belonging, free to perform their manhood outside the confines of the feminized home and unburdened of the thought that their mothers had in any significant way shaped their identities as men.

Chapter 4 examines how changing attitudes about the body and racial identity influenced French Canadians' responses to the rising tide of imperialism in English-speaking Canada. Although many French Canadian leaders pointed to Canada's participation in the South African War and the Great War as evidence of the country's dangerous turn toward greater imperial unity, these wars also convinced many French Canadian men of the need to accelerate their efforts to redefine manhood within a retooled and reinvigorated national identity. At the heart of this process was an effort to position the French Canadian man at the centre of a vigorous and martial historical narrative. Chapter 5 focuses on nationalists' efforts to rewrite French Canada's historical narrative in an effort to bring the past into line with the more muscular and aggressive form of manhood that they promoted in the early decades of the twentieth century. During these years, French Canadians broke from the writings of nineteenth-century historians who had often portrayed them as a passive and simple people, content to let others determine their fate. In the wake of French Canadians' failures to prevent the rise of English Canadian imperialism, to thwart the passage of anti-French and anti-Catholic legislation in Manitoba and Ontario, and to block military conscription, the simplicity that historians had upheld in the nineteenth century as a virtue came to be regarded as a liability in the twentieth century. French Canadian writers thus began purging from the historical narrative any hints of weakness or passivity and replacing them with examples of individual acts of heroism and military glory. This new historical narrative was intended to legitimize the more militant and aggressive manhood that nationalists promoted in the 1920s and 1930s by pointing to its deep roots in the French Canadian past.

Not everyone supported such efforts to bolster manhood by encouraging men to embrace their national identities. An increasingly vocal group of critics emerged during the 1930s to complain that nationalism had done little to attenuate the effects of the Depression or to improve the state of manhood. Chapter 6 focuses on this emerging critique of the effort to link manhood to national identity. Whereas some men turned to nationalism as a means of reinvigorating manhood, these critics attempted to disentangle manhood from national identity, arguing that nationalists had gone too far when they claimed that manhood could be achieved only through a man's immersion in his national identity. Insisting that this placed too great a burden on the province's boys, they suggested that the emphasis on national identity was distracting boys from their primary task of becoming men. By rejecting the nationalist suggestion that manhood was something that flowed from a person's sense of national belonging, these critics recentred the person, privileging individual values above the community and the nation. In this way, they articulated an alternate version of manhood that insisted men should develop their national identities only after they had established their identities as men.

As French Canadian men turned to nationalism as a means of bolstering their sense of manhood and securing their position in the early-twentieth-century urban and industrial world, women became increasingly marginal in Quebec's cultural and social consciousness. Even as women were steadily joining the workforce during these years, they were also being excluded from a national debate that was framed by men intent upon using nationalism to consolidate their own economic and political power as well as their authority over women. Although women had never exercised much real power or influence in a society dominated by the Roman Catholic Church and organized along strict patriarchal lines, the late nineteenth and early twentieth centuries marked an important moment of cultural remasculinization in the province. During these years, women lost some of the influence they may have had over racial destiny and were removed from the province's historical consciousness as men rewrote history in ways that emphasized episodes of manly heroism and violent conflict and that cleansed it of any hints of supposedly feminine passivity. By the middle of the twentieth century, women had become expendable in the nationalist struggle since they were no longer needed to perpetuate the race and were more easily overlooked if they were seen to stand in the way of men's nationalist aspirations, which were emerging as central to their identities as men.

This study thus opens in the closing decades of the nineteenth century, a period when a group of leading French Canadian men were taking the first steps to remasculinize the cultural and economic landscapes of the province. The bulk of the analysis focuses on the interwar years, when efforts to consolidate French Canadian manhood intensified. It ends in the 1940s, the decade that saw women win the right to vote in Quebec provincial elections, thus putting an end to the process of remasculinization. With the vote, women regained some of the influence that they had lost when French Canadian culture was being remasculinized during of the first decades of the century.[55] As a result, the year women won the right to vote in Quebec stands as a critical moment in the history of manhood and nationalism in the province, bringing to an end the monopoly those men held in the political sphere. In the years after the Second World War, of course, men continued to dominate politics, and women were only very slowly and grudgingly welcomed into the public realm. But if the postwar years were marked by a more aggressive and more obviously gendered rhetoric of nationalism, it was in part because women's formal re-entry into the political world threatened to weaken the connections between manhood and national affirmation that men had drawn in the previous decades.

The late nineteenth and early twentieth centuries, then, were an important period in the history of manhood in Quebec, one that represented the last opportunity of French Canadian men to turn to an exclusively male political world in order to advance a particular idea about manhood. By turning to the state and national identity as central to the meaning of modern manhood, French Canadian men gave shape to a nationalist movement that would emerge as an instrument to promote men's identities as men and to bolster their political and economic power in the province. When the rest of the country had granted women the right to vote following the Great War, the Quebec government had refused to grant women that same right in provincial elections. This stance had permitted men to continue their dominance of the public sphere in a manner that was no longer available to men in the rest of the country. Influential French Canadian men spent these years redefining manhood for the twentieth century, which meant tying it ever more closely to national identity. Although women would be allowed back into the political process in the second half of the twentieth century, the province's political culture as well as its nationalist movement remained resolutely male-centred because French Canadian leaders had so effectively tied manhood to political power and national identity in the first half of the century.

1 The Roots of National Manhood

NATIONAL MANHOOD DIFFERED from earlier ideas of manhood in Quebec. Until the middle decades of the nineteenth century, the province's lay and ecclesiastical leaders encouraged French Canadian men to conform to a model of manhood that was rooted in the land and defined by sobriety, self-control, emotional restraint, and domesticity. Men had been warned to resist the temptations that existed in the province's cities and to remain wary of industrialization. As the industrialized city came to be associated in the public mind with poverty, overcrowding, disease, loose morals, and unhealthy bodies, this agrarian ideal of manhood was presented as a more desirable alternative to the dissolute man found in the province's urban centres. The Catholic Church and much of the rest of the French Canadian elite in Quebec promoted a rural way of life, warning French Canadians that the survival of their community in North America depended on their ability to resist the values associated with industrial capitalism. The industrious and self-reliant farmer who presided over a large family and who was faithful to the church remained the model of French Canadian manhood until the middle years of the nineteenth century.

THIS DOMESTICATED VERSION of manhood existed alongside a more unruly type, one that was said to be characterized by rowdiness, gambling, excessive alcohol consumption, and violence.[1] This tradition, which was said to be deeply ingrained in Quebec society and to have its roots in the eighteenth century, when the *coureurs de bois*, with their tales of adventure in the Northwest, loomed large in the colonists' imaginations, persisted into the early nineteenth century.[2] By then, French Canadian men had begun to express a level of independence that tapped into this earlier tradition and that also dismayed a number of priests who found that some men appeared especially intent upon testing the authority of the church. This type of behaviour, which was common in an early-nineteenth-century urban environment that lacked a strong state to enforce laws, produced a harder-edged manhood in the province's urban centres.[3] Men sometimes bristled under the strict authority of the church, for example, and occasionally asserted their independence by testing the authority of priests. During the first decades of the nineteenth century, in fact, some priests encountered considerable resistance to their authority and often complained about the behaviour of their parishioners.[4] Such seemingly harmless – albeit disruptive – acts, like walking out of church during the sermon or spreading salacious rumours about priests, in fact constituted passive forms of resistance to church authority.[5]

In the minds of some church leaders, such behaviour could no longer be considered harmless by the middle years of the nineteenth century. Instead, it came to be regarded as a serious threat to the survival of French Canada. This independent and disorderly manhood had, according to some observers, produced a restless population of men who proved to be insufficiently deferential to the church and were thought to be susceptible to dangerous and foreign ideas such as democracy, liberty, and secularism.[6] The Rebellions of 1837 reminded the church leadership in Lower Canada of just what might occur if French Canadians abandoned their traditional deference to authority and simple way of life in order to embrace what they called foreign ideas such as democracy and liberty.[7] The Rebellions marked the culmination of a movement that had begun in the early nineteenth century when a number of reform-minded French Canadian leaders began to push for greater power for the elected assembly in the affairs of the colony. Although the Constitutional Act of 1791 had provided French Canadians with an elected assembly for the first time, ambitious members in the Legislative Assembly of Lower Canada very quickly discovered that they had little real power because the governor retained the right to reject bills emanating from the assembly. This realization on the part of an increasingly dynamic French Canadian middle class, whose members were intent upon exercising greater control over their own affairs through the instruments of the state and were becoming much more interested in the ideas about liberty and democracy that were circulating in the Atlantic world at this time, prompted calls for much more authority to be vested in the assembly itself. Those calling for reform were seeking to make the people the source of power in the colony and to transform the unelected Legislative Council into a body that served primarily to enact and enforce the will of the assembly. More radical leaders, including Louis-Joseph Papineau, would go further, suggesting that true popular sovereignty would exist only when all public officeholders were elected by the people and only when the colony achieved independence from the British Empire. Independence from Great Britain would be necessary, of course, because popular sovereignty could not be achieved within an imperial system that rested upon the idea that the British Parliament was supreme.[8]

If the desire for reform was widely shared by the colony's emerging middle class as well as grounded in the larger intellectual currents of the time, the violent Rebellions that this desire precipitated turned out to be less well thought out and less popular among the masses than was perhaps expected.

The British put down the Rebellions easily enough and sent the liberal-minded statesman and administrator John George Lambton, the First Earl of Durham, to the colony to investigate the causes of the disturbance. In his soon to be famous *Report*, Lord Durham observed, "I expected to find a contest between a government and a people: I found two nations warring in the bosom of a single state: I found a struggle, not of principles, but of races."[9] He was critical of the British for what he described as "misgovernment" in the colony, including the failure to create the most basic educational and political institutions necessary to ensure adequate social order and stability.[10] But he reserved his harshest criticism for the French Canadians themselves: "There can hardly be conceived a nationality more destitute of all that can invigorate and elevate a people than that which is exhibited by the descendants of the French in Lower Canada, owing to their retaining their peculiar language and manners. They are a people with no history, and no literature."[11]

Although the church in Quebec did not share Durham's dim view of French Canadian culture, it would have agreed with his suggestion that French Canadians had become "ungovernable."[12] The violence of the Rebellions, it suspected, was a symptom of a larger state of disorder in the colony. The inhabitants of Lower Canada lacked structure and had become undisciplined, which made them susceptible to the demagogic appeals of men like Papineau. Even if some members of the clergy privately sympathized with some of the nationalist aims of the rebels, the church nonetheless condemned the Rebellions because some of the leaders exhibited anti-clerical sentiments or promoted republican ideas that challenged the institutional framework that propped up the colony's power.

In the years following the defeat of the Rebellions and the passage of the Act of Union in 1840, which united Upper and Lower Canada, the church consolidated its position and emerged as the dominant influence over the institutional and political life of the French-speaking eastern part of the newly united Canada. It then took the lead in defending French Canadian culture in a manner that it felt would best ensure the community's survival on the continent. The church took on its expanded role in large part due to the fact that the leadership that had come to dominate the political affairs of the colony prior to the Rebellions had left the political stage and in some cases gone into exile. And those *patriotes* who had not taken a leading role in the violent uprising or in the political affairs of the colony prior to the Rebellions very quickly resurfaced in the political arena as moderate reformers in the aftermath of the violence. Led by Louis-Hippolyte Lafontaine, and then George-Étienne Cartier, who had sympathized with some of the objectives of the rebels in the years leading up to the crisis, these figures sought political reform after the

Rebellions by working within the framework provided by the Act of Union. When Louis-Joseph Papineau returned to the colony in 1845 after an exile spent in the United States and France, he was elected to the assembly in 1848 but could do little to challenge the moderate coalition that Lafontaine had built during his absence. Papineau led a small group of followers in the assembly and continued to speak out against the union and to call for reform. But a decade after the Rebellions had fizzled, Papineau failed to arouse much interest in his cause. Instead, he served more as an icon of an earlier age than as an effective or relevant voice for reform.

The passing from the scene of the radical leadership, as well as the success of Lafontaine in assimilating former radicals into his moderate reform movement, permitted the church to consolidate its position in the colony. Lafontaine had secured his hold on power in part by forging a close alliance with the church. If his political moderation appealed to the church, it also disappointed many former rebels, who continued to regard the church as one of the primary obstacles to reform in the colony. This rapprochement with the church allowed Lafontaine to consolidate his own hold on power and also provided the church with continued access to the political world of the colony.

The church leadership had always supported those individuals who wielded power in the colony. In Lower Canada this support had been extended to like-minded members of the appointed Legislative Council rather than to the members of the popularly elected Legislative Assembly. The church had supported the British leadership because it represented the constituted authority and was thus crucial to providing the social stability that it cherished. The church also supported the British conquerors because it recognized that social order, and its own position near the top of that order, required the maintenance of social and political hierarchies. In the decades leading up to the Rebellions, individual members of the clergy may have sympathized with the *patriotes*, but they did not support their specific calls for reform, which threatened to destabilize the existing social hierarchy. Under the leadership of Joseph-Octave Plessis, who served as the first archbishop of the newly created Roman Catholic Archdiocese of Quebec from 1806 until his death in 1825, the church encouraged French Canadians to fall in line behind British officials and institutions. It had been these officials and institutions, according to the church, that had permitted French Canadians to survive in the years since the Conquest. It was thus as political realists that church leaders helped to ensure French Canadian loyalty to the British Crown.

But in the years following the Rebellions, there was a perceptible shift in the clergy's attitudes toward British political leaders. Mindful that the emergence of responsible government in the colony might shift power away from the governor and toward the assembly, the church began to align itself much more closely with the moderate French Canadian leaders in that assembly. Its attitude about its place in the political hierarchy also evolved during these years. Jean-Jacques Lartigue, who became the auxiliary bishop of Montreal in 1821 and then the first bishop of the newly created Diocese of Montreal in 1836, had opposed the Rebellions because they threatened to disrupt social order. Like Plessis, Lartigue recognized that the state played an important role in the maintenance of order in the colony. But whereas Plessis had limited himself largely to ecclesiastical affairs, Lartigue sought a larger role in the affairs of the state and also embraced ultramontanism, which privileged the authority of the pope above local-government officials. By turning to Rome for spiritual direction and diminsishing the status of the state as the preeminent institution in the colony, Lartigue was contributing to a transformation of the social hierarchy in Canada. The church sought to elevate itself above the state in order to become the main centre of power in the colony. Lartigue was not interested in completely subverting state power. Rather, he hoped to become much more directly involved in state affairs, viewing the state as an important instrument to advance the church's agenda.

The church emerged from the Rebellions in a stronger position than it had occupied before the crisis, but it continued to encounter resistance from those who were concerned about its growing influence. Although the influence of former rebels and their supporters in the assembly was declining, these figures found other outlets outside of government. The most troublesome organization, according to many members of the clergy, was the Institut canadien. Established in 1844 in Montreal, the Institut canadien was a debating society and reading club that offered its members the opportunity to read material that was condemned by the church and thus provided a means for opponents of the church to express their dissatisfaction with the clergy's growing power in society. The Institut canadien appeared to challenge the order being established by the church and thus was seen as an outlet for the type of disorderly manhood that was thought to have contributed to the outbreak of the Rebellions. By circulating works that had been placed on the church's index of forbidden books, and discussing liberal ideas, the Institut canadien threatened to undermine the type of orderly society that the church was seeking to establish.

But the Institut canadien proved to be more of a nuisance to the church than a serious threat to its authority. The defeat of the Rebellions had eliminated the major popular threat to the church, and the rise of ultramontanism would only increase its power by aligning it much more closely with the state. The church now worked to restore the order that it believed was missing prior to the Rebellions. And the basis of this order would be the home. The church began to promote much more vigorously a domesticated version of manhood that would both restrain men's rougher instincts and strengthen an institution – the family – that was thought to be central to the maintenance of social order. To counter the less easily controlled type of manhood, the church promoted a more disciplined form of manhood that would be characterized by sobriety, fatherhood, and piety. This manhood would be expressed most fully on the land, where patriarchy could be preserved within the home and where the church could continue to exercise its authority at the top of the social hierarchy. Of course, the intention was to uphold a hierarchical society that could preserve the cultural and religious values of the society. The household, headed by the father, thus emerged as a central institution in the effort to prop up religious authority and to monitor individual men and keep them from becoming too autonomous in an urbanizing environment. The church's own authority also came to rest upon the stability of the family and the household.

The rural, domestic, pious father served as a tool for a church that was seeking greater control over the domestic realm since this type of man was also imagined to be much more easily monitored. The problem with the industrial city was that it supposedly weakened the bonds of the family, releasing men into an unsupervised and disorderly urban space that was further beyond the reach of clerical influence. The domesticated man was not presented as a nostalgic throwback to an imagined simpler time. Rather, the domesticated and rural man was promoted as a resolutely *modern* figure. According to the journalist and member of Quebec's Legislative Assembly Guillaume-Alphonse Nantel, the agrarian life provided an appealing alternative to the monotonous and "effeminizing" factory work found in the industrial city.[13] This rural manhood, which centred upon a domestic patriarchal arrangement within a larger social hierarchy dominated by the clergy, was regarded by its defenders as part of a profoundly *modern* ordering of society. It was the industrial city, with its dissolute morals, unsupervised leisure time, and lack of order, that appeared old-fashioned and anti-modern, harkening back to an earlier type of manhood that thrived on the frontier and that was beyond the control of the church.[14]

The rapid pace of industrialization during the latter part of the nineteenth century only encouraged more people to embrace this domesticated version of manhood. As the industrialized city came to be associated in the public mind with poverty, overcrowding, disease, loose morals, and unhealthy bodies, this agrarian ideal of manhood was presented as preferable to the dissipated man found in the province's urban centres. The church and much of the rest of the governing elite in French Canada promoted a rural way of life, warning French Canadians that the survival of a French-speaking and Catholic community in North America depended on their ability to resist the values associated with industrial capitalism. In their view, the industrious and self-reliant farmer who presided over a large family and remained faithful to the land and the church was to be the model of French Canadian manhood in the middle years of the nineteenth century.

In the later decades of the nineteenth century, French-speaking Canadians living in Quebec were told that their way of life was increasingly under threat. Such warnings were nothing new, of course, and had been a constant in French Canadian thought since at least the British Conquest. In the years following the Conquest, once the immediate fears about the intentions of the conquerors subsided, with the British leaders in the colony displaying a relative degree of toleration for their new subjects, many of the French-speaking Canadians who remained came to accept the reality of their new circumstances. This acceptance turned into relief for many people with the news of the events surrounding the French Revolution, which demonstrated especially to the church leadership that the Conquest may have been an act of providence that shielded Canadians from the secularizing forces in France. The church, which had embraced the British presence if only because it had permitted it to survive, could now point to the Revolution in France as evidence that the Conquest was not necessarily a catastrophe.

But concern about survival increased dramatically in the years following the Rebellions, especially following the passage of the Act of Union, which united the two Canadas into one political entity seemingly with the intent of assimilating the French-speaking inhabitants of Lower Canada. Fears of assimilation would subside somewhat in 1867 with the passage of the British North America Act, which restored Quebec's autonomous legislature and provided the French-speaking population with control over such areas as education and culture, which were seen as crucial to the survival of the French Canadian community in North America. The church had been a key supporter of Confederation, especially since it raised the possibility that its own power might be enhanced with this move. But in the decades following Confederation, French Canadians once again felt under siege. Support for Confederation was weakened with the hanging of Louis Riel in 1885, which served to remind French Canadians of their limited influence within the new dominion. Riel was, of course, an imperfect figure. There had been some support for his cause in the West as well as a sense that he was fighting to defend a just cause. But it was not until they were confronted with the possibility that Riel might be executed that French Canadians in Quebec really took notice and championed his cause. Thus his death served as a sharp reminder that they had little influence within the new country that they had so recently championed.

At the same time, French Canadians could only watch as French-language and Catholic rights were being stripped away in provinces like Manitoba and Ontario. As the number of immigrants to Canada increased, moreover, and as these immigrants integrated overwhelmingly in the English-speaking community, it became very clear that Canada was being transformed into a predominantly English-speaking country. Westward expansion and growth, therefore, came to be perceived as threats to French Canadian survival since they would ultimately dilute French Canada's political influence at the federal level.

Moreover, French Canadians were, like other Canadians, coming to terms with the realities of industrialism. Although the church and its allies promoted the virtues of rural life and emphasized the benefits of a domesticated version of manhood, most French Canadians found the idea of remaining on the land to be neither realistic nor particularly appealing.[15] But after years of being told to remain true to the land and resist reforms that might have prepared them for the new industrial reality, many French Canadians found that the province offered them few opportunities, so they left in search of work in the textile mills in New England. According to some estimates, as many as 900,000 people, the vast majority of them French Canadians, left the province between the 1830s and the 1930s.[16] For those French Canadians who did not leave the province, it appeared increasingly likely that they would find themselves falling behind English-speaking Canadians in the new economy.

In the past, obstacles that were thought to prevent French Canadians from fully enjoying the benefits of industrialism had been easier to overlook because people were said to be able to find refuge in an agrarian lifestyle, which was promoted, in any case, as the real source of survival. But with the decline of the family farm, and the realization that industrialization was not going to go away, French Canadian leaders could no longer encourage people to simply turn to the countryside as a release from the pressures of urban industrialism. They were forced to reconsider their opposition to industrialism as well as rethink the means by which they could ensure French Canada's continued survival on the continent.

There had long been calls during these years for greater openness to industrialism. These voices often framed their concern about Quebec's economic difficulties by attacking the church, which many of them blamed for the province's ills. Such concern followed in the tradition of Étienne Parent, a liberal member of the Institut canadien, who warned French Canadians in 1846 that their antipathy to industrialism would merely ensure their eventual cultural extinction.[17] By the close of the century, critics had become more impatient with the failure of the province to modernize its institutions in such a manner as would permit French-speaking Canadians to participate in the industrial economy. According to some of these critics, the source of the province's problem was an educational system dominated by the clergy and failing its young men and an industrial economy directed from outside the province. The province may have been industrializing, but because of its weak political leadership, it came to be regarded as rather effeminate in its lack of control over its own destiny. They blamed the church for its failure to adapt to the modern realities of the period and for failing to guide boys into proper manhood. French Canadian men had become so feminized and physically weak, critics charged, that they were unable to compete in the Anglo-Saxon world of business and commerce. This critique persisted well into the twentieth century. The economist and sociologist Victor Barbeau, a professor at the École des hautes études commerciales in Montreal, argued that this economic inferiority was perpetuated by a "divirilizing" and "emasculating" curriculum in Quebec's schools that "proletarianized" the province's boys.[18] If nothing was done, critics like Barbeau warned, French Canadians would find themselves becoming low-paid labourers with few opportunities to advance in the new economy and with little hope of surviving as a French-speaking and Catholic community on the continent.

Such anxiety pervaded much of North American thought during the closing decades of the nineteenth century. As the nineteenth century progressed and industrialism became ever more entrenched in Canadian society, many English Canadian leaders expressed a level of anxiety about industrialism that was possible only because of their relatively privileged status in society. Like the French, many English-speaking observers were struggling to come to terms with the effects of industrialism, particularly its effect on their position in North America and on their understanding of manhood.

Although many people in Quebec tended to equate industrialism with Anglo-Saxonism and also implied that the benefits of the new economy accrued largely to English-speaking Canadians, most English Canadians, in fact, found themselves in the exact same circumstances as French Canadians. Like French Canada, English Canada was going through the same process of urbanization, which raised many of the same concerns about how this would affect the social order that had prevailed until that time. For one thing, industrialism tended to sharpen the distinctions between the public and private spheres. Even with the growing number of women who participated in the workforce, the distinction between home and work became more pronounced. Besides, the presence of women in the workplace, even if they were not performing the exact same tasks as men, appeared to diminish the value of the work that men performed and thus further chipped away at the sense of manhood that men had derived from their work. As men increasingly moved from the countryside to the cities, and as more and more of these men gravitated toward industrial jobs that were to be performed indoors and that thus followed the artificial prompts of the clock rather than the natural rhythms of nature, a number of concerned citizens began to wonder whether this change might not be a threat. As living conditions in the city and repetitive tasks on the job threatened the health of male bodies, a number of people became anxious that the nation's men were being sapped of the strength that they were thought to have had in the past.

The middle classes were not immune from the threats associated with the age. By the closing decades of the nineteenth century, many middle-class Canadians had become concerned that their professional working lives as well as their comfortable domestic existence were draining them of their strength and manhood. The fineries of the home, as well as the comforts associated with the modern age, had removed them from their supposedly rugged and thus more natural environment, which was thought to have prevailed prior to the advent of industrialism. Modern industrial society, too, was said to be producing a generation of men who were too comfortable, filled with doubt, and susceptible to physical and mental decline. For those employed in factories, the repetitive and mindless work was said to produce automatons who would be unable to think for themselves and who would find themselves limited by their bodies, which were susceptible to an accelerated physical decline as a result of industrialism.

And so the virtues of progress and civilization that had made industrialism possible were now said to be estranging men from their supposed natural environment, which was said to be found closer to nature and to involve greater physical exertion than could be found in the modern workplace. In the United States, men like Theodore Roosevelt had become concerned with what they believed was Americans' increasingly comfortable civilization, and they would challenge themselves physically in a seeming attempt to prove that they had not succumbed to the effeminizing influences of the age. In a series of books and essays, Roosevelt warned that Western civilization was doomed to extinction if nothing was done to halt its slide into decadence. In one of the many essays he wrote on this theme, Roosevelt warned that "a certain softness of fibre in civilized nations, which, if it were to prove progressive, might mean the development of a cultured and refined people quite unable to hold its own in those conflicts through which alone any great race can ultimately march to victory."[19] Roosevelt's fear that America's manly virtue was being lost prompted him to promote a much more robust role for the United States on the world stage and compelled him to take a much more belligerent tone when it came to describing other civilizations, which he now viewed as representing threats to American and Western survival.

The American neurologist George Beard came up with the term "neurasthenia" to describe all sorts of ailments, such as anxiety, fatigue, and depression, associated with what some individuals were beginning to describe as overcivilization.[20] In the American mind, the Western frontier was said to have served an important function as a safety valve for an increasingly urban and industrial nation, a space where men could go to regenerate their minds and their bodies and to reclaim their racial vigour. But the so-called closing of the frontier in the 1890s – that is, the realization that there was no longer any land available in the American West for would-be farmers – precipitated an intellectual crisis for some because men would no longer have an outlet for their racial and manly energy. America's more aggressive foreign policy and its acquisition of empire was an outgrowth of this desire of American men to prove that they still had the fighting spirit of a great race and that they had not become overcivilized.[21]

In Canada, too, there developed a concern about racial degeneration, precipitated by increasing numbers of supposedly "undesirable" immigrants, by the rise in urban poverty, in disease, and in sexual immorality, as well as by industrial work, which was increasingly seen to cause the dissipation of bodies, thus leading to racial decline and the end of the civilization. There were calls for restrictions on immigration, as well as campaigns to promote eugenics in order to prevent supposedly undesirable members of society from passing on their traits to the next generation. A growing number of English Canadians also became critical of prevailing notions of domesticity and self-control, which had come to define a certain type of manhood in the industrial age. Confronted with a much more feminized domestic sphere, a number of English Canadians yearned to reconnect to a more rugged form of manhood, which they imagined had prevailed prior to the advent of industrialism.

Many English-speaking Canadians had also become as concerned as some French Canadians about the disappearance of a rural way of life that had for so long been considered central to their own ideas of manhood. Some English Canadians expressed an admiration for French Canadians who appeared to have succeeded in staving off the supposedly effeminizing effects of the city and industry by staying true to a presumably more masculine version of life found in the countryside.[22] Some English Canadians responded to the perceived degenerative effects of city life by promoting outdoor activities for boys and men as well as encouraging them to participate in competitive sports that might reinstill the virtues of courage, physical strength, and camaraderie that were said to be lost in the industrial workplace or office.

This desire to express a more vigorous form of manhood impelled a growing number of English Canadians to turn toward militarism and to call for a larger role for Canada within the British Empire. As Britain came to be involved in imperial adventurism, many English Canadians yearned to play a greater international role, which meant, of course, a larger role within a newly empowered British Empire. When the South African War broke out in 1899, many English Canadians embraced the cause, and some men jumped at the opportunity to sign up in order to showcase on the battlefield the strength and courage that they had learned on the playing field.

The decision of Prime Minister Wilfrid Laurier's government to permit Canadian volunteers to join the war effort, however, angered many French Canadians, who tended to oppose such imperialist wars. Most French Canadians had grown accustomed to British institutions, and many had come to regard the Conquest as providential because it had sheltered Lower Canada from the effects of the French Revolution and continued to protect Quebec from American absorption. But many also recoiled at the prospect of closer imperial integration if it meant promoting Anglo-Saxon values and participating in distant wars that were framed as tests of imperial loyalty as well as manhood.

The imperialism of the time was often expressed in optimistic terms as a means of catapulting Canada to the very centre of the empire and fulfilling a civilizing mission. But this discourse was also expressed in the context of larger fears of racial and cultural degeneration during the closing years of the twentieth century. If imperialism was, as the historian Carl Berger has suggested, "one form of Canadian nationalism," it was also reactionary in its desire to shore up a perceived loss of manhood and racial decline.[23] Although the political crises that defined late-nineteenth-century Canadian political life alienated many French Canadians, making them less likely to turn to the federal government for leadership and more likely to focus on their own province, they also served to displace French-speaking Canadians from the English Canadian consciousness. English Canadians after Confederation, like French Canadians in Quebec, would have their own provincial legislatures and would dominate the federal Parliament in a manner that altered English Canadian views of French Canadians, effectively transforming them into a minority group. The end of the union period thus limited English Canadian contact with French Canadians, and with that isolation came both a distance between the two groups at home and a renewed desire to rekindle the old imperial connection. If Prime Minister John A. Macdonald, who had famously declared in his last election campaign, "A British subject I was born – a British subject I will die," was more than willing to express his fondness for Britain, he also did little to pursue greater ties between Canada and Britain. But much had changed since Macdonald died. The cultural division between English- and French-speaking Canadians, coupled with English Canadians' growing concern about the effects of industrialism on their racial and masculine vigour, prompted a renewed interest in the British Empire.

Thus, when Laurier became prime minister in 1896, he was confronted with an altered political landscape. As the first French Canadian to hold the office, he was more vulnerable than Macdonald had been to attacks on his loyalty to the empire. Although he was a great admirer of British institutions, and accepted a knighthood on his visit to England during the imperial conference of 1897, he nonetheless would find it more difficult to reject a greater Canadian role in the empire than Macdonald had. In Quebec he was burdened both by his radical past and by his apparently moderate political incarnation as Liberal leader. As a one-time *rouge*, he had been caught up in the radicalism of the age and attracted the ire of the church, which was not afraid to interfere in political debates or in warning its followers that heaven is found in the blue (Conservative) sky and that hell is (Liberal) red. At the same time, once he became prime minister, he was confronted with a revivified imperial spirit in English-speaking Canada that pulled him into local disputes about language and schooling. As a believer in process, he upheld the principle of separation of powers in refusing to disallow legislation that would have restricted francophone rights in Manitoba. By upholding provincial autonomy, Laurier felt that he was doing more to maintain national unity and the principle of law, as well as protecting Quebec and French Canadians. If he intervened on behalf of French Canadians over the issue of language, what was to stop a future government from intervening in the internal affairs of Quebec and overturning a law emanating from Quebec's legislature? Even though he had the power to do such a thing with the disallowance clause of the Constitution, he knew that this power was toxic and would ultimately make a mockery of provincial autonomy – a central feature of the British North America Act that Quebec had clung to in the years since Confederation. Such long-term considerations did not appear to concern those within Quebec who felt that Laurier was failing to stand up for French Canadian rights in the West. Thus Laurier, who had for so long been attacked by conservative voices in the province for being too radical, was now being attacked for political timidity and for demonstrating an insufficient willingness to stand up for French Canadian rights outside Quebec.

Although Laurier was admired by many French Canadians who felt a certain pride that a fellow French Canadian had ascended to the very top of the country's political power structure, he also took office at a time when the political landscape appeared much less amenable to the type of moderation that he was promoting. If Laurier had by the last decades of the nineteenth century refashioned himself as a moderate in the tradition of Louis-Hippolyte Lafontaine, he also found himself governing within a political landscape that had been transformed by nationalists like Quebec premier Honoré Mercier, who led the province from 1887 to 1891 and who was focused more on the survival of French Canadians living within the province of Quebec than across the country. And by creating the Quebec legislature in 1867, the British North America Act effectively diverted French Canadians' attention away from Ottawa and toward Quebec City. The death in 1873 of George-Étienne Cartier, the dominant Quebec politician at the federal level, would only further alienate the province from Ottawa.

The growing estrangement between English- and French-speaking Canadians arising from the creation of separate institutions that appeared increasingly to compete for the public's affection and loyalty meant that common experiences would be understood differently. Industrialization, for example, affected most workers in the same ways, but since English and French Canadians rarely looked to one another as constituting a single class of people, French Canadians appeared particularly susceptible to the hardships associated with industrialism. To be sure, there were differences between English- and French-speaking Canadians because ambitious French-speaking Canadians found it difficult to compete in the new industrial system given that they had not had the benefit of a schooling system and social and political infrastructure that would have placed them on a leadership path in this new economy. There was also, of course, the reality of English Canadian discrimination against French-speaking Canadians, which was rooted in an English Canadian attitude that tended to view English Canadians as much more suited than French-speaking Canadians to managerial positions.

But when it came to the masses in the new urban environment, there could not be said to be any significant difference in the manner in which English and French Canadians experienced industrialism. Because English was the language of business, and since industrialism was presented as an outgrowth of Anglo-Saxon values, there did develop the perception, of course, that French Canadians were worse off than English Canadians. The degradations of French-speaking workers in Montreal, therefore, were understood to be less the product of the new industrial landscape that was shared by all workers and more a particularly cruel fate that was reserved for French Canadians. The explanation for this turn of events differed, as did the blame, but there remained a suspicion that French Canadians were considerably worse off than English Canadians in this new industrial landscape.

Thus industrialism, as well as Louis Riel's execution and Manitoba's passage of laws that limited the rights of French-speaking Catholic students, occurred against the backdrop of a narrative of cultural decline in Quebec. Moreover, French Canadians' political influence appeared to be shrinking in the same way that their economic power was declining in the new industrial order. And Laurier, who is so often associated with optimism, was caught between competing forces of pessimism and competing fears of cultural, national, and racial decline. Both French Canadians' *survivance* and English Canadians' imperialism were, in their own ways, appeals for greater power as well as for greater control over their own fates. Both sides were driven by a fear of racial degeneration, as well as by the perceived existence of a crisis of manhood, and each side struggled to find ways to increase its community's power.

If French Canadian fears of decline were in line with the fears shared by many English-speaking Canadians, the domesticated and agrarian ideal of manhood that many French Canadian thinkers were promoting as a means of arresting this supposed decline was increasingly out of step with the rest of North American thinking. Industrialism was transforming Quebec at a much faster rate than anybody might have imagined, placing an enormous strain on the ideal of domesticated manhood. The province's leaders were promoting this domesticated version of manhood at the same time that the rest of the continent was moving away from this model and toward a more militaristic and aggressive version of manhood. The idea of domesticated manhood served the interests of a church hierarchy intent upon maintaining social and political order in the province, but it also came under increasing pressure as the century wore on. In addition to promoting a return to the land, the church also encouraged men to return to the domestic sphere. But these domestic spaces were becoming, according to some observers, more and more feminized as the nineteenth century wore on. During the 1830s, when nationalist leaders like Louis-Joseph Papineau promoted a type of nationalism grounded in the concept of male citizenship rights, there developed a sharper division between the public and male world of politics and the private and feminine domestic realm.[24] Women had participated in the public world of electoral politics since the passage of the Constitutional Act of 1791, which had imposed property requirements but had not explicitly limited voting on the basis of sex. The distinction between the private and feminine world of the home and the public and masculine world of politics would become more pronounced after 1849, when the legislature formally stripped women of the right to vote.[25]

To ensure that the home could serve as a refuge from the harsh and disordered public world that they envisioned with industrialism, the clergy became more intimately involved in family life. The surest means of gaining access to the home, it turned out, was by forging close relationships with the women of the household. The church had come to view women as important agents of stability, responsible for running the household as well as for raising children and providing a comfortable refuge for men. Ties between the clergy and women were forged as many women became ever more involved in the religious life of their communities. Excluded from any meaningful roles within the formal structure of the church, and with the public sphere largely out of reach, many women became involved in lay Catholic organizations. The church encouraged women's involvement in religious organizations, pointing to women's supposedly natural piety. Women's increased involvement in such activities, moreover, solidified the position of the church in the social affairs of the community. It also heightened women's visibility in the area of social services, which was controlled by the church, creating the impression in the minds of some men that religious observance, church attendance, and charitable work were feminine endeavours.[26] This association was perilous for a church that was attempting to convince men to return to the domestic sphere.

By the end of the nineteenth century, the traditional view of domestic manhood had become overwhelmed by the rise of imperialism as well as the relentless pace of industrialization in the province. These pressures challenged the assumptions about domestic manhood that the church had been promoting for some time. Indeed, a growing number of critics focused on the deteriorating quality of manhood as the primary reason for the province's supposed backwardness. Men like Victor Barbeau pointed to an attachment to the older version of manhood – one that privileged the land, the church, and the family – as the primary obstacle to French Canadian survival. Others like the nationalist leader and member of Parliament Henri Bourassa framed their opposition to the South African War and then the Great War as evidence of their superior manhood, which would in turn give shape to a definition of manhood that became inextricably tied to a man's sense of national identity. For Bourassa, true manhood would be achieved only when Canada dissociated itself from the mother country and exercised greater political independence. Confronted with an increasingly militaristic attitude on the part of English Canadians, many of whom accused anti-imperialists of disloyalty and cowardice, critics of the war, like Bourassa, responded with claims that their own manhood was in fact superior to any imperial version of manhood being promoted in English Canada. Bourassa mocked English Canada's support for the war, suggesting that it revealed the country's immature and emasculating dependence on the mother country. He pointed to French Canadians' opposition to these wars as evidence of their superior manhood because it demonstrated their lack of subservience to the imperial centre.[27]

Bourassa would be marginalized following the Great War, as the conscription crisis discredited his vision of pan-Canadian nationalism, but his ideas about national loyalty would persist. Lionel Groulx would not go so far as Victor Barbeau in defending industry, nor would he embrace Bourassa's brand of Canadian nationalism. But he did share Bourassa's view that manhood had to become central to the question of survival. And he integrated Bourassa's ideas about Canadian independence into his own version of nationalism, which was much more clearly focused on the province of Quebec. According to Groulx, French Canadian men could overcome the difficulties associated with industrialism, and exhibit a proper manhood, only if they demonstrated complete loyalty to their nationality. Groulx, perhaps the most influential leader following the Great War, warned that French Canadians were being "proletarianized" in this new economy.[28] The primary cause of French Canadians' inferiority in the workplace and in the economy as a whole, according to Groulx, was the absence among men of a strong national consciousness. French Canadians' economic backwardness could be explained less as the result of an inadequate educational system or of a cultural environment that discouraged men from embracing industrial work and more as a symptom of this absence of national sentiment. According to Groulx, French Canadians' economic inferiority could be overcome only when French Canadians exhibited a greater sense of national consciousness, suggesting that the province's challenges could be overcome only if, "like a normal people, we possessed a strong national feeling." Groulx lamented, "The main problem with French Canadians, it must be said, is that there are no French Canadians."[29] Only a reinvigorated nationalism, according to Groulx, could revive a French Canadian manhood that was said to be undermined by the English Canadian models being promoted at that time.

National manhood, which was embraced by disparate figures such as Barbeau, Bourassa, and Groulx, privileged a man's independence above his membership in his family, his community, or his parish. National manhood emerged as a response to the pressures of industrialism and as a way of ensuring that French Canadians could compete as men without adopting English attitudes about individualism or materialism. For French Canadian nationalists, then, individualism promised to release men from the constraints of the land, family, and church without leading them on a path toward materialism or secularism, as was said to have happened with English Canadian men. Instead, the individual would become free to cultivate his national identity. This national identity would both define men's identities as men and ensure French Canada's survival as a community. Like the English Canadian rhetoric about manhood at the close of the nineteenth century, French Canadian rhetoric was liberating in its promise that men could embrace industrialism as well as survive as a French-speaking Catholic community without succumbing to the problems associated with industrialism. But such rhetoric was also laced with a pessimism that reminded French Canadians that they were essentially doomed if they did not embrace this new national manhood. To ensure that national manhood prevailed, French Canadian intellectual and religious leaders took a much more active interest in men's lives and turned increasingly to state power in order to monitor and ultimately control men's activities.

2
Reinforcing Heterosexual Manhood

During the late nineteenth and early twentieth centuries, heterosexuality emerged as a central part of national manhood. The growing emphasis on a person's sexuality would become part of a larger effort by many leading members of the province's religious, cultural, and political worlds to restore a degree of social order in the face of the perceived upheaval associated with industrialism. The consolidation of an industrial and urban economy during these years was seen to disrupt this order as well as to threaten the type of manhood that was thought to be necessary for its maintenance. Since the middle years of the nineteenth century, many of the province's secular and religious leaders had been promoting a particular version of manhood, characterized by self-control and expressed most fully through fatherhood, in part to counter the seemingly disordered manhood that they imagined had prevailed in the first half of the century. But this domesticated manhood, which these leaders had also believed would serve as a bulwark against the disorder of modernity, was coming under increasing pressure from the industrial city, which had come to be associated with poverty and overcrowding and was said to compromise men's physical health and thus their ability to fulfil their duties as fathers, husbands, and efficient workers in the new economy. The industrial city was also presented as a threat to male sexuality because it was home to a large number of men living and working in the homosocial male spaces that developed there, which critics warned would lead men on a path toward homosexuality. In response, the province's leaders began to place much greater importance on sexuality when defining the terms of what was thought to be normal manhood and as a means of controlling this population of single men in the city.[1]

An important reason for this emphasis on heterosexuality was the desire to maintain social order. The unattached man living in an industrial and urban environment, it became clear, was less easily controlled than the domesticated man living in a rural or small-town setting. Because manhood had come to be measured by domesticity and self-control and because that domesticity in turn was regarded as necessary for the maintenance of social, economic, and political stability in the face of industrial upheaval, the changing makeup of the family in the later nineteenth century and the release of men from the oversight of their families were regarded as a threat to that order and thus to manhood.

There was a greater sense of urgency surrounding the issue of sexuality in Quebec because French Canadian survival depended upon the physical reproduction of the race. The added pressure of ensuring the survival of a people led to a greater degree of consensus than might have been expected from individuals and groups who were seeming ideological foes. Catholic priests, for example, who had clung tightly to agrarian and religious models of manhood, found a common purpose with some of the era's scientific experts, who appeared more comfortable with the new urban environment as well as with the rationalism of science. Experts and priests, as well as social reformers, shared a desire to ensure French Canadian survival and to impose order on the new industrial and urban environment.

With the rise of industrial capitalism, it became much more difficult for anyone to cling to the notion that true manhood could be found only on the farm or defined primarily within a family unit, or even that the family could serve as the basis of social stability. Instead, lay and religious leaders turned their attention to the individual man, singling out heterosexuality rather than membership in a family unit as key to what they described as normal manhood. Of course, heterosexuality had always been assumed to define proper manhood. But by the late nineteenth century, heterosexual desire had become much more explicitly tied to notions of proper manhood. Although fatherhood, family, and self-control would still be regarded as hallmarks of manhood, heterosexuality emerged in the late nineteenth century as the crucial marker of normal manhood in Quebec. Because heterosexuality became the indispensable mark of normal manhood and thus a key to social order, the question of sexuality emerged as a matter of considerable public interest. The declining importance of the family as an agent of social control, as well as the rise of the homosocial spaces in the industrial city, had thrown into doubt the presumption that men would naturally gravitate toward heterosexuality and had prompted the state to assume a much greater role in monitoring and ultimately regulating men's sex lives.

The industrial and urban environment turned out to present a considerable challenge to the domesticated ideal of manhood that had taken shape beginning in the middle decades of the nineteenth century. As men began moving in large numbers from the province's rural areas to its urban centres in search of work, they often lived in rooming houses in densely populated areas of the city, raising concern among a growing number of reform-minded individuals about such things as the spread of disease.[2] In 1897 the civic reformer and soon to be Montreal alderman Herbert Brown Ames described the living conditions in Montreal's Sainte Anne ward in his book "*The City Below the Hill*." In this landmark study, Ames revealed that more than half the residents of Griffintown, the district just down the hill from Westmount, one of Canada's wealthiest neighbourhoods, relied on "that insanitary abomination, the out-of-door-pit-in-the-ground privy," which he feared posed a "danger to public health and morals."[3] Reformers like Ames were concerned that such poor sanitation led to the spread of disease and produced social problems and that such conditions were taking a toll on the area's men. According to Ames, "Death and disease have so crippled the family group that it can no longer unaided keep up in the fierce struggle for subsistence."[4]

Although Ames was interested in helping the poor by improving their living conditions, he was also concerned about the effects that the city's slums might be having on the larger community. In an effort to convince the general population to care about the plight of the industrial poor, Ames emphasized what he called the "interdependence of society," reminding his readers that "no portion of the community can be allowed to deteriorate without danger to the whole."[5] Others shared this view, including the Montreal judge Stanley Weir, who wrote, "the body politic is like the human body in that the infection of any one part causes the whole to suffer."[6]

These sentiments reflected such progressive ideals as social justice and community solidarity. They also signalled changing attitudes about the poor. It had long been assumed that the poor were responsible, either through laziness, immorality, or poor decision making, for their own destitution. Although this attitude certainly persisted into the twentieth century, it competed with the idea that the urban poor were not necessarily entirely responsible for their plight. The sheer number of poor people in the industrial city, as well as the inescapable fact that so many people lived in squalor, convinced reformers that poverty and destitution were perhaps symptomatic of the industrial city rather than of any moral failings on the part of the impoverished worker. A number of reformers came to focus on the larger causes of poverty, identifying structural deficiencies in the market-driven industrial system, and called for greater state regulation to mitigate the harsher effects of industrialism. But this desire to help the poor also revealed an authoritarian impulse within the reform movement. The campaign for reform was not simply about improving the lives of the urban masses. It was also about preserving a social order that was thought to be imperiled by poverty, urban slums, and unregulated industrial capitalism. This desire to maintain order, along with the belief that individual actions had profound social implications, would serve to justify the reformers' and ultimately the state's efforts to monitor and regulate people's private lives.

By taking the position of rational and modern figures, scientific experts and civic reformers presented themselves as uniquely qualified to address the problems caused by modern industrial capitalism. They promoted their ideas in a number of professional trade journals during these years, including the monthly *Journal d'hygiène populaire,* established in 1884 as the official organ of the Société d'hygiène de la province de Québec, and *Le journal pour tous,* founded in 1906 to reach a more popular audience. In these publications, experts embraced modernity, framing social and medical problems using the industrial language of the time. It was common for urban reformers and medical experts, for example, to approach the male body as a machine, suggesting that men could be improved in the same rational and efficient manner that the machine had improved and rationalized production. By describing the human body as a "very well-made machine," in the words of one observer, "where each part has its own function," these experts were at once depersonalizing the individual in the spirit of the age and revealing their supreme confidence in society's (as well as their own) ability to fix the broken, or inefficient, body, just as any broken machine could be fixed.[7]

But although these experts appeared to embrace modernity, many also saw themselves as providing the moral guidance they believed to be necessary to reconcile industrial capitalism with a set of values they felt were being challenged by modernity.[8] For some experts, this role meant working closely with religious figures.[9] As much as they embraced the modern age, experts, it turned out, often craved ecclesiastical support for their work. Dr. J.-I. Desroches, the editor-in-chief of the *Journal d'hygiène populaire,* was delighted, for example, when the Comité catholique du conseil de l'instruction publique gave his book on private hygiene its seal of approval, believing that such an endorsement confirmed that he was engaging in a "useful science."[10] There were, of course, practical reasons for developing close ties with priests. Experts recognized that a priest's endorsement could pave the way for a wider dissemination of their ideas due to the Catholic Church's institutional reach across the province. But the sometimes-close relationship between experts and priests also reveals the motivations of some of these experts and reformers. These experts had little difficulty aligning their goals with the moral teachings of the church because both experts and priests were seeking to impose order on a society that they both found to be increasingly disordered.[11]

One of the primary threats to social order arising from industrial capitalism was the supposed blurring of gender lines. For those men who had tied their sense of manhood to their ability to control women and to keep them confined to the domestic sphere, the industrial city presented a considerable threat to the world that they had known. In many ways, industrialization reinforced the lines that divided men and women by introducing a much clearer demarcation between the public and private spheres. It also perpetuated gendered distinctions in the workplace, as women were integrated into a system of patriarchal capitalism that paid them less than men and very often segregated women into jobs that were deemed feminine. But as more women entered the industrial workforce, enjoyed the new leisure culture of the era, and delayed marriage and motherhood, some men became increasingly concerned that these women presented a serious challenge to patriarchal authority and thus to their sense of manhood.

The influx of American popular culture into the province following the Great War also threatened to destabilize accepted gender roles. By the 1920s American magazines, movies, and books, many of which depicted carefree young men, and especially women, in sexually suggestive or explicit ways, were flooding into the province. Following the trends in American movies and magazines, French Canadian women began to dress in more revealing clothes, smoke cigarettes in public, and challenge gender divisions by dressing in what some critics believed resembled men's fashions.[12] According to one observer, such behaviour was evidence that women were seeking to overturn traditional gender roles. Georges Panneton, a priest from Trois Rivières, denounced the new woman who "turned into a man" by dressing in men's clothing as "a hybrid type created by a depraved, warped, desexed feminism."[13] Borrowing the term from the influential novel *La garçonne* (1922) by the French writer Victor Margueritte, Panneton described this phenomenon as *le garçonnisme* and accused the new woman of turning her back on her maternal duties.[14]

Feminism came to be seen by these critics as the most pernicious of all the foreign cultural imports to the province. Like Panneton, Henri Bourassa, one of the most eloquent and influential French Canadian leaders of the period, grew distraught over the manner in which feminism was supposedly disrupting society's proper and natural sex roles. He warned that society would fall apart if women turned their back on marriage, motherhood, and womanhood.[15] Bourassa also opposed extending the franchise to women, suggesting that such a move would compromise women's ability to be effective mothers and strip them of their ability to "remain as women."[16] Accusing feminists of wanting to become men, he described them as being "desexualised" and as "monsters, in every sense of the word."[17] Others, like Father Georges Courchesne of Rimouski, criticized the new industrial economy for attracting women "without sex" to work in factories, and he dismissed the idea of a coeducational school system as an "education for hermaphrodites."[18]

Although critics like Bourassa and Courchesne directed their attacks against women and feminism, there was also considerable doubt about men's ability to adjust to the freedom that they encountered in the city. The anonymity of the city allowed men to establish lives beyond the controlling reach of their parents as well as the prying eyes of a close-knit community. It was precisely this anonymity that worried the critics. Reformers worried that institutions such as the tavern, which remained an important feature of urban life as a site of working-class culture, could become a breeding ground for vice. Despite the efforts of political and religious leaders to domesticate men, a rougher version of manhood persisted into the later nineteenth century. In Montreal, establishments such as Joe Beef's Tavern, a working-class establishment on the city's waterfront that opened in 1869, served up entertainment and, of course, alcohol, making it a material and commercial expression of this rough male culture.[19]

To its critics, the tavern was a holdover from an earlier era, when manhood was measured by the rougher standards of a frontier society. By the later nineteenth century, this type of manhood came to be associated with the loss of social order and was said to compromise men's ability to support their families. The church had been promoting a domesticated form of manhood, which was centred on the family, as part of a larger effort to deal with the threats presented by industrialism and to exert greater control over men. But the persistence of the rough manhood that was found in the tavern undermined the reformers' efforts to define manhood by sobriety, moderation, and self-control. And the male social world that thrived in the urban and industrial environment provided young men with the autonomy from parental authority that they craved, as well as a considerable degree of anonymity that permitted them to pursue sexual relationships with women or men.[20]

By the later part of the nineteenth century, there were a number of well-known hangouts in Montreal for men who were interested in having sex with other men, including Moise Tellier's apple and cake shop on Craig (now St. Antoine) Street, which opened in 1869 and is reputedly Canada's first gay establishment.[21] But it would be the public spaces carved out of the industrial city that purportedly offered men the most opportunities to find other men for sex.[22] One of the most famous of these spaces was Champs de Mars, the public square directly behind Montreal's City Hall and the Court House, which served as a popular cruising area for men. The men who gathered in the square attracted widespread attention in 1886 when a reporter for the Montreal daily *La Presse* wrote about the "effeminate" men who gathered there.[23] The men who congregated in the square did so largely in public view and encountered minimal interference from the police. This particular reporter, however, expressed dismay that the police were allowing these men to carry on as they did, complaining that they were handing out light sentences that did little to discourage these "men-women" from returning.

The growing anger directed toward men who congregated behind City Hall as well as calls for greater police action against those men represented an apparent shift in the general public's attitudes toward men who had sex with other men. French Canadians appear, until the later decades of the nineteenth century, to have been largely unmoved by the idea of men having sex with other men. This view has arisen in part because there is little evidence that men were brought to trial on charges of sodomy or what might have been considered sexual immorality. If the absence of such evidence has prompted some historians to claim that there existed a level of tolerance in the colony, others have suggested that such a paucity of evidence is more reflective of the limited resources of a colonial legal system than of a widespread tolerance among the population.[24] To be sure, the supposed tolerance of French Canadians existed only so long as men were discreet about their sexual activities and also rested upon the presumption that such encounters between men were uncommon.[25] At the same time, although colonial officials may have been limited in just how vigorously they could apply the law, it was also true that in those cases that did go ahead, the punishment very often fell well short of the maximum possible sentence, which in the case of sodomy, was death.

Such apparent tolerance was evident in the early years of the French regime in North America. In 1648 a military drummer in Ville Marie, present-day Montreal, was accused of engaging in "crimes of the worst kind" with another man. The drummer was found guilty of the crime with an unidentified person and sentenced to death. But the Jesuits intervened on behalf of the drummer, asking for lenience and a reduced sentence. This request was granted when officials offered the man the opportunity to escape death if he agreed to become the colony's first executioner. In another case, in 1691, Lieutenant Nicolas Daucy, Seigneur of Saint-Michel, was accused of engaging in sodomy with two soldiers. Following a trial, the two soldiers were sentenced to two years of hard labour, and Daucy was fined and banished from the colony. These men thus received relatively light sentences considering the maximum punishment.[26]

The Daucy case reveals the lengths to which governing officials sought to avoid imposing harsh punishments on men who had sex with other men, especially if these men were members of society's leadership class. Class almost certainly played a role in this particular case, where there was clearly a desire on the part of the governing elite to protect one of its own members. There was also a concern that if such cases were pursued too vigorously or publicized too widely, they might leave the public with the impression that such acts were more common than they actually were. If the military, moreover, which was already regarded as an erotic space, became even more firmly associated in the public mind with supposed sexual immorality, then respect for and deference to government or military officers could be further eroded. Leading Canadians thus appear to have been hesitant to come down hard on men in positions of authority who engaged in morally questionable sexual acts because widespread revelations of moral transgressions within the governing elite might have weakened respect for public institutions and possibly undermined public order.[27]

This reluctance to apply the full force of the law against men who were caught engaging in sodomy continued during the British regime. In one high-profile case, George Markland, the inspector general of Upper Canada, was accused in 1838 of having sex with another man. An enquiry was called, but the case was quietly dropped when Markland agreed to resign his position and to retire to Kingston. Although Markland's public career was certainly ended by the allegations of his affairs with men, forcing him to spend his remaining years in quiet exile, and his reputation was undoubtedly tarnished, the legal proceedings against him were dropped. The reaction to this case has prompted one historian to claim that there was "a more liberal attitude toward homosexuality among Upper Canada's educated governing elite," where "such activity was, if not countenanced, at least tacitly accepted unless done in the streets."[28]

If the elite felt compelled to downplay instances of sexual impropriety within their ranks, there appears to have been little appetite for delving too deeply into the sexual lives of poor or working-class men either. It turns out that sex between working-class men failed to arouse widespread comment because evidence of such activities merely affirmed the elite's already low regard for working-class morality. This view of working-class and poor men was on display at Montreal's Juvenile Delinquent's Court, which was established in 1912 to deal with crimes committed by boys and girls under the age of sixteen. Court workers exhibited very little interest in boys' sexual lives unless boys were thought to have been violent, engaged in incestuous sex, or had sex with other boys.[29] But even if boys were found to have engaged in same-sex acts, the court often downplayed the seriousness of the transgression. This was especially the case if a boy was said to have had a sexual encounter with an older man. In such instances, the court tended to view the boys as victims of abuse within an unequal power relationship.[30] As a result, the court chose to look past the sexual acts themselves and to provide these boys with the rehabilitation that they supposedly needed. The court was somewhat protective of boys because they were seen to represent the future of the nation. As these boys were future citizens who would enter into marriages with women who would then reproduce the race and thus ensure French Canadian survival on the continent, the court felt compelled to help them rather than simply punish them.[31] Even a same-sex encounter during a boy's adolescence could not be permitted to stand in the way of his path toward full heterosexual citizenship.

The court's apparent lack of interest in boys' sexual experiences contrasted sharply with the considerable importance that it placed on the sex lives of girls. Although the court also tended to view delinquent girls as the products of dysfunctional domestic arrangements and poverty, it did not tend to view girls as sexual innocents. Instead, it believed girls to be much more responsible for contributing to their own delinquency, especially if they happened to be sexually experienced. This attitude prevailed even when girls had sex with older men.[32] The reason for this double standard is that the court tended to view any form of sexual encounter by girls to be a threat to the nation because it supposedly endangered a girl's ability to one day contribute to the survival of the nation by producing a baby. In contrast, a boy who had sex with a girl or who had sex with a man did not present the same threat to the nation because his acts were not seen to imperil his ability to eventually become a productive citizen and father. For these reasons, a girl who engaged in heterosexual sex was perceived to be a much greater threat to the future of the nation than a boy who had sex with a man.

The different attitudes toward adolescent boys and girls suggest that class was not the only factor at play in the court's response to same-sex activity. These attitudes also reflected larger assumptions about male adolescent sexuality. Some experts tended to regard childhood as a period of asexuality and early adolescence as a stage of sexual confusion and even bisexuality.[33] It was considered normal, for example, for boys to develop sexual attractions to their male friends.[34] It was seen to be perfectly acceptable for a boy to form deep bonds with other boys. Such bonds had been encouraged, in fact, by priests and others who tended to discourage too much interaction between boys and girls until adolescence.[35] Well into the twentieth century, men like Georges Panneton could still be heard warning against interaction between the sexes outside of marriage, and Father Victorin Germain reminded parents that close interaction between girls and boys could lead to "illicit familiarity."[36] A boy's primary interaction with girls was to be restricted to members of his own family, which, it was hoped, would produce in the boy a nonsexual response to the female body.[37] By late adolescence, boys were expected to leave the confines of their homosocial youth, to abandon whatever homosexual urges they may have experienced, and to enter into relationships with women that would lead to marriage.

Canadians in general and French Canadians in particular appeared rather tolerant of men who had sex with other men. Under certain circumstances, and in certain places, sex between men was, in the words of one scholar, a "socially tolerated and accepted fact of life."[38] This attitude, along with the supposed shock of sexual transgressions among the elite, as well as the elite's belief that members of the working class were especially and inevitably immoral, conspired to keep the issue of sex between men out of the public discourse. But this tolerance existed only because such acts were thought to be rare and only because they remained out of public view. During the late nineteenth and early twentieth centuries, however, the increasing visibility of men in urban spaces who appeared to be advertising a desire to have sex with other men made these acts much more difficult for the public to ignore. And the boldness with which men appropriated public spaces behind Montreal's City Hall and Court House – monuments to civic order – convinced a general public already feeling anxious due to industrialism that the number of men who wished to have sex with other men was on the rise. Once visibility increased, it became clear that French Canadians had never really tolerated sex between men as much as chosen to close their eyes to what they had thought were rare instances of sexual transgression.

The growing reaction against homosexual sex was in part a response to the perceived increase in homosexual activity in the city, but it also reflected changes in the way that people had come to understand men who had sex with other men. Until the second half of the nineteenth century, sex between men had in many instances been tolerated – or at least overlooked – because although the sexual act itself was said to be deviant, the individuals engaging in such acts were not necessarily regarded as deviant. That is, engaging in sodomy, for instance, was regarded as a vile and deviant *act* but not as a mark of a person's larger sexual identity. Men like George Markland could escape harsh punishment because they continued to enjoy the support of their community even as they were accused of engaging in such acts. Markland may have lived out the rest of his life in political exile, but he escaped incarceration, or the death penalty, because he was regarded as normal despite his sexual activities.

As the century progressed, however, and with the increasing visibility of an identifiable group of men who were said to be having sex with men, there emerged a stronger link in the public mind between a person's behaviour and his sexuality. It was, in particular, the growing association between men who had sex with men and effeminacy that aroused hostility among many French Canadians. In very many cases, it was the violation of gender norms that appeared just as threatening to many people as the sexual acts themselves. By the 1860s the Montreal police had begun to crack down on individuals who violated society's gendered assumptions, arresting a number of men, for example, because they were seen in public spaces wearing women's clothes.[39] The growing anger being directed against those men who congregated behind Montreal's City Hall can be explained in large part by the fact that these men were in a very public way flouting society's gender norms.

The level of hostility directed toward men who had sex with men was also very often determined by the degree to which society's gendered norms had been violated during a particular sexual encounter. A man who had assumed a supposedly passive role while having sex with another man, for example, was more likely to be said to be engaging in deviant or unmanly behaviour because he was seen to have taken on a feminine posture by being dominated. In contrast, a man who remained in control during the sexual exchange with another man could more easily retain his claim to normal manhood because he was thought to have fulfilled the masculine role by dominating his partner.[40] That is, the sex of a man's partner mattered less when determining a man's sexuality than the gendered role that he assumed during the sexual encounter.

By the late nineteenth century, however, such distinctions began to fade away as medical professionals started describing sexual encounters between men as symptomatic of psychological disorders. In an address to an American medical society in 1892, Dr. James G. Kiernan used the term "homosexual" to describe a person whose "mental state is that of the opposite sex" and one who suffered from "psychical hermaphroditism," suggesting that he showed "inclinations to both sexes." And Dr. Richard von Krafft-Ebing, one of the leading psychologists of the era, used the term "heterosexual" to describe a person who was attracted to members of the other sex.[41] Such labels meant that sodomy, for example, which had often been regarded as an "unimaginable crime" or an "unthinkable act" or sometimes dismissed as a momentary lapse of judgment, would now be considered a symptom of a larger homosexual *identity*.[42] And as soon as a same-sex encounter came to be regarded as a sign of a larger pathology, and an expression of an identity, it became much more difficult for a man who had sex with another man to retain his claim to normal manhood. The sex of a man's sexual partner became the key indicator of his own sexuality and crucial to his identity as a normal man. As a result, sex between men could no longer be regarded as a relatively harmless act, even if the act took place in private and even if a man retained a position of dominance during the sexual encounter. Instead, these men emerged in the public mind as serious threats to public order. By arguing that sex between men was an expression of a larger identity and a symptom of a larger pathology, medical experts fuelled the public's growing fear of men who had sex with men and also provided the impetus for greater state regulation of men's sex lives.[43]

When French Canadian political leaders took up the issue of sex, they tended to follow the English lead. The English state signalled its entry into the realm of sex with the passage of the Buggery Act in 1534. Prior to this act, the issue of sex was considered a moral one and thus left largely to ecclesiastical courts. But the growing sense that sex between men was becoming a larger social problem, especially in the navy, encouraged the state to take on a much more active role on the question of sex. Although the act did not explicitly define "buggery," it was interpreted to mean sodomy with humans as well as with animals. Conviction under the act could lead to loss of property or even a sentence of death. In the 1860s the death penalty for sodomy would be removed first in Britain and then in Canada and be replaced with a two-year jail term.

By the last decades of the nineteenth century, however, it had become clear that a law against specific acts like sodomy was no longer adequate in a cultural landscape altered by the categorization of sexual identities. By focusing on particular acts rather than on general behaviour, the law was of limited use when it came to any conduct that fell outside the strict definition of "sodomy" but that was said to be symptomatic of a homosexual identity. The growing sense that men who had sex with men were psychologically deviant in some way, as well as the growing anxiety over the conspicuousness of homosexual men, prompted state officials to rethink the wording of the law.

In 1890 Canada's minister of justice, and future prime minister, John S. Thompson, signalled his desire to broaden the scope of the law to include behaviour that might be overlooked under the existing law on sodomy. Speaking in the House of Commons, Thompson observed, "We have upon that subject very little law, and we have no remedy for offences which are now notorious in another country, and which have made their appearance in this country."[44] In the new Criminal Code of 1892, which Thompson championed and was instrumental in passing, buggery "either with a human being or with any other living creature" remained a crime. But it also stated, "Every male person is guilty of an indictable offense and liable to five years' imprisonment and to be whipped who, in public or private, commits or is a party to the commission of, or procures or attempts to procure the commission by any male person of, any act of gross indecency with another male person." This section is practically identical to the Labouchère Amendment of the Criminal Law Amendment Act of 1885, except that the maximum penalty in England was a prison term of no longer than two years. The precise meaning of "gross indecency" in both the English and Canadian laws was not more clearly defined, although it did clearly target what was thought to be homosexual behaviour. Some lawmakers expressed concern that the law was too vague. But Thompson dismissed such complaints: "It is impossible to define them any better, for the reason that the offences which are aimed at are so various." It was precisely this vagueness that appealed to the framers of the code because it would provide the state and the police greater discretion when dealing with individuals who were not necessarily engaging in sodomy but who were nonetheless seen to be part of a new homosexual subculture. By including the term "gross indecency" in the new Criminal Code, the state was endorsing the new sexual categories being promoted by the medical experts at the time. It was also effectively criminalizing homosexuality.

By the twentieth century, then, normal sex was being defined much more narrowly as an act between a man and a woman. Any behaviour that did not conform to what was expected of heterosexual men was denounced as deviant and even prosecuted. The hardening of attitudes was evident at the Montreal Juvenile Court during the interwar years, when officials began looking much more closely at the sexual lives of boys and became less tolerant of conduct that it might have once chosen to ignore or to downplay. Homosexual encounters, for example, were no longer rationalized away as often. Masturbation, too, which had not raised too many concerns just a few years earlier, was now seen as a threat to a boy's normal sexual development, especially if it occurred in groups, where it was thought to lead to homosexuality.[45] By the Second World War the Juvenile Court had adopted a more limited view of normal adolescent sexual behaviour, treating any deviance from the new heterosexual norm as symptomatic of a larger psychological deficiency.

This growing reaction against men who had sex with men during the second half of the nineteenth century grew out of the deeper anxieties of a population struggling to come to terms with industrial capitalism. For those men who were already feeling besieged by changes in the workplace, as well as by women's more assertive presence in the public sphere, the conspicuousness of those seemingly effeminate men in Montreal's urban spaces like Champ de Mars only heightened their anxieties about modernity. The modern industrial city, which was already linked in many people's minds with disorder and gender confusion, was now increasingly associated with homosexuality. Thus, when experts suggested that men who had sex with other men were not simply engaging in simple sexual acts but were in fact acting upon a set of desires that made them homosexual in identity and deviant in psychological makeup, the public did not need to be convinced that the state should step in to regulate this type of sexual activity more strictly in order to protect social order.

Consequently, at the very moment when men were feeling liberated from the confines of the province's small towns and rural communities and embracing the freedoms that they encountered in the city, there was a general decline in the tolerance for same-sex sexual encounters. It was the very openness with which men exercised the freedom to pursue these encounters that provoked such a strong response from the larger community and that would ultimately place these men's lives under greater scrutiny and legal surveillance. The freedom that the city afforded men thus proved to be fleeting since calls to suppress this freedom were heard as soon as it was exercised too openly.

The demands for stricter laws against the newly designated homosexual were made in the context of a larger push for more state involvement in other areas of people's lives. A growing number of French Canadians were beginning to accept the idea of increased state activism because they had come to the conclusion that their society had become disordered as a result of industrialism and that this disorder threatened the very survival of the French-speaking Catholic community on the continent. And by the late nineteenth century, one of the primary causes of this disorder was the perceived rise of homosexuality. In fact, the state had long exercised a degree of control over people's lives in the name of cultural survival. French-speaking Canadians have perhaps been more acutely aware than other Canadians of the degree to which their survival as a community in North America has depended on heterosexual sex. During the early years of French settlement on the continent, colonial officials worried that too many men chose to follow the life of a trader rather than to settle down with a wife in a settlement. But even for those men who might have wanted to settle down, one of the major obstacles to the creation of a viable settlement was the absence of women. So in the decade following 1663, officials secured the passage of more than 1,000 young single women and girls, known as the *filles du roi,* to the colony from France to serve as wives for the colonists.[46] Even so, the lure of the West persisted, and men who craved adventure and the wealth to be made from the fur trade exhibited very little interest in abandoning their freedom to settle into a heterosexual family life. In response, colonial officials attempted a number of measures, such as restricting the ability of single men to travel into the wilderness.[47] The viability of the whole colonial enterprise as a settlement depended on men's willingness to settle down on a farm with a woman in a domestic and heterosexual arrangement.

In the years following the Conquest, French Canadians found that their new British rulers appeared content to leave their new subjects largely to themselves. With the departure of much of the colony's French colonial leadership, the Catholic Church emerged as the primary social institution in the province. For the next century and a half, the church concentrated on ensuring the survival of a Catholic and French-speaking population on the continent. As

French Canadians were coming to terms with their minority position within British North America and then with the limits of their political power within Confederation, survival came to depend heavily on the physical reproduction of the race. During the late nineteenth and early twentieth centuries, lay and ecclesiastical authorities began to encourage couples much more explicitly to produce large families as a means of perpetuating the French Canadian way of life. Unlike people in the rest of Canada, which was growing rapidly in large part due to immigration, French Canadians could not fall back on large-scale immigration to bolster their community's economic and political clout. Few French-speaking immigrants settled in Quebec, and most of those immigrants who did settle in the province tended to integrate into the province's English-speaking community, which effectively swelled the minority population's numbers and increased its economic and political influence even more. French Canadian survival on the continent thus came to depend almost exclusively on the population's natural increase – a principle that, when encouraged, came to be known as the "revenge of the cradle."[48]

Anything that threatened the physical reproduction of the population, including sex between men, was seen not only as unnatural and pathological but also as a threat to the very survival of a French-speaking community in Canada. The belief that homosexual activity was on the rise, coupled with fears about declining birthrates, convinced a growing number of people that more needed to be done to monitor boys' sexual development. The belief that boys would instinctively grow into heterosexual men, ready to assume their roles as husbands and fathers, began to fade as the province industrialized. Thus it became necessary to monitor a boy's sexual development much more closely. Parents and teachers were told to monitor boys' activities in those homosocial spaces, such as school dormitories, showers, and gymnasiums, where boys might be drawn toward other boys.[49]

There was also a sense that boys needed to be much more firmly steered toward heterosexuality. Because childhood was thought to be a person's pre-heterosexual stage, it was seen to be all the more important that boys be taught about proper sexuality. Reformers thus increased their calls for sex education in the province's schools as a means of ensuring that boys and girls grew up aware of the heterosexual roles they were expected to play when they entered adulthood. Prior to the First World War, many people were wary about introducing sex education in school, fearing that too much talk about sex would encourage young men to become sexually active. But the flow of American popular culture entering the province also convinced many experts that keeping children in the dark when it came to sexual matters was no longer possible or even desirable. Experts advised parents that it would be preferable for their children to learn about sex at home or at school rather than from imported magazines or on the streets from friends or strangers. The silence and ignorance surrounding sex and sexuality were no longer seen as satisfactory responses to a boy's inquisitive mind, as it was becoming increasingly clear that a boy could easily learn about sex from other outlets if he was not taught about it at home.[50] Experts suggested, moreover, that the surest way to quell sexual urges was actually to teach children about sex. Proper sex education thus came to be seen as a necessary response to rapidly changing cultural circumstances.

Experts presented themselves as the people who could most effectively uncover the mysteries of the body and of sexuality. Encouraging parents and teachers to teach children about sex and sexuality as early as possible in a boy's life, they told parents to take the initiative on this subject, to be open and honest, and to use the correct words when referring to the sexual organs.[51] They also warned boys that any form of sex outside of marriage or for reasons other than reproduction, including masturbation, which they said would lead to physical and mental degeneration, constituted deviant behaviour.[52] Adolescents were told that sex should be confined to marriage for the sole purpose of reproduction, thus reinforcing it as a purely heterosexual act. Through sex education, then, experts reinforced the ties between sex and reproduction, thereby privileging heterosexual desire over all other forms of sexual expression. In this sense, sex education became a means of promoting heterosexuality and a defensive reaction to a child's curiosity about sex.[53]

The church, for its part, remained divided over the issue of sex education. However, a growing number of lay Catholics as well as a number of priests came to embrace it, recognizing that it could be a useful means of ensuring boys' development into heterosexuals. Before long, Cardinal Jean-Marie-Rodrigue Villeneuve, the archbishop of Quebec, would be lamenting, "Too many children fall into immorality because they have not been taught in time about the mysteries of life."[54] The church came to recognize that ignorance of sexual matters would not guarantee sexual morality and accepted sex education as a useful tool to guide a boy toward heterosexuality. In the end, church leaders recognized that their vision of society could be implemented more easily if they were seen to be associated with scientific experts, who appeared to command considerable public attention in an increasingly materialistic age. Working with experts to promote proper sexual conduct also allowed the church to retain a degree of influence over the expert, who threatened priests' dominant role in the community as moral leaders.[55]

Some Catholic leaders also revised their attitudes about marriage for the same reasons that they had embraced sex education. During the first decades of the twentieth century, the idea that men and women should enter marriage as partners and that they should derive emotional and sexual fulfilment from one another was beginning to take hold. For much of the previous century, the church had viewed marriage as an institution that would serve to both domesticate men and to transform women into mothers who would provide the nation with the babies it needed to survive. Feelings such as personal fulfilment, mutual affection, or even love appeared entirely beside the point when national survival was at stake. But by the first decades of the twentieth century, a growing number of lay Catholic leaders, as well as priests, especially ones involved in the Catholic Action Movement, appeared more receptive to the idea that marriage could also be a partnership between a man and a woman who found fulfilment and happiness in their union.

This new type of companionate marriage was not without its detractors. Its emphasis on individual happiness over reproduction left some people wondering whether this new type of marriage was simply incorporating the hedonism of the age and transforming itself into just another consumer product offering a superficial sense of happiness without responsibility. Moreover, for many women, this new companionate marriage did offer the possibility of escaping a patriarchal model of marriage. But the idea of a companionate marriage was not without perils for women. For one thing, it made women much more dependent on their husbands for their emotional and intellectual fulfilment, thereby binding them much more firmly to an institution that remained patriarchal in the eyes of the law. At the same time, it created sometimes unrealistic expectations of what could be found in marriage. Finding and then keeping a partner who could provide intellectual, emotional, and sexual fulfilment proved to be difficult. And if the promise of marriage was not fulfilled, it might collapse under the weight of frustrated expectations. The idea of the companionate marriage also raised expectations of what it meant to be a good wife and mother and thus increased the burden on women, who were expected to meet ever-rising standards.[56]

In order to help women to fulfil their new roles as companions to their husbands and to fulfil their duties as wives and mothers, some priests and experts began offering courses to train young women in the science of marriage. A number of marriage-preparation courses appeared during these years to provide women and men the skills that they needed for married life. One of the most famous of the marriage-preparation courses was initiated by Henri Roy, the chaplain of the Jeunesse Ouvrière Catholique, a group founded in 1932 to help the unemployed and to offer night classes for those workers who wished to continue their education or training. Roy had become concerned about the state of marriage and was motivated to do something about it by Pope Pius XI, who had written, "In order to bring about the restoration of marriage, it is indeed of the utmost importance that the faithful should be well instructed concerning matrimony."[57] So, with the help of doctors, nurses, lawyers, and other priests, Roy designed a twelve-month marriage-preparation course that would teach young couples about everything from proper social etiquette and gender roles to sex and reproduction.[58] Young couples who completed the course successfully could then enter into marriage confident that they had the skills necessary to make their unions succeed.

The culminating event of Roy's year-long program occurred on July 23, 1939, when the first 104 couples to complete the program gathered in front of a crowd of 25,000 people at Delorimier Stadium in Montreal to participate in a mass wedding ceremony. It was an event unlike any seen in the city. The couples began their day with breakfast at the Windsor Hotel before being driven to the baseball stadium.[59] As the couples arrived at the park and made their way to the special altar that had been set up at centre field, cheerleaders entertained the crowd. Archbishop Georges Gauthier delivered his sermon over loudspeakers that had been placed throughout the stadium. Following the ceremony, members of the crowd streamed out of the stadium and made their way to Saint Helen's Island for the official wedding reception, which featured a six-foot-tall wedding cake. By then, the crowd had swelled to around 40,000 people. Although 400 spectators collapsed that day due to the heat, the event was deemed a major success.

The year-long preparation program revealed the extent to which attitudes about marriage were changing. Marriage had become something for which couples trained, much like they would train for a job. And because a successful marriage required skill and effort, it was not to be entered into lightly. The mass wedding in the park, meanwhile, revealed just how much marriage was being transformed into a commodity to be marketed and purchased just like any other good in the consumer society taking shape during these years. This mass wedding, too, was intended as an advertisement for marriage; it transformed what had usually been a religious ceremony celebrated in front of friends and family into a depersonalized piece of heterosexual theatre packaged for public consumption. This dimension of the event was not lost on those who covered the wedding for the press. The city's newspapers, which featured the ceremony prominently in their pages, emphasized the festive nature of the event by referring to it as a "spectacle."[60] The French-language daily *La Presse,* for example, observed, "The ceremony would no doubt have been more pious if it had been held in the historic Notre Dame Church, but would it have been as impressive, or as inclusive of the masses?"[61]

Marriage became during these years an important marker of a man's normality. Just as consumers purchased goods to signal something about themselves, marriage in interwar Quebec became a potent marker of one's sexual normality. In his sermon that day, Archbishop Gauthier stressed that the ceremony was conceived as an advertisement for heterosexual marriage.[62] He defended the event, describing it as a means of countering "all the unfavorable publicity marriage is getting from the world's divorce court."[63] Reflecting on the wedding two decades later, Father Henri Roy, too, described the wedding as "propaganda for happy marriage to counteract the other side of marriage, divorce and broken homes, which now gets most of the publicity."[64] As the crowning achievement for a year of preparation, marriage here became both the reward for the couples' successful immersion in heterosexual training and the ultimate badge of normality in a society that had become much more self-consciously heterosexual. With this spectacle in the park, the church helped to transform heterosexuality into a commodity to be negotiated, contested, and finally displayed on public ground for all to see. The ceremony combined religious tradition and solemnity with modern commercial entertainment to create an appealing advertisement for heterosexual marriage. The couples who took part in the mass wedding in the park that day in July, as well as any other couple that entered into marriage in front of their families, friends, and communities, were proclaiming their normality and signalling their intention to live their lives as heterosexuals.

The promotion of companionate marriage, much like the embrace of sex education, was thus in part a defensive reaction on the part of experts and priests against the threats associated with the modern industrial city. Among the greatest perceived threats were those women who were said to be enjoying the freedoms available to them in the cities. There developed a fear that women were in fact beginning to turn their backs on marriage. Some men began to blame women for Montreal's persistently high infant mortality rate, accusing them of taking their responsibilities as mothers too lightly.[65] Others warned those women who turned their backs on their maternal destinies that they faced increased risks of developing serious nervous disorders. Some priests, meanwhile, turned to experts in order to support their campaign to reassure women that they had nothing to fear from childbirth.[66] This supposed fear of giving birth prompted some observers to worry that marital breakdown led to declining birthrates and that this decline in turn reduced French Canadians' political influence in Canada.[67]

The companionate marriage, then, was promoted in part to lure women back to the domestic sphere with the promise that they could find just as much happiness and fulfilment within marriage as they might as single women in the city's public spaces. By making marriage the primary source of individual happiness and emotional and sexual fulfilment, it was hoped that women and men would find little need to look for gratification outside the home. So, although the new companionate model being promoted in these marriage-preparation courses appeared to be progressive by emphasizing individual happiness and giving women an enhanced role in the relationship, the primary intention of these new arrangements was to promote heterosexual unions, not to advance women's equality.

The notion that couples needed to be trained for married life suggests that priests and experts acknowledged the artificiality of marriage and that the skills that couples needed to make a good marriage did not come naturally to people. In the same way that boys needed to be steered toward heterosexuality, couples needed to be taught how to live as husband and wife. Heterosexuality and marriage thus needed to be propped up if French Canadian society was expected to survive.

As French Canadians worked to defend heterosexual manhood in the face of challenges arising from industrialism, no issue proved to be as vexing as the question of female prostitution.[68] Many of the public's anxieties about modernity, sexuality, and manhood would be played out in the debate over what to do about a figure who so openly flouted expectations of proper feminine behaviour. Like the campaigns to promote companionate marriages, the debate over what to do about prostitutes had less to do with the prostitutes themselves and more to do with finding a way to promote male heterosexuality. Although the prostitute was hardly the product of the new urban environment, she did fit seamlessly into the narrative of the city as a site of sexual danger. One of the major concerns about the city was that it was said to promote a level of sexual immodesty among girls and women who might then fall into lives of prostitution.

It was also believed that prostitutes threatened to lead men astray. In addition to concerns about venereal diseases, there was also the feeling that prostitutes provided the opportunity for men to break free of their well-ordered lives and to indulge their sexual desires. For this reason, according to some of her critics, the prostitute represented a serious threat to the orderly manhood that was being promoted as an antidote to the disorderliness of the city. Like a boy who masturbated alone or with his male friends, a man who hired a female prostitute was surrendering to his lust and exhibiting a failure to restrain his passion. The prostitute came to represent, like the city in which she worked, degeneracy and disorder.[69] And like the city, she was said to threaten a heterosexual manhood that was thought to be built upon rational self-control. But unlike masturbation, which Montreal's Juvenile Court had begun to discourage in the belief that it might lead boys toward homosexuality, prostitution would never be seriously restricted by the state or police during these years. The reason was that heterosexual desire was increasingly coming to be seen as a more important marker of normal manhood during these years than self-control. The sexual exchange between the female prostitute and the male client would still be regarded as a decadent abandonment of the norms of an ordered society, but it remained a *heterosexual* exchange. Thus the female prostitute emerged as one part of a broader effort to reclaim the city as an ordered heterosexual space by becoming a bulwark against male sexual deviance.

Montreal had become well known by the 1920s as a "wide-open" city with no fewer than 300 houses of prostitution and as many as 3,000 prostitutes.[70] The city's emerging reputation as a centre for vice worried a number of people, including Louis Coderre, a leading conservative judge who would head a commission of enquiry in 1924 investigating corruption in the Montreal Police Department. In his final report to that commission, Coderre wrote, "Prostitution, the trade in human flesh ... functions and flourishes in Montreal like a perfectly organized commercial enterprise; I would even dare say that few industrial or commercial enterprises possess so perfect an organization ... and enjoy such rigorous internal discipline."[71] The Reverend E.I. Hart, for his part, identified prostitution as one of five "master evils" and claimed that it represented a "national peril."[72] He had also referred to the city as a "modern Sodom."[73] One American observer remarked that Montreal was "the rottenest town I have ever been in,"[74] and Nathan Gordon, a lawyer and a member of the Anglo-Protestant moral-reform group, the Committee of Sixteen, claimed the city was a "leper amongst cities of the Western world."[75]

During the late nineteenth century, the City of Montreal did little to stop prostitution. According to *Montreal by Gaslight* (1889), an exposé of the city's nightlife, "It [Montreal] legislates against the social evil. But the law is a dead letter. It is seldom put into practice."[76] The Recorder Court, it was true, did little to enforce the law. Judges John Sexton and Benjamin-Antoine Testard de Montigny, for example, endorsed regulation over suppression, and Judge F.-X. Dupuis instructed the police to follow a policy of tolerance. The Rainville Enquiry into police corruption in 1894 also came out in favour of regulation.[77] The Recorder Court's willingness to tolerate the "social evil" prompted critics to accuse it of encouraging prostitution and of contributing to the moral decay of society. These critics complained that judges had allowed the spread of immorality by issuing small fines to brothel owners rather than tough prison sentences. According to the Reverend Hart, "The very thought of prostitution as a necessary evil should be anathema, and inspired by the lowest depths of hell when tolerated by a community and employed as a civic revenue producer."[78] In 1905 Sir Henri Taschereau, the future chief justice of Quebec, reminded the police that the laws to suppress prostitution were already in place and were quite clear and that all that was lacking was the will to enforce them.[79] Tolerance had become so widely accepted as a means of dealing with prostitution that Judge Lawrence Cannon, in a 1909 report on police conduct, deemed it necessary to remind everyone that tolerance was, in fact, illegal.[80]

By the late nineteenth century, then, Montreal had in place an unofficial policy of tolerance.[81] The Recorder Court defended its policy of tolerance by arguing that it would simply be impossible to eliminate prostitution from the streets of Montreal. The court's leniency can be partly explained by the fact that the law made it difficult to suppress prostitution. Although the law made it a criminal offence to own or to be found in a brothel, it did not directly single out prostitutes.[82] A police officer could not charge a prostitute or her client on the basis of the sexual acts themselves, and since it would be difficult to prove that an exchange of money for sex had taken place, the police relied upon vagrancy laws to charge women who were found to be walking on the street without a valid reason or who could not explain their reasons for being found in a brothel. The sexual act between the female prostitute and her client, in other words, was rarely a decisive factor in a woman's arrest. Rather, it was a female prostitute's gendered transgression on the street or her presence in a brothel, not her private sexual performance, that made her vulnerable to arrest.[83]

In 1924 Montreal's police superintendent, Pierre Bélanger, explained the difficulty of enforcing ambiguous laws in his testimony to the Coderre Commission, one of the many enquiries established during these years to investigate police corruption. Headed by the respected judge Louis Coderre, the enquiry was established to investigate police involvement in a robbery. But for six months beginning in September 1924, lurid tales about police officers who frequented houses of prostitution, and sensational revelations about the collaboration between brothel owners and police officers to keep the Red-Light District running, dominated the city's newspaper headlines. The public learned that some police officers were regular visitors to certain houses of prostitution and that these officers participated in elaborate schemes to shield prostitutes from arrest. The enquiry concluded predictably with a scathing indictment of the city's policy toward prostitution. In his final report, Judge Coderre pointed out that the city neither suppressed nor regulated prostitution but rather tolerated a "hybrid" system.[84]

Bélanger told the committee that his hands were tied, suggesting the he could do little to stop prostitution until the law was changed.[85] But Bélanger's failure to crack down on prostitution was not, as he claimed, simply a reflection of inadequate laws. Brothel owners did find ways to avoid prosecution, but the police were more than willing to help them stay one step ahead of the law. Police officers, for example, might alert the owner of a brothel of an impending raid. Also, although brothel owners were routinely charged with running houses of ill fame, they usually paid small fines and would return to work "sometimes in half an hour in that house."[86] Bélanger was not interested in cracking down on prostitution because many of his own officers routinely frequented brothels and offered protection to brothel owners.[87] Corruption, as well as the legitimate complaint that the law made it difficult to crack down on prostitutes, explained why municipal and police officials often chose to tolerate rather than suppress prostitution.

The city's policy of tolerance also reflected a larger cultural ambivalence about prostitution itself. By the late nineteenth century, the female prostitute's body had become an important site upon which male sexuality was negotiated. As long as a female prostitute solicited male customers, especially respectable middle-class male customers, her transgression arose from breaking the social codes that had defined where sex should occur and for what reason it should be tolerated. Although the female prostitute's acts conscripted men into her own presumed moral decay, weakened the ties between sex and reproduction, and transgressed the boundaries of proper femininity, the sexual act between a female prostitute and her male customer did not in itself subvert any laws of sexuality and was thus not considered sexually deviant.

The female prostitute's open display of her sexuality challenged the belief that women should remain in the private sphere, where they were to exhibit only the slightest interest in sex, and then only for the purpose of procreation. That the prostitute did so as part of a commercial exchange in the public sphere offended middle-class sensibilities even more. It was the prostitute's blurring of the public and private worlds, the increasingly public nature of prostitution, and the fact that it challenged socially enforced assumptions about female sexuality that most troubled reformers.[88] Henri Taschereau captured this attitude when, in 1905, he explained, "All agree that prostitution is immoral." But, he continued,

> The law, no doubt, cannot always reach it, because there is the private domicile, the inviolability of which must be respected. But as soon as this evil, moral and social, takes, so to speak, a concrete form, a public aspect, a scandalous appearance, it becomes accessible to the law, which must repress it without weakness and without compromise, prevent it from exhibiting itself, arrest the guilty parties and close the houses where this evil is indulged in openly and cynically.[89]

The Montreal recorder Stanley Weir agreed that sex between a man and a female prostitute within the privacy of the home was tolerable, writing, "Private prostitution ... is not a legal crime and can only be combated by moral influences and its own bitter fruit."[90]

Even those who fought vigorously against regulation and in favour of suppression made the distinction between public and private prostitution. Owen Dawson, secretary of the Boys' Farm, a reform school in the Laurentians, and a member of the Committee of Sixteen, claimed, "There are some people who think that the Committee was organized to suppress prostitution and generally reform the morals of the city. This is not the object of the Committee. The Committee was formed to suppress commercialized prostitution."[91] The law, in other words, did not treat private prostitution as a crime, and few people saw anything abnormal or particularly threatening about such private sexual exchanges. It was, instead, the public nature of prostitution that most disturbed men like Taschereau and Weir, transforming it into a "social evil."

By the early twentieth century, a number of factors contributed to a developing sense that the city's unofficial policy of tolerance was becoming untenable. The growing visibility of prostitution on the streets of Montreal during the early twentieth century prompted city reformers to take a closer look at the city's policy. Dawson targeted the Red-Light District because it could no longer be hidden and because it had become an advertisement to the outside world that Montreal was a wide-open city. It was also feared that the increasing visibility of the prostitute who could pursue her trade with near impunity would send the wrong message to society at large and to children in particular about women's sexuality. Dawson explained that his call to shut down the Red-Light District was based in part on his desire to protect the "hundreds of respectable families living in this district." He argued that the children who lived in or near the area "have nowhere to play but on the streets in the midst of all this filth."[92]

Growing awareness about venereal disease also placed the city's approach to prostitution under greater scrutiny.[93] As fear surrounding the spread of venereal disease increased, the prostitute's sexual acts came to be regarded as weapons with the potential to cripple French Canadian manhood and to undermine the family and Western civilization in the process. The passage of the Contagious Diseases Act in England in 1864, which gave police officers the power to force women to undergo examinations for venereal disease, contributed to the transformation of the prostitute in the public mind into a threat to public health.[94] The sexual exchange between the female prostitute and her male clients evolved from a simple economic agreement to temporarily forsake moral values into a threat to healthy and vigorous manhood. A man's once-private attraction to the prostitute as a marginal social and moral figure was being transformed into an act of public recklessness that threatened the nation's health.

Judge Amédée Geoffrion of the Recorder Court in Montreal, an outspoken supporter of regulation, told the Coderre Commission that the government's priority on the issue of prostitution should be to halt the spread of venereal disease.[95] Geoffrion was preoccupied with French Canada's racial health and feared that if prostitution remained unregulated, it would endanger the vitality of the race. In 1923 he wrote to Lomer Gouin, the federal minister of justice, pleading for the passage of a law that would allow him to incarcerate infected female prostitutes indefinitely. He wrote, "I trust that the state has the duty to pursue all necessary means to keep the national life from being poisoned," and he claimed, "I am thinking of the future of the race, of the health of future generations."[96] Abbé Philippe Perrier, meanwhile, from the parish of L'Enfant-Jésus du Mile End, which bordered the Red-Light District, called for the suppression of prostitution before it could do any more to corrupt young men and destroy their physical health.[97]

Evolving perceptions of the prostitute also put pressure on city officials to change their policy. The female prostitute had long been portrayed as the victim of the harsh male urban world who had, through little fault of her own, slid into the world of vice. This perception continued to resonate among a number of individuals during the early twentieth century. Dr. Alfred K. Haywood, superintendent of the Montreal General Hospital, for example, described women in disorderly houses as slaves and claimed that some had been drugged and forced into these houses, where they remained out of fear of returning home to face their parents.[98] By the late nineteenth century, however, the female prostitute was just as likely to be portrayed as a predator who aggressively pursued vulnerable men in order satisfy her own sexual appetites.[99] The Montreal journalist C.S. Clark was instrumental in shifting public opinion against the plight of the prostitute. In his book *Of Toronto the Good* (1898), Clark dismissed the notion that female prostitutes were victims, arguing instead that these women had chosen their own fates. He suggested, "the great majority have entered from motives of pure licentiousness and at the same time gratify a taste for an easy life."[100] No longer portrayed as a victim of her industrial urban environment, the female prostitute was being transformed in the public imagination into a deft manipulator of her surroundings capable of exploiting the sexual freedom available to her in the city. Observers also came to view prostitution as an extension of the sexual mores of the period and as a reflection of poor parenting in the home. Judge Geoffrion, for example, argued that parents who allowed their girls too much liberty were setting them up for a life of prostitution. He charged that too many young women were permitted to go out "with dresses low-necked, short skirted and most of the time armless," and he warned that dance halls and hotels were leading girls on a path of destruction: "This is the plague that is eating into the vitals of our society. This is the starting point for the disorderly house for these girls."[101]

Once the public came to view the female prostitute as the sexual aggressor who had chosen her own path in life, it became much easier to turn away from the idea that she could ever be reformed. Although a number of people, including Joseph Tremblay, the former chief of police in Montreal, held out hope that girls who became prostitutes would choose the path to virtue if only they were provided with the opportunity to do so, others began to doubt that a prostitute could ever be reformed. John Swaill, who worked as a pianist in the Red-Light District, doubted that these women could be rehabilitated or reintegrated into society. He told the Coderre Commission that these girls could not be reformed since one could "never cure a bad egg," explaining, "You cannot change a woman. She is a woman."[102] Whereas people might have once been more open to the possibility that a virtuous woman might temporarily fall into prostitution in order to overcome difficult circumstances, by the late nineteenth and early twentieth centuries, people were just as likely to regard prostitution as a lifestyle choice.[103]

By the early years of the twentieth century, therefore, the prostitute had evolved in the public mind from being the victim of male exploitation into the aggressive carrier of venereal disease who lured young men toward moral and physical ruin. Increased awareness about venereal disease and evolving attitudes about women convinced most people that the city's hybrid system of official suppression and unofficial toleration was no longer acceptable. One side called for a full system of regulation whereby prostitutes would be monitored by the police and public health officials. The other side identified prostitution as a moral stain on the city and called for its complete suppression. Both sides exhibited little but contempt for the female prostitute herself and worked instead to find a solution that could benefit her male customers. The debate, in other words, focused primarily on men.

As with many issues in Montreal's history, the debate over prostitution was at least partly defined by the city's language tensions. The campaign to suppress prostitution in Montreal was led by reform groups such as the Committee of Sixteen, a group established in 1917 by English-speaking Protestant Montrealers to challenge the city's unofficial policy of toleration. It argued that a policy of toleration "results from an attitude of mind which fails to conceive of prostitution as more than the immorality of two willing individuals, and which neglects to take into account prostitution as involving physical and moral ruin to some, and ill-gotten profit for others."[104] Members of the committee were concerned primarily with the role prostitutes played in the spread of venereal disease but couched their calls for suppression in moral terms. Although this call had its roots in Protestant moral-reform movements in English Canada and English-speaking Montrealers dominated the ranks of the Committee of Sixteen and were at the forefront of the move to suppress commercial vice in the city, a number of prominent French Canadian leaders also spoke out against the policy of toleration. Henri Taschereau, for example, had written in 1905, "the human body is a sacred trust committed to the soul by the creator," and he had called for the complete suppression of this "plague" of humanity.[105]

Nevertheless, in spite of Taschereau's views, there remained a general feeling that reform activity in general, and the campaign to suppress prostitution in particular, was the work of elite English-speaking Montrealers.[106] In 1914 Médéric Martin capitalized on this perception to propel himself into the mayor's office in what many observers regarded to be an anti-English campaign against the forces of reform.[107] From a working-class background, Martin transformed municipal politics into a series of battles between working-class French Canadians, with whom he identified as a former cigar maker, and powerful and wealthy English Montrealers, primarily from the west end of the city.[108] His victory that year, the result of strong support from the city's predominantly French-speaking east end, would halt reform initiatives at City Hall and also bring to an end the convention of alternating between English- and French-speaking mayors.[109] Martin came out in support of a segregated Red-Light District in 1918 and in the process helped to polarize the debate over prostitution along class and language lines.[110]

Although Martin opposed the work of reformers in part to protect the patronage machine that he used to reward his working-class supporters, his position also reflected the general feeling in working-class circles that the wealthy reformers were unrealistic in their desire to suppress prostitution and were motivated by a desire to interfere in their lives. The labour leader Gustave Francq supported regulation over repression because he claimed that larger social changes had to take place if one wanted to eliminate prostitution. The journalist Julien Saint-Michel, too, rejected suppression as impractical, writing that efforts to curb prostitution would be like "trying to calm the Lachine rapids."[111] These self-styled realists argued that since it would be impossible to eliminate prostitution from the streets of Montreal, a system of regulation would be more effective in controlling the spread of venereal disease. Judges and police officers, who claimed to possess a greater knowledge of the problem because they dealt with the issue every day in the city's courts, also tended to support regulation. Judge Charles Langelier from Quebec City, for example, came out in favour of regulation in 1919 as the only means of slowing the spread of venereal disease.[112]

Judge Geoffrion, too, called for regulation because he believed it would be futile to attempt to eradicate what he termed an "unavoidable evil" that was the common curse of all big cities.[113] But his push to control prostitution also stemmed from his desire to halt what he claimed was French Canada's racial degeneration. Geoffrion proposed that doctors should establish programs to certify clean prostitutes and decide which women would be permitted to continue their trade. Those prostitutes found to be infected with venereal disease, Geoffrion argued, should be imprisoned indefinitely in an effort to keep them away from unsuspecting male customers. He argued that the system of fines in place at the time amounted to nothing more than a tax on prostitution.[114] He wanted to give court officials the authority to imprison prostitutes and to "keep them there until they no longer present a threat to public health."[115] He reasoned that the fear of prosecution had deterred prostitutes from seeking treatment for venereal diseases and thus made prostitution more difficult to control.

Critics of such plans pointed out that other countries' attempts to regulate prostitution had ended in failure and done little to halt the spread of venereal disease. Others suggested that Geoffrion cared little for the health and well-being of the female prostitutes and seemed concerned only that their male clients were receiving value for their money. Dr. Gustave Archambault, a public health officer, for example, pointed out that any plan to incarcerate infected female prostitutes would simply punish the unhealthy prostitutes, who needed medical care the most, and reward the healthy prostitutes, who should be the ones incarcerated.[116] In the process, Archambault added, such a plan would simply remove infected prostitutes from the streets and brothels and leave a supply of healthy prostitutes for men, thus doing little to help the female prostitute.[117] But helping the prostitute was never Geoffrion's intention, and ensuring a clean supply of prostitutes for men was precisely the point. Geoffrion made no secret of the fact that his primary concern rested with public health and with the men who were vulnerable to venereal diseases from prostitutes.

Those who called for suppression faced an uphill battle. One reason why it proved more difficult to suppress the "social evil" than it did to control gambling or the consumption of alcohol, for example, was that, according to one observer, "the number of men who desire to practise these customs themselves is much larger than that of gamblers and drinkers."[118] In reality, although prostitution may have been perceived during the second half of the nineteenth and the early twentieth centuries as the ultimate form of female deviance, it was far from considered deviant for a man to pay a woman for sex.[119] In fact, paying a prostitute for sex was often regarded as a rite of passage and a mark of one's manhood. During the 1920s some men, according to testimony heard at the Coderre Commission, even felt that "gonorrhoea established their manhood."[120] The idea that the heterosexual exchange between a young man and a female prostitute was an important affirmation of normal manhood became even more attractive during this period as fear of homosexuality increased. This fear transformed the female prostitute into an important site upon which a man could perform his heterosexuality.

The female prostitute was already seen to fulfil an important social function by providing men with the means to release their sexual energies. In this sense, she was seen to be protecting so-called honest women from men's unwanted sexual advances.[121] Judge F.-X. Dupuis of the Recorder Court had warned in 1909 that "on the very day when the last prostitute disappears there will no longer be any honest women."[122] In the same way that prostitutes were thought to fulfil a man's sexual needs while protecting the virtue of respectable and virtuous women, they were thought to serve the useful role of ensuring that men did not act out their sexual desires on other men.

Those reformers who favoured regulation over suppression tapped into the public's anxieties about deviant manhood in their effort to portray the female prostitute as central to normal manhood and as necessary to prevent man's slide into homosexuality. As sodomy came to be viewed as a symptom of a larger homosexual identity and as an illness rather than an isolated transgression that any man might commit, some reformers pushed to have prostitution treated as an acceptable transgression in order to prevent this more serious sexual transgression. Many people believed that prostitution should not merely be tolerated but should be protected as a necessary means of promoting male heterosexual desire. C.S. Clark, for example, wrote that houses of "ill-fame" were a necessity in any urban environment. He favoured the system of toleration found in much of Europe and denounced leaders in England, Canada, and the United States for taking a moral position on the issue. He asked those moralists who considered tolerance to be "a frightful outrage" to remember that England, which pursued a policy of repression, "has produced a Somerset and an Oscar Wilde." He also noted, "I can take you to places in New York and Chicago, where acts of the most appalling bestiality are committed, of so vile a nature that the English language does not supply words to express them, and in comparison with which the inmate of a house of ill-fame might consider herself almost saintly."[123] By arguing that it was preferable for a man to "visit such a place than that he should ultimately become the inmate of an insane asylum," Clark tapped into this fear of homosexuality.[124]

French Canadian leaders would echo Clark's views in their own efforts to present the female prostitute as an important release for male heterosexual urges. Judge Dupuis, for example, who had warned that the suppression of prostitution "would present a grave danger to public morals," suggested that although the female prostitute may have been a blot on the community, little could be done to restrict her activities.[125] He argued that a well-regulated and clean world of prostitution would offer men a safe outlet for their heterosexual urges and shield virtuous women from unwanted sexual attention from those men. Without easy access to prostitutes, men would turn their attention to innocent girls and honest women.[126] The removal of such an outlet, he argued, would prompt frustrated men to direct their sexual energies toward virtuous women, or worse, toward other men.

Like Clark and Dupuis, Amédée Geoffrion skilfully exploited the public's anxiety over deviant manhood in his defence of regulation. Challenging the Reverend Hart's allegation that Montreal was a "modern Sodom," he argued that commercialized prostitution could hardly be compared to the vice associated with Sodom.[127] Instead, Geoffrion argued that the female prostitute was a useful instrument in upholding heterosexual manhood because she discouraged men from the temptation of engaging in sodomy with other men. He defended disorderly houses because "they fulfill the function of the moral sewer of a big city," and he criticized the Committee of Sixteen for being "narrow-minded" in its drive to suppress prostitution and for being composed of "people born blind who have never faced the realities of life."[128] He argued,

> If the Committee of Sixteen does not know where Mr. Gordon's fine band would go to satisfy the "unnameable need which makes us do so many silly things," St. Augustine, St. Thomas Aquinas, Jeremy Bentham, ... etc., know. That is why those men and many others, counsel statesmen and legislators to tolerate those houses, so as to prevent the solicitation of honest women, adultery, the seduction of young girls, sodomy, pederasty, etc. To the wisdom of those thinkers, I shall add that of nations, which says: "Of two evils, choose the lesser."[129]

Referencing Saint Thomas Aquinas, Geoffrion argued, "God tolerates certain evils because their suppression might harm the greater good or, worse, could lead to a greater evil."[130] Geoffrion's turn to Catholic thinkers to make his case for the regulation of prostitution was not unusual at this time. Much of the debate in Quebec over prostitution revolved around the writing of Aquinas on the subject, which some observers interpreted as offering support for toleration.

Although the church believed that sexual acts between a man and a woman within the confines of a marriage and for the purpose of reproduction were the only acceptable form of sexual expression, it did not consider all transgressions of this ideal to be equally wrong in the hierarchy of sins. Paying a female prostitute for sex, for example, was not considered the worst sexual transgression because in doing so the man also displayed all the signs of normal sexuality and manhood. Sodomy, in contrast, which was clearly not intended for reproduction, was considered a greater evil because it violated natural sexual law. According to sexual law, therefore, a man paying a female prostitute for sex was to be preferred to a man engaging in sodomy with another man.[131]

Although theologians bristled at Geoffrion's appropriation of church teachings to bolster his case for regulation, they were forced to acknowledge his larger point. For instance, Abbé Adélard Dugré, professor of theology, agreed that heterosexual contact between a female prostitute and her male customer was to be preferred to sex between men.[132] He did challenge Geoffrion's claim that Aquinas was willing to tolerate prostitution under any circumstances, pointing out that he did so only under exceptional conditions, such as when men were away from home for long periods of time while serving in the army. Dugré argued that Aquinas believed that "if we deny them [soldiers] access to women, they will seek out other men." He concluded that Aquinas would prefer that men have sex with prostitutes rather than engage in "crimes against nature."[133]

But although Dugré reaffirmed that sex with a female prostitute was wrong, he conceded that it was not as wrong as sex with another man. Dugré's concession illustrates the degree to which heterosexual sexual activity had become the essential marker of normal manhood. Reformers who sought to regulate prostitution as well as those who fought for suppression emphasized that men who paid a female prostitute for sex were, in the end, normal. Nathan Gordon, the Crown prosecutor of the Recorder Court, for example, reminded the Coderre Commission that "houses of prostitution were used not just by the scum but also by elite of society."[134] Years later, the reformer Pacifique Plante would point out that "abnormal people only very rarely frequent brothels."[135] Although a man who paid a female prostitute for sex may have exercised poor judgment or displayed moral laxity, he emerged from the exchange with his manhood intact. A man's sexual encounter with a female prostitute, therefore, was constructed as a normal expression of heterosexual desire and would always be regarded as preferable to so-called perversions of nature.

The belief that only "normal" men paid for sex with a prostitute helps to explain the municipal courts' reluctance to prosecute men found in houses of prostitution. Judge Geoffrion, for example, scoffed at the suggestion that men caught in brothels should be subjected to the same punishment that he proposed for the female prostitute. He claimed that it would be cruel and unreasonable to expect the courts to send men who were caught in brothels to jail and suggested to the Coderre Commission, "There could be found in these houses men who ended up there in a moment of weakness, or husbands, or fathers."[136] Geoffrion was simply one in a long line of judges on the Recorder

Court to hold this view. Sixteen years earlier, Dupuis had argued that sending a man to jail for visiting a prostitute could "ruin an honest man's future, tarnish a reputation, cause pain and discord in the family home, and produce anger and hatred between spouses." Dupuis claimed that one of his duties on the bench was to show compassion for those men who had made mistakes, pointing out that "when I was promoted to the bench, I did not stop being a man."[137] This sexual double standard meant that women who performed sexual acts for men in exchange for money were seen to have violated sexual and gendered boundaries, but the men who paid for these acts were excused, both in the public mind and in the courts of law, from what were labelled momentary transgressions. It also meant that men were not targeted for medical examinations because they were not deemed to have done anything wrong or to be the sources of venereal diseases.[138]

In the end, and as everyone who was following the enquiry had expected, Judge Louis Coderre called for the suppression of prostitution in his final report. He was adamant that "prostitution should not be tolerated in any way," and he implored municipal authorities and the Montreal Police Department to work toward the elimination of prostitution from the city's streets.[139] The enquiry, as it happened, turned out to be the last great public discussion of these issues before larger forces intervened to shape the ultimate course of the debate. The concerns over masculine health and vigour that arose during the First World War, for example, resurfaced during the Second World War. Moral crusaders hoping to eradicate prostitution from the streets of Montreal were handed a partial victory in 1944 when the Red-Light District was shut down in an effort to protect soldiers from the debilitating effects of venereal diseases.[140] This victory, however, proved to be short-lived. Shutting down the Red-Light District simply sent prostitution underground, beyond the easy reach of social reformers and the police. By the late 1940s and the 1950s, Montreal had reclaimed its reputation as a wide-open city.[141] Prostitution became only one part of a larger heterosexual sex industry that included the open selling of sex at strip clubs and peep shows. The city also attracted some of the continent's most famous stripteasers, such as Lili St. Cyr, who visited Montreal often to perform her famous act. It also projected a heterosexual façade with commercial signs depicting women's naked bodies in sexually suggestive ways, which encouraged men to come and stare at women as a means of feeding their heterosexual fantasies and desires.

The idea that it was normal for men to visit prostitutes either to break up the tedium of sex with their wives or as a young man's rite of passage into heterosexual manhood was consolidated during the early decades of the twentieth century.[142] The perception that the female prostitute provided men with the means to express their normal heterosexual passions without the fear of violating a proper woman's prescribed role as a virtuous and respectable figure, or without the need to seek out other men for a sexual release, ensured that she remained an attractive figure. As the fear of homosexuality spread during the late nineteenth and early twentieth centuries, the female prostitute became an integral part of a society working to defend a social order that was said to depend on heterosexuality. Amédée Geoffrion had argued before the Coderre Commission that the government's role in society should be restricted to safeguarding individual liberty and ensuring public order. Since he and many others who supported regulation believed that prostitution did not threaten public order, and in fact solidified that order by reinforcing male heterosexuality, complete suppression remained an unattractive option for most people.[143] In an urban setting that reformers worked hard to define as a heterosexual space, the female prostitute thus emerged as a useful instrument to uphold codes of male heterosexual conduct. Both sides in this debate occasionally claimed to be fighting to protect the female prostitutes themselves. But it was clear that both sides were concerned primarily with upholding heterosexual manhood. One writer has pointed out that the various attempts to regulate or suppress prostitution amounted to little more than a "male pact" designed to control women and protect masculine vitality.[144]

Although neither side would be satisfied completely that prostitution was sent underground following the Second World War, both sides could claim victory by knowing that they had helped to consolidate male heterosexual identity in the province. By emphasizing a man's heterosexual private life as the key to public happiness and national vitality, experts had blurred the line between the public and private worlds in the province. The church played a crucial role in transforming male heterosexuality into a public duty during these years as it positioned itself as a modern practitioner of its values with such spectacular events as the mass wedding it helped to orchestrate at Delorimier Stadium. As men defined their manhood through such public displays of heterosexuality, the community came to judge their performance, leaving little room to dissent from publicly staged and enforced standards of normality. As heterosexuality moved to the centre of a French Canadian manhood that was to be first learned, then practised, and finally nurtured within the parameters of an increasingly well-defined heterosexual social structure, the female prostitute also emerged as an important element in propping up the heterosexual French Canadian nation. A man's heterosexuality, more than his domesticity, self-restraint, or work, came to define his manhood during these years. Anything that could further that idea would be encouraged, including, it turned out, female prostitution.

3
The Decline of the French Canadian Race

At the beginning of the twentieth century, it was common for French Canadians to claim that they possessed genetic and physical attributes that distinguished them as a race.[1] In *La naissance d'une race* (1919), Lionel Groulx described French Canadians as being distinct in their "political allegiance, history, and tradition," as well as in "physical and moral character, which has already been set and that has been transmitted from the end of the seventeenth century."[2] And in 1926 Groulx pointed out that a nationality describes a group of people who share an identity "based on blood" and who share certain "physical, psychological, and moral" similarities.[3] Ten years later, he continued to insist that French Canadians "are born with psychological predispositions" and that "by our birth, by the blood that flows in our veins, by heredity, we are predestined to think and feel in certain ways."[4] Many others echoed these sentiments, including the journalist Léo-Paul Desrosiers, who wrote, "Every individual in this nation is more or less a perfect reproduction of that first image [of the race]; there are always essential traits."[5]

Despite the persistence of such ideas during the interwar years, a number of men began to retreat from their claims of French Canadian physiological distinctiveness. It turned out that if biology played such an important role in determining a person's racial character, then women, by virtue of the fact that they produced children, exercised considerable influence over the future of the race. This realization was especially alarming during the interwar years because a number of men suspected that women were turning their backs on their supposed duties as women by joining the workforce and having fewer children. If women were producing fewer children – and more importantly, according to these men, fewer boys – they were failing to transmit those virtues that were said to have characterized the original French settlers and that were also said to be so necessary for ensuring the continued survival of the French Canadian community on the continent. In addition, women's perceived failure to produce the number of children that men wanted represented a significant challenge to an idea of French Canadian manhood that had come to depend very heavily on the maintenance of patriarchal authority in the home.[6]

French Canadian men who were concerned about the survival of the community responded to these perceived threats by redefining women's role in racial regeneration. Eager to regain control over their racial destinies, and emboldened by the evolution of scientific thinking at the time, which was becoming increasingly skeptical that cultural characteristics could be passed on through heredity, leading French Canadian men retreated from their claims of biological difference and emphasized, instead, the cultural dimension of their racial character. By disentangling racial identity from biology, these men claimed the right to decide who could call themselves a true French Canadian man, and they proceeded to measure manhood according to one's adherence to a retooled racial identity that had been purged of biological, and thus feminine, influence and that they would control fully. French Canadian men appeared particularly receptive to evolving theories about race that forced them to abandon their claims of biological difference because these theories permitted them to reassert their authority over women and in the process to reclaim their identities as men.

The preoccupation with the physical distinctiveness of French Canadians had grown out of a larger concern about survival as a French-speaking and Catholic community on the continent. Since the British Conquest, French Canadians had lived a somewhat insular existence. Cut off from their ties to France, and separated from their new English-speaking leaders along linguistic, religious, and cultural lines, French Canadians turned inward and would come to rely on the Catholic Church, the only familiar institution that also continued to be run by French-speaking and thus accessible leaders, for direction. The church served a useful function in the aftermath of the Conquest, working closely with English leaders in a manner that permitted it to retain its own position of power within the colony. The church also secured for the English a loyal population in return for guarantees that the French-speaking community could continue to speak its language and practise its religion. When the Rebellions broke out in 1837, one of the reasons that the church and others would oppose them was that they threatened to end the community's isolation and to expose it to liberal and thus dangerous ideas from the outside world. This turn inward, and the resistance to outside influences, was thought to be necessary for the survival of the French Canadian community in North America. Indeed, one of the primary assumptions about survival was that it could be ensured only if French Canadians remained different and apart from the rest of the continent. For much of the rest of the nineteenth century, this desire meant that men would be encouraged to remain close to the land and to reject the materialist values associated with industrial capitalism. The French-speaking population in Quebec would remain a cohesive and largely self-contained community for the rest of the century, and it was this isolation from the outside world that had come to be regarded as necessary for the population's continued survival on the continent.

That French-speaking Canadians had been living under British rule since the middle of the eighteenth century turned out to matter very little to those who stayed behind after the Conquest. Because the British had made few real efforts to limit the rights of Catholics to practise their faith and left the population largely to itself, few French-speaking Canadians appeared to mind being governed by English-speaking rulers. By the end of the eighteenth century, in fact, as France experienced the disruptions of its Revolution, many French Canadians would come to regard the Conquest as an act of providence because it had shielded the province from the tumult in France. The British Conquest thus emerged as the event that permitted French Canadians to continue to live their lives largely untouched by the radicalism associated with the French Revolution. By the nineteenth century, a growing number of church leaders would promote much more forcefully the idea that French Canadians had a particular destiny to fulfil as a Catholic and French-speaking community in North America. The French Revolution, and the American Revolution before it, therefore, stood as vivid reminders of the threats emanating from the outside world, and the British Conquest emerged much more prominently in the public mind as a form of divine intervention that had preserved the French Canadian community so that it might fulfil its destiny.

The classic statement of this idea comes from L.-F.-R. Laflèche, who wrote "The Providential Mission of the French Canadians" in the spring of 1866, just before being named bishop of Trois-Rivières. Laflèche states, "Providence has allotted each and every nation its own mission to fulfil, its own predetermined goal to attain. Every nation is bound to succeed, so long as it faithfully answers God's calling: for God, in his power and his wisdom, always apportions the necessary means to a given end."[7] According to Laflèche, French Canada's survival was assured as long as it fulfilled its destiny by remaining faithful to Catholicism. This idea was taken up by the priest and theologian Louis-Adolphe Pâquet in a sermon delivered in Quebec City in 1902 entitled "A Sermon on the Vocation of the French Race in America." In that sermon, delivered on the eve of Saint-Jean-Baptiste Day, Pâquet suggested that God had "created different races with varied tastes and aptitudes; and also how, within the hierarchy of societies and empires, He has assigned to each one of these races a distinct role of its own." He continued, "History both ancient and modern proves this: there are peoples dedicated to the soil, there are industrial peoples, merchant races, conquerors, there are peoples versed in the arts and the sciences, and there are also races of apostles." According to Pâquet, "Our mission is less to handle capital than to stimulate ideas; less to light the furnaces of factories than to maintain and spread the glowing fires of religion and thought, and to help them cast their light into the distance."[8] Many French Canadians were willing to concede Anglo-Saxon success in finance, industry, and commerce, therefore, because they had come to believe that their own spirituality and humanism were evidence of their racial superiority.[9] Pâquet linked this providence to blood as well, telling the audience, "Through a happy and providential combination we have French blood and Christian blood circulating in our veins. French blood alone leads quickly to corruption, perhaps more quickly than any other; but mixed with Christian blood it produces heroes, disseminators of fruitful spiritual doctrines, glorious craftsmen and the most beautiful and divine works."[10]

This isolation persisted well into the twentieth century even as the province faced large-scale immigration and continued to experience a level of industrial transformation that integrated it more fully into the continental economy. Unlike the rest of the continent, however, French Canada largely escaped the anxieties usually associated with the influx of large numbers of immigrants. The immigrants who arrived in the province tended to settle in Montreal, and once there they usually gravitated toward the city's English-speaking community. This trend was not viewed as entirely unwelcome by French Canadian leaders, who saw little need for immigration to sustain the community's numbers as long as the French Canadian birthrate remained high. Moreover, since many French Canadians had wished to maintain their insularity from other communities as well as to preserve the purity of the French Canadian race, the fact that immigrants integrated into the English-speaking community permitted French Canadians to preserve their racial purity.

Although the desire for survival and isolation may have appeared defensive and to be characterized by a deep suspicion of most things associated with the outside world, it also reflected a considerable degree of confidence on the part of French Canadian leaders. Many French Canadians had derived a great deal of comfort from their community's isolation from the outside world. It was this isolation, some observers said, that had prevented the type of racial mixing that was said to be plaguing other societies during those years. Indeed, for observers like Groulx, French Canadians had inherited "a pure blood" that would provide them with "the moral virtues needed to continue the transmission of life."[11] Survival on the continent was assured, according to Groulx, because French Canadians possessed "neither sick blood, nor a blood that had been exhausted by the ancient or decadent civilizations."[12] Groulx was thus optimistic about French Canadians' prospects for survival because they had "French blood in their veins."[13] In 1918 Abbé Edmond Lacroix echoed this sentiment about the purity of blood when he reminded French Canadians in *L'Action française* that "not a drop of foreign blood courses through your veins."[14]

THE FOCUS ON THE PURITY of one's blood as well as the concern about racial degeneration placed French-speaking Quebecers in the mainstream of North American thought at this time. By the end of the nineteenth century, it had become quite common for members of the middle classes, especially those professionals who came to make up the burgeoning healthcare fields, including medical doctors, psychologists, and sociologists, to lament that Western civilization and the Anglo-Saxon race were entering a period of decline. The modern era, many of these experts warned, which was characterized by new technology and industrial change, had produced anxiety among men, who had been forced to adjust to the new competitive realities of a market economy. In addition, the domestic realm, which was described as having become overly feminized, provided a world of sedentary comforts at odds with what was thought to be a man's natural state of mind, which drained men of their physical and mental energy and produced debilitating levels of angst. According to the eminent American psychologist G. Stanley Hall, the president of the American Psychological Association, American men had become "over-civilized."[15]

For those observers who shared Hall's concerns about racial decline, the solution to this supposed excess of civilization was to encourage men to escape the effeminizing clutches of modern society and to refamiliarize themselves with their more primitive instincts. Many of the ailments that were said to afflict modern men, including fatigue, anxiety, and depression, were seen to be symptoms of "neurasthenia," a term first used by the American neurologist George Miller Beard to describe what he claimed was a nervous disorder arising from the stresses associated with urbanization and modernity.[16] Although neurasthenia was said to affect both men and women, the treatment prescribed for each sex differed. Women who were afflicted with the disorder were usually advised to take to their beds and to rest, sometimes for up to several weeks at a time. Men, in contrast, were often encouraged to escape the comforts of the home by immersing themselves in the fresh air of the outdoors and to engage in physical exercise in order to reinvigorate their bodies and spirits. For Hall, the solution to overcivilization, and thus to its primary symptom, neurasthenia, was to encourage boys to embrace their supposedly more primitive natures. Because Hall had lamented the fact that men had been told to restrain their supposedly natural instincts in order to conform to certain assumptions about Victorian propriety, he believed that the surest means of reversing this process of overcivilization was to encourage boys and men to exhibit more aggressive and passionate behaviour. This behaviour could include anything from simple physical activity to organized sport or violent encounters with other men.

Although Hall was influenced by ideas associated with evolutionary biology, he was not deterministic in his thinking. Nor was he pessimistic about modern life. He was confident, after all, that the decline of Western civilization could be reversed. For the decline of civilization to be stopped, however, society needed to rethink the ways that it conditioned its boys. Hall is best known for his work on "adolescence" – a term that he coined – as well as for his theory of recapitulation, which suggested that an individual's life course mirrored the evolutionary stages of a civilization, with childhood and adolescence associated with a society's more primitive stages and adulthood reflecting a group's attainment of civilization. Since the precivilized, or primitive, stage was thought to be a necessary step on the road to achieving a state of civilization, so too was a child's primitive stage thought to be a necessary step in the process of developing into a civilized and normal adult.[17] Hall had grown increasingly concerned that boys and young men were being forced to suppress their natural inclinations toward violence, aggression, and conflict, which he suggested was a threat to the life of a civilization because a boy who enjoyed a privileged and pampered upbringing would fail to pass through the necessary evolutionary stages of life and thus never become properly civilized. Thus Hall called on parents as well as school teachers to grant boys greater freedom to act in ways that corresponded to the civilization's more primitive stages. Boys who were caught fighting with other boys were to be permitted to experience this more aggressive side of their personalities because it was seen to be not only a way that these young men connected to their supposedly more primitive pasts but also a means of preparing them to grow up to be men who were capable of defending civilization.

But if the privileged existence enjoyed by the more affluent members of society was said to be compromising racial vigour, there was also a growing concern that the race was being imperilled by the working conditions found in the industrial factories. Some observers noted that the work being performed in factories was disrupting men's supposedly natural rhythms by forcing them to work indoors as well as in long and gruelling shifts. Moreover, this type of work was often repetitive and did little to exercise a man's body or challenge his mind. The growth of crowded cities and the emergence of slums, meanwhile, raised fears about the spread of disease as well as fears about productivity in the workplace. Such conditions also led to social problems since poverty was said to lead to moral laxity as well as family breakdown, juvenile delinquency, and infant mortality. The conditions in the province's cities, then, were hardly ideal for promoting racial vigour.

Underlying much of the talk of racial decline during these years was the growing fear that the wrong people were having too many children. This belief was rooted in an assumption that a person's mental aptitude or physical fitness was an inherited trait. For those people who believed that feeblemindedness was biologically transferred from one generation to the next, it became society's responsibility to step in to prevent the transference of those traits that were said to contribute to poverty, social problems, and ultimately racial decline. In the United States the notion that racial decline could be reversed gained traction as activists like Margaret Sanger, a pioneer in the birth control movement of the early twentieth century, promoted the limitation of births as a means of preserving the race by limiting the number of children born to so-called undesirable elements of society. Such ideas were rooted in the ideas of the economist Thomas Malthus, who warned in the late eighteenth century that the world's population would grow faster than the food supply could support. For activists like Sanger and Marie Stopes, another pioneer in the birth control movement, the solution to this demographic threat was to be found in limiting the number of what they considered undesirable children through various birth control methods. In Canada the idea that the race could be saved by limiting the number of children being born to the poor or supposedly unfit members of society gained in popularity during the late nineteenth and early twentieth centuries, especially among reform-minded individuals who believed that scientific methods could be used to improve society.[18] Emily Murphy, the pioneering women's rights activist and a member of the "famous five," who argued that women should be recognized as legal persons, would embrace eugenics as a means of controlling population growth in order to limit the transmission of undesirable traits to the next generation.[19] By the 1930s Murphy would become an enthusiastic supporter of eugenics legislation, campaigning in support of a law in Alberta that called for the sterilization of those members of society who were deemed to be mentally unfit.[20]

These ideas were circulating within an intellectual environment shaped by Darwinian notions of evolution as well as Spencerian arguments about the survival of the fittest. "Eugenics," a term coined by Francis Galton, a cousin of Charles Darwin, grew in popularity during these years in the United States and Canada. The prospect that a society could control the transmission of those physical and mental traits that were at this time believed to be hereditary proved to be very appealing to progressive-minded reformers who were seeking to improve society. Those who embraced eugenics thus did so out of a profoundly optimistic sense that modern scientific knowledge might be marshalled in such a way as to ensure that only those who were deemed to be the fittest members of the race would survive. What this involved, in very many cases, was an attempt to prevent so-called undesirable elements of society from having children, ensuring that they did not pass on those traits that were draining the strength of the entire race. The means toward racial improvement varied widely and could include improved education, greater access to birth control, or in more extreme cases, sterilization. Interest in eugenics grew during the late nineteenth and early twentieth centuries when the squalid living conditions of the urban poor became widely known and persisted during the interwar years. The presumed high birthrate among the poor, as well as among newly arrived immigrants, sparked fears of what was termed "race suicide" among some English Canadians, who turned to social engineering as a solution.[21]

Many French-speaking Canadians shared these concerns about the enervating effects of modern industrial capitalism, but they generally did not embrace the types of solutions being forwarded by English-speaking North Americans. For instance, they did not endorse the calls by men such as G. Stanley Hall to return to the primitive.[22] Although French Canadians certainly promoted a return to the land in part as a means of escaping the effeminizing influences of the industrial city, those individuals who had promoted the ideal of the rural and domesticated man did so as part of a larger effort to restore social order and bolster institutional authority in the province. This return to the land was to take place under the close supervision of the church, and it was to be done in an orderly and rational manner. There was little appetite to revive the rougher type of manhood that was thought to have existed during an earlier era. The church had devoted considerable energy to encouraging men to become domesticated, so it was not about to celebrate the more primitive image of manhood being promoted elsewhere. Moreover, the calls for a return to the supposedly more natural and primitive environment reminded many French Canadians of persistent stereotypes about French Canadian primitivism that they had been struggling to overcome for some time. Many observers had gone to great lengths to challenge the stereotypes that suggested that French Canadians were a backward people. Lionel Groulx, for example, had taken issue with the influential American historian Francis Parkman's portrayal of the inhabitants of New France as "semi-savage" or "semi-barbaric"[23] and would devote much of his own historical writing to challenging these assumptions.

Nor did French-speaking Canadians embrace eugenics to the degree that others outside the province might have. Although many French Canadians pointed to their own blood purity as evidence of their racial superiority, few would support birth control or sterilization as means of achieving social reform. To be sure, the preoccupation that many French Canadians exhibited with maintaining the purity of their blood was a form of eugenics.[24] But French Canadians exhibited little enthusiasm for the more extreme forms of population control, including sterilization. The opposition of the Catholic Church to eugenics played a significant role in limiting its appeal in the province. According to the botanist Abbé Louis-Marie Lalande, eugenics was to be opposed simply because it interfered with God's plan.[25] For others, the danger of limiting births for the purpose of improving the race was that it would inevitably be followed by the wider availability of birth control, which would simply lead to promiscuity in the general population and thus to moral decline.[26]

But French Canadians had another reason to be skeptical of eugenics. Eugenics was associated with the English-speaking Protestant world, and there was some suspicion that French Canadians might be targeted with birth control information because their own high birthrates represented a threat to the Protestant population. There was also some question about how French Canadians might measure up within a racial taxonomy devised by English-speaking Protestants.[27] French Canadians had for some time struggled to overcome English Canadian assumptions about their fitness. In the closing decades of the nineteenth century, French Canadians encountered discrimination as stereotypes about their lack of intelligence and civilization proliferated. The mass migration of French Canadians into the New England states in search of industrial work had aroused significant anger among some Americans, who did not think very highly of these workers. Many Americans came to resent the emergence of these *little Canadas* – communities of French-speaking Canadian workers – that appeared throughout the northeastern United States. In 1881 the head of the Bureau of Statistics of the Massachusetts Department of Labor and Industries captured the unease that many Americans felt at the presence of these newcomers in the state when he referred to French Canadians as "the Chinese of the Eastern States." According to his report, French Canadians were, supposedly like the Chinese, not easily assimilated into the larger culture and cared

> nothing for our institutions, civil, political, or educational. They do not come to make a home among us, to dwell with us as citizens, and so become a part of us; but their purpose is merely to sojourn a few years as aliens, touching us only at a single point, that of work, and when they have gathered out of us what will satisfy their ends, to get them away to whence they came, and bestow it there.

Although the report did acknowledge that French Canadians were eager to work, this positive assessment was tempered by the fear that their eagerness would make life more difficult for the American workers: "Now, it is not strange that so sordid and low a people should awaken corresponding feelings in the managers, and that these should feel that, the longer the hours for such people, the better, and that to work them to the uttermost is about the only good use they can be put to." The report warned that the French Canadians were raising managers' expectations of what other workers could do on the job, which could lead to harsher conditions for all workers. In the end, the report concluded, "Society should be shaped to the better portion of the people; and where the case requires it the laws should be so amended and enforced that these people will either be coerced to conform to our established ways, or else go where the already established ways of the country do please them."[28]

Three years earlier, George Miller Beard had also raised questions about the mental aptitude of French Canadians. In a report to the American Neurological Association in 1878, Beard noted that a large number of French Canadian lumbermen working in the northern part of Maine appeared to suffer from a condition that prompted them to jump when they became suddenly excited. Beard explained, "If one of these persons be suddenly told to strike another, he strikes right out, even if it be his own mother whom he hits." They have, he said, "no inhibitory power after sudden excitation." Describing it as "a psychological and not a pathological state," he suggested that it was "a survival of the habits of the Middle Ages" and was "the result of a psychical condition among a people of a low order of intellectual development."[29]

These assumptions lingered into the twentieth century and placed French Canadians on the defensive, making them much less likely to embrace racial ideas being promoted from outside the province. French Canadian leaders then, were largely immune from these outside influences when it came to eugenics. Few felt any attraction to returning to the frontier in order to rediscover some primitive ideal by which to revive a flagging manhood. And most French Canadian leaders were more interested in encouraging French-speaking Quebec women to have as many children as they could than in discouraging or even preventing others from having children. Although it is true that the persistently high rate of infant mortality in the province tempered this faith in the community's survival, French Canadians felt confident that their high birthrate would be sufficient to ensure the survival of the community.[30]

Because survival depended so heavily on a high birthrate, as soon as women appeared to challenge prevailing assumptions about their proper roles in society by participating in the public and male world, and most frighteningly when the birthrate itself began to fall, French Canadian leaders began to worry much more than they had in the past about the community's survival on the continent.[31] The confidence that many people felt about their prospects for survival waned as they came to the realization that French Canada's survival had come to depend very heavily upon women's continued ability and willingness to produce children. Some observers noted that French Canadians were uniquely dependent on women's bodies for racial survival. According to Dr. Raoul Masson, a professor of pediatrics at the Université de Montréal, this dependence was a matter for concern because the province had been "deprived of the aid that French immigration would provide ... To ensure our national future we are reduced to our own resources – in other words to our birthrate and the survival of our children."[32]

If English Canadian leaders and others approached the issue of their supposed racial decline within the framework of a larger competition between races and focused on preventing those so-called unfit members of society from having too many children, French Canadian leaders directed much of their anxiety toward women, who were seen as playing a crucial role in the physical perpetuation of the race.[33] English Canadian fears of racial decline were expressed through efforts to limit immigration and to restrict those deemed unfit from physically reproducing the race and thus from passing on those traits that were said to be a threat to racial vigour. The French Canadian leadership, in contrast, which remained much more isolated from the outside world, turned against women, who came to be regarded as the primary threat to the survival of the race because of the perception that they were turning away from their duties as mothers.

WOMEN HAD LONG OCCUPIED a privileged position within the narrative of French Canadian racial survival. It was women's roles as mothers or potential mothers that ensured that they would be venerated by those men who placed a great deal of importance on producing the next generation capable of carrying on the racial mission of the community. Although women's political power narrowed considerably in the 1840s, they were expected to contribute to the national life of the province. French Canadian women had been venerated as mothers of the race precisely because they were seen to play an important role both in transmitting those racial characteristics that were thought to have defined early Canadian settlers and in nurturing male children to fulfil their destinies as men. During the nineteenth century, the image of the French Canadian mother had emerged as central to a racial narrative that emphasized the purity of blood and the miracle of the community's survival.

With the emphasis on French Canadian survival, women emerged as central characters in the province as the cultural and spiritual guardians of the nation. In 1921 Henriette Dessaulles Saint-Jacques, who contributed to the women's pages in *Le Devoir* under the penname "Fadette," spoke for many people when she wrote, "The mother is the primary influence over the soul of her small children."[34] She went on to note, "It is the woman who creates the nation, as a mother, educator and social authority" in her community.[35] A number of prominent men, too, argued that women exercised considerable influence over French Canada's fate. Joseph Gauvreau, the first director of *L'Action française*, for example, promoted the idea that women had "done more than men to develop and Christianize the human race."[36] And Henri Bourassa, the nationalist leader and conservative founder of *Le Devoir*, suggested, "It is the Christian family, formed by the Christian woman, that has saved French Canada."[37] The journalist Errol Bouchette understood that French Canadian economic empowerment rested upon women's abilities to produce many children, noting in his novel *Robert Lozé* (1903), "Whoever rocks the cradle rules the world," by which he meant that French Canadians would become strong largely through women.[38] But it was especially women's role as the physical reproducer of the race that accounted for their exalted standing in the French Canadian imagination.[39] The belief that cultural traits and mental abilities were inherited meant that the physical reproduction of the population was absolutely vital to survival.

Mothers had also become synonymous with the race itself, and men's love for their mothers occasionally blurred into their love for their race and their nation. French Canadian men would often frame their affection toward their mothers by expressing gratitude for their mothers' role in transmitting to them the pure blood of their hardy ancestors. Father Henri Guay, using the name Lambert Closse, described this slippage between mother and nation in his 1936 book *La réponse de la race*: "How must we consider a child who does not love its mother?/It is a monster./And he who doesn't love his nation?/A national monster./What is the nation for the French Canadian?/A mother."[40] This close association between nation and mother meant that a person's betrayal of his race could be interpreted as a form of matricide.

Before they became mothers, women stood as the objects of desire that served as the means for men to express their love for their race. Joseph Gauvreau put it in this way: "When we love a woman, we love her language. When we love a language, we love a race. When we love a race we perpetuate it."[41] Women had come to dominate the narrative of French Canadian survival in their role as mothers to such an extent that there sometimes appeared to be little room left for men. The cultural critic Elspeth Probyn has observed that French Canadian culture had "given an account of the spatial configurations of early Québécois nationhood that places men off cutting wood or working in the north. We are accustomed to a telling of the past wherein men just were not very important – to women or to the national project. It is a strangely empty space of the past, peopled by women and priests."[42]

Although women were venerated for their role in reproducing the race, they did not possess any actual power in society. The historian Ruth Roach Pierson has suggested that there often exists an "inverse relationship between the prominence of female figures in the allegorizations of nation and the degree of access granted women to the political apparatus of the state."[43] A number of women understood that whatever power they were said to possess was illusory and warned that the continued veneration of motherhood could only delay their eventual access to formal power. The journalist and activist Idola Saint-Jean, for one, was intent upon translating women's symbolic influence as mothers into real political and legal power. Representing a new generation of feminists who were no longer content to acquiesce to the role of submissive mothers, Saint-Jean used her column in the *Montreal Herald* to attack the province's treatment of women. In one column she wondered how women were to be expected to raise children who could serve the interests of the nation and the race if "the wise counsels of the mother are discounted by the child, owing to the fact that she is placed in the same position as imbeciles and interdicted persons in the eyes of the law."[44]

This type of talk worried men like Henri Bourassa, who could not understand how women could be anything but content with their assigned roles in society. Women already possessed considerable power, Bourassa contended, pointing out that their biological destiny had provided them with enormous social and political influence. Bourassa reminded women that they had provided the nation with 3 million people through their "generous" acts of regeneration. Moreover, Bourassa argued, "the principal function of a woman is – regardless of what the suffragettes say or do – motherhood." It was this role that made women, in Bourassa's mind, "the equal to man ... and even his superior."[45] Because he was convinced that women possessed even more power than men, Bourassa was quick to dismiss any calls for reform as the misguided work of women who had fallen under the spell of Anglo-Saxon and Protestant feminist propaganda.[46] He pointed out that "French Canadian women understand that they have little to gain and much to lose" if they followed such a feminist path.[47] Thus he warned women that feminism "would bring about the destruction of the family, lead to social disorder, and lead to the degradation of women themselves."[48]

Men had venerated women because they depended on women's bodies, and the so-called "revenge of the cradle," for their own ability to compete in the political and economic realms.[49] Women's supposed rejection of motherhood represented a troubling development for men, who had pinned their hopes for survival on women's reproductive lives. Although men controlled the legal and political machinery of the province, and constantly emphasized the importance of a father's authority in the household, they now concluded that women possessed too much power over the physical survival of the race.[50] If women had been regarded as central to the survival of the race, it was understood that they could easily become a destructive force as well. Women were, as Fadette reminded her readers, "all-powerful" when it came to the question of national survival.[51] The literary critic Patricia Smart has identified this fear of women's power as a recurring theme in French Canadian literature, where "maternal love almost inevitably turns into its opposite, the mother being driven by the force of circumstances towards the temptation of being the destroyer as well as giver of life."[52] At the same time, men had come to regard their dependence on women's bodies as a serious threat to their authority as well as an obstacle to the survival of the community.[53]

This dilemma can be detected in Harry Bernard's novel *L'Homme tombé* (1924), one of the most celebrated and popular works of fiction of the era. Bernard, who edited the weekly *Courrier de Saint-Hyacinthe,* and who would go on to become the founding editor of the influential *L'Action nationale* in 1933, illustrates in this novel the anxieties of a population coming to terms with an industrializing economy and shifting gender roles. In the novel, which won the Prix David, inaugurated the previous year by Provincial Secretary Athanase David to recognize the year's best literary works, Étienne Normand, a cultured French Canadian doctor, falls in love with Alberte Dumont, a woman who works in a factory. But when the dutiful Étienne informs his mother of his intention to marry Alberte, he is disappointed by her reaction. "Why is it," his mother wonders, "that our educated men, those who are the most cultivated, our lawyers and our doctors, our public men ... remain on the whole mediocre?" Offering her own response, she claims it is because "nine times out of ten, they marry women who are beneath them."[54] Étienne ignores his mother's warning, however, and marries Alberte anyway.

Their initial happiness as a married couple quickly evaporates as Étienne realizes that Alberte appears to be more interested in pursuing a life of frivolity and travel than in staying at home to raise children. Since Alberte is frequently away from the home, it falls on Étienne to raise their son on his own. But since he is unaccustomed to this role, he flounders and begins his gradual fall. As Étienne's resentment toward his wife grows, Alberte hints that he should abandon his medical practice in Saint-Hyacinthe so that they can move to Montreal in order to enjoy the pleasures of the big city. Because Étienne has become so weak and unable to resist his wife's demands, his medical practice collapses, and he realizes the truth in his mother's warning that women too often crush men's spirits and weaken the race. He laments that French Canada's long history of struggle and survival has been in vain: in one generation, women such as his wife have destroyed three centuries of hard work. The fight to preserve the race, he concludes, is no longer worth continuing because for every man who fights for survival, there are many more who do not.[55]

Although Étienne is eager to preserve his race, he lacks the strength needed to fight what he realizes is ultimately a losing battle. He begins to feel like a "fallen man" who "had neither the strength nor the courage to stand up."[56] Étienne's great potential has been extinguished by his wife's insatiable desire to have a good time in the city and by her decision to turn her back on her race. By stepping into the public world, and choosing to produce for her husband only one son (a disappointment for Alberte, who hoped for a girl),[57] Alberte fails to perform her duty as a French Canadian woman and mother. In the novel, Alberte comes to represent all that is wrong with French Canada. Étienne's manhood depends on his ability to protect and control his wife and his race. In the end, he can do neither.

If concern about survival and the suspicion that women were no longer up to the job of being good mothers had prompted medical professionals to intervene more directly in the lives of women and to medicalize childbirth and motherhood, there also developed a sense among some people that society needed to move away entirely from the idea that women were so important to racial regeneration and survival. Some men had begun to imagine a world in which they would be freed entirely from their dependence on women's bodies for the community's survival.[58] Lionel Groulx, who had placed an enormous degree of importance on maintaining the purity of French Canadian blood, would come to reframe the issue of survival in a manner that had the effect of appropriating for men the regenerative power of birth by casting them in the traditionally feminine role of life giver. Groulx was willing to concede that a woman might give birth to a child, but he argued that children needed to undergo a "second birth," marking their racial entry into the world.[59] At other times, Groulx eliminated women altogether from the process of racial regeneration, such as when he wrote, "Like the past, like history, the country is our master. We are the sons of our native land, like we are the sons of our race, of our time."[60] He appears to imply that French Canadian boys were the sons of just about everything – except of their mothers. So prevalent had such rhetoric become during these years that François Hertel, a priest and a professor of literature at Jean-de-Brébeuf College in Montreal, felt it necessary to remind his readers, "Before we were the sons of a homeland, we were the sons of a woman."[61]

By appropriating the language of birth, men were undermining the role that heredity was thought to play in the perpetuation of the race. Groulx would further downplay the physical transmission of cultural traits when he observed, "Without a doubt, our first duty is to populate our homes, but populating them will not suffice. We must also raise the children that we produce." He wondered, "What good is it to bring children into the world if we don't arrange to take care of them?"[62] This shift away from blood was a major development in the evolution of racial identity in the province. It allowed men to downplay women's role in the perpetuation of the race, diverting power from women's bodies to the cultural realm, which they controlled.

For some men, the surest means of obtaining this freedom from women was through the colonization of the north, which at this time generally meant the area northwest of Montreal, stretching from the Ottawa Valley to northern Ontario and on toward Winnipeg. The idea of the north had particular resonance for French Canadians, who were worried about the exodus of people to New England in search of work and who chafed under the growing influence of foreign capital within their own province. The north was particularly attractive to some because it seemed to offer French Canadians the opportunity to start over following years of political setbacks.[63] In 1895 Guillaume-Alphonse Nantel, the editor of the newspaper *Le Nord* in Saint-Jérôme and a member of the Legislative Assembly for Terrebonne, described colonization as a form of rebirth and imagined it as an opportunity for men to create a new race of men in the north.[64] The north offered men who had grown weary of the effeminizing influence of the city an opportunity to re-energize their manhood and to do so without relying on women's bodies.[65] Although women would play an important supporting role in the colonization campaigns, and would be expected to produce the next generation of men, it was the rugged north itself that most appealed to these men. The environment, then, not women's biological role, was going to regenerate manhood and, in the process, strengthen the race.[66] Many French Canadians saw the north as an alluring site for racial renewal and viewed colonization as a means to forge a new and virile race of northern men.[67]

Unlike those men on the rest of the continent who saw the West as a site of wilderness that would allow men to immerse themselves in a primitive environment, French Canada's push for the colonization of the north was part of a larger process of modernization in Quebec. The turn to the north had little to do with any desire to rediscover a primitive form of manhood that was thought to have been lost in the modern world. Instead, escaping to the north was part of a larger dream to escape women's influence over the direction of the race by making the environment as important a factor in ensuring the vitality of the race as women. The primary appeal of the north was that it offered French Canadians the opportunity to reassert control over the direction of the race by downgrading women's influence over racial regeneration. In this way, the turn to the north was part of a larger modernization effort in the province. One pamphlet extolling the virtues of northern expansion characterized colonization as an act of an advanced and mature civilization that was ready to reproduce an entirely new society in its own image.[68]

This dream of regeneration in the north and of a masculine world freed from women's influence found its clearest expression in one of the period's most significant novels.[69] In the utopian *Pour la patrie* (1895), Jules-Paul Tardivel, the editor of the influential ultramontane newspaper *La Vérité,* imagines a future where women have been disentangled from the narrative of French Canadian racial survival and where men have been released from their supposed dependence on these women. Set in the year 1945, the novel points to a time when men's allegiance to their national and racial identities has become increasingly incompatible with their loyalty to and love for women.

The novel traces Joseph Lamirande's fight to protect his race and religion in the face of English Canadian efforts to impose a legislative union on French Canada. But Lamirande's effort to defeat the initiative is almost derailed when his wife becomes ill after mistakenly drinking a poisoned drink that had been intended for him. He prays to Saint Joseph for his wife's recovery but is dismayed by the response he receives: "If you insist on the temporal grace you ask for, it will certainly be granted. Your wife will live. But if, on the contrary, you leave everything to the will of God, the sacrifice of your domestic happiness will be repaid by the triumph of your homeland." Lamirande's wife insists that he let her die: "God is promising to save everything if the two of us will sacrifice a few years of happiness ... think what good can be accomplished in return for a few years of a miserable life!" She exults in the thought that "it is not often that a woman can save her country by dying."[70]

Lamirande faces a similar dilemma when Marie, his only daughter, also becomes ill and dies. Soon after Marie dies, however, she reappears to her father. Her apparent return to life is fortuitous because in doing so she makes a convert of her father's friend, who witnesses the event. This friend just happens to hold the vote needed to defeat the proposed constitution that Lamirande feels will spell the end of French Canada. Lamirande thanks God for "the blessing You have bestowed upon us. In return for one small sacrifice, You have granted the conversion of my friend, and, through his conversion, assured the future of our beloved country. In fact, to a faithful soul, the sacrifice is a slight one."[71]

In the novel Lamirande loses both his wife and his daughter, but their deaths become necessary for the survival of French Canada. In the case of his wife, who is sacrificed for the greater good of the community, a woman has become a potential obstacle to racial survival and thus has to be sacrificed. She has become expendable. Both mother and daughter save the race by dying, yet neither receives much recognition for her sacrifice. Instead, Lamirande's friend, the journalist Paul Leverdier, becomes the president of a new country called New France. Tardivel recentres men as heads of and saviours of the race and removes women from the narrative altogether. When given the choice between one's wife and one's race, moreover, a man is expected to follow his one and only true love. Lamirande thus performs his manly duty to his race by letting his wife die. In this way, Tardivel's novel served as the literary fulfilment of men's fantasy to forge a nation without women's help.

If this vision of displacing women in the racial narrative was a literary fantasy in the nineteenth century, it appeared much more within reach in the 1920s and 1930s as attitudes about racial identity evolved in ways that made it more difficult for French Canadians to claim that they constituted a distinct biological race. By the interwar years, a growing number of anthropologists were beginning to challenge widely held assumptions about race by rejecting the commonly held view that a person's character, culture, or identity was in any way determined by one's biological inheritance.[72] By the 1930s Otto Klineberg, a psychologist born in Quebec City and raised in Montreal, was at the forefront of the effort to disentangle culture and race. In his book *Race Differences* (1935), Klineberg traced the evolution of the word "race" and concluded, "Whatever else it includes, it must at least refer to certain physical characteristics." He was adamant that it remain separate from culture, and he defined race as "a large group of men possessing in common certain physical characteristics which are determined by heredity" and must be "independent of environmental influence."[73]

The drift away from a biological definition of "race" accelerated during the interwar years as a growing number of French Canadian intellectuals spoke out against any form of national identity based on blood. The influential priest and teacher François Hertel, for example, rejected any form of national identity that was tied to racism.[74] And in the fall of 1936, the small but influential literary and political journal *La Relève* denounced the link between blood and national identity. Influenced by French personalism and concerned about the rise of extreme ideologies in Europe, it rejected the blood basis of national identity and privileged, instead, the individual's role in shaping his own identity.[75] European politics also had a profound impact on a young André Laurendeau. After spending some time in France, he returned home to Montreal and turned away from the nationalism steeped in blood that he had embraced as a youth. In an article for *L'Action nationale*, which he had taken over as editor from his father in 1936, he attacked the connection between blood and racial identity:

"According to modern ethnology there is no longer any pure race in this world, whether Saxon, Slavic, or Germanic." He then declared, "we oppose any superiority based on blood."[76]

The retreat from a biological understanding of race meant that the quality of French Canadian children became much more important than how many of them there were. Some members of the clergy even stepped back from their earlier insistence that large families were necessary for French Canadian survival, becoming more tolerant of so-called natural methods of birth control.[77] The church was very much in step on this issue with the medical community, which had also been downplaying the biological function that women were thought to have played in the perpetuation of the race. In 1940, for example, Dr. Albert Guilbault reminded parents to move beyond simply ensuring the physical health of the child and to pursue what he called an "an educative procreation."[78] And Dr. Hector Palardy purported to offer scientific proof of women's irrelevance in racial formation by showing that women played no decisive role during sexual intercourse or in the biological transmission of physical characteristics. He wrote, "We once believed, and some still incorrectly believe, that women played an active role in regeneration." But, according to Palardy, a woman was a mere carrier of the race: "The male has, in regeneration, the essential role." The female, Palardy continued, "is a mere receptacle."[79] This attitude was summed up in a 1931 editorial in the Quebec City daily *Le Soleil,* which called for greater protections for women because they were responsible for providing "a man to the homeland."[80] Women, it appears, had become mere carriers of their husbands' sons.[81]

Groulx could not ignore this trend, nor could he dismiss the conclusions of the scientific community, so he retreated from some of his earlier claims that French Canadians constituted a distinct biological race. In the revised second edition of his *La naissance d'une race* (1930), he downplayed the physiological distinctiveness of French Canadians that he had emphasized in the first edition of that work. In the new edition, he noted that some people had taken issue with his use of the word "race" in his works. He claimed that he had never presented French Canadians as a biologically distinct race. To do so, he said, would be "improper and pretentious." He addressed those critics who had taken him to task for his use of the word "race": "I never meant to suggest that French Canadians constituted a race in an anthropological sense."[82]

Groulx's evolving views about race were evident in his bestselling novel *L'Appel de la race* (1922).[83] Although this novel is usually approached as a political work warning of the dangers of a "mixed marriage" between an English Canadian woman and a French Canadian man,[84] it also provides a revealing look at the difficult transition from a racial identity steeped in biology to one that is to be determined largely by cultural and national factors. It explores one man's struggle to regain control over his racial identity, as well as over his children's racial identities, which he fears he has abandoned to his wife.

The novel follows Jules de Lantagnac, a successful French Canadian lawyer, as he embarks upon a journey of cultural rediscovery that ultimately forces him to choose between his wife and his race. As a graduate of McGill University with a respectable English Canadian wife, Maud Fletcher, who converted to Catholicism when she married him, Jules has assimilated into the Anglo-Saxon world in the nation's capital. In spite of his social and professional successes, however, Jules grows increasingly restless and comes to regret that he turned his back on his French Canadian heritage. So at the age of forty-three, he undertakes to sharpen his rusty French and seeks to reconnect with his culture.

The story takes place in the years following the passage of Regulation 17 in Ontario, which curtailed the rights of French Canadian children to be educated in their own language. This attack on the rights of Franco-Ontarians spurs Jules into action. He contests, against Maud's wishes, and wins a by-election on the platform of minority language rights. Jules' growing interest in his own heritage and his entry into the political world locks him in a power struggle with his wife. But he dismisses Maud's concerns about his growing militancy and then comes to resent the influence she has on their four children.

The more that Jules becomes reacquainted with his French Canadian heritage, the more alarmed he becomes about his children's "mixed blood." At one point, he says, "My sons and daughters have, through their mother, English blood in their veins; but from me they have received the venerable blood of the Lantagnacs."[85] This race mixing has produced physical differences between his children:

> The strange thing was that this mental dualism showed itself particularly in William and Nellie, the two in whom the well characterized type of the Fletcher heritage stood out as clearly dominant. Wolfred and Virginia, on the other hand, revealed almost exclusively features peculiar to the French: the fine tanned features of the Lantagnacs and the well-balanced physical conformation, whereas the elder girl and the younger boy, both of whom were fair of hair and complexion, rather slender and a bit lanky, had a striking resemblance to their mother.[86]

Wolfred remains inscrutable throughout much of the novel, but his affinity for his French Canadian heritage is never in much doubt. His ultimate embrace of his father's race and cultural heritage comes as little surprise to the reader because he has been described throughout the novel as a "tall young man with dark, energetic features." Wolfred's admirable physical and mental traits stand in sharp contrast to William's "obstinate [and] testy" personality, which explains why he rejects his father's culture. Reflecting on the loss of William, Jules laments, "As the younger boy grew older, Saxon characteristics became sharper in the face and the whole body of this lanky adolescent. The line of the brow became more taut, the pout of the lips more arrogant; he would generally amble along, his neck pulled back, his fists half closed, with the gait of a rugby player."[87]

As much as Jules resents Maud for turning his children into Anglo-Saxons, he acknowledges that he is partly to blame. He concedes, "I relinquished to her the education of my children; she alone chose a college for my sons, a convent for my daughters." But he also feels that Maud went further and "made it her purpose to appropriate more fully what I abandoned to her."[88] When he learns of William's decision to attend the English-language Loyola College rather than the French-language University of Ottawa, he blames Maud and suspects that there might be "a conspiracy between mother and son." As for Nellie, his other "Anglo-Saxon" child, he laments that she is "a terribly stubborn child whom her mother has completely taken control of, what can one expect of her?"[89]

Jules blames his wife so completely for the loss of at least two of his children that he resolves that he has little choice but to remove them from her influence. At the same time, he is unsure of his own ability to regain control of his family's racial destiny. He wonders, "Shall I manage to free myself entirely? If you only knew how weak I feel as I face the return to my old milieu, inwardly a different person. And then, between my children and me there is someone ... Alas, I know only too well that in taking them away from their English upbringing, I shall be taking them away from their mother." But Jules concludes that to be "the true man, the unified man," he has to leave his wife and fight to protect his race. He thus faces "the moment of maturity when he resolves to take possession of his full strength, when he seeks to unify his thoughts and his moral being." Jules confronts Maud in their bedroom, "the setting of their most complete intimacy" and the very place where he has feared "he would be dangerously weak."[90] In choosing the bedroom, Jules attempts to restage the moment of his children's conception. He hopes to wrest control of his children from his wife in the very room where years before he abdicated authority to her, a room that he has come to associate with his weakness and failure as a man.

This confrontation with Maud precipitates a series of events that ultimately permit Jules to regain full control over his racial destiny. Maud announces that she is leaving him and that she intends to take William and Nellie, their two

"Anglo-Saxon children," with her. At this point, Wolfred, the long-wavering son, announces his loyalty to his father. He has undergone a type of conversion and has been reborn into his father's race by immersing himself in French Canadian history. It was on a pilgrimage to the Long-Sault, the site of Dollard des Ormeaux's heroic last stand, that everything became clear for him. As he contemplated French Canada's heroic past, he says, "I stretched out my arm towards the monument of the hero. There, I tell you, yes, there, I swore it aloud; I shall be on my father's side, French like him and my ancestors, wholly and enthusiastically French!" Wolfred then declares that the "Anglo-Saxon mirage was almost at an end for me." As if to prove his rebirth as a French Canadian man and his commitment to perpetuate the race, he announces to his father that he has decided to break off his engagement to an Anglo-Saxon woman: "Since yesterday, my fiancée is none other than yours."[91] Jules, too, realizes that Maud's departure will leave him "with one fiancée, perhaps: the cause to which I shall henceforth devote my life."[92] The transfer of racial power from the woman to the man in the novel is completed when Virginia, the only daughter who has remained loyal to her father throughout her life, declares, "children should belong to the same ethnic group and speak the same language as their father."[93] The racial connection between a mother and her children has thus been severed.

In the end, Jules' mistake was not simply that he married an English Canadian woman. The consequences of this decision, it turns out, are reversible because of the realization that his children's racial identities depend less on their biological inheritance and more on how they choose to live. Rather, Jules' error was to relinquish to his wife his parental duty to teach his children about their racial heritage. It turns out that Groulx was less interested in condemning mixed marriages (although he did this, too) than in demonstrating that a people's biological inheritance alone did not determine their racial identity. The novel was thus an appeal for men to take on a larger role in the lives of their children and an effort to marginalize women in the process of racial formation.

French Canadian nationalist leaders were ready to move away from a racial identity defined by a person's biological inheritance because such a move permitted them to exercise greater control over the direction of the race. As long as race had been linked in the public imagination to blood and biology, women could be said to play an important role in determining the fate of the French Canadian people through their reproductive capabilities. As the birthrate fell and a growing number of women were said to be sidestepping their assigned role as mothers, however, these men worried that they could no longer depend on women's willingness to produce enough children to maintain their own economic and political position. But if blood could no longer be said to form the basis of a distinct French Canadian identity, men could limit women's influence by diminishing the importance of the one area over which men had little control: reproduction. By severing the link between racial identity and biology, men regained control over their racial destinies and in the process displaced women in the narrative of French Canadian survival.

The evolving meaning of the word "race" may have deflated French Canadians' conceit about their biological distinctiveness and even superiority, but it also permitted men to assert greater control over a racial identity that they feared they had abandoned to women. French Canadian leaders seized upon the fluctuating meanings of the word "race" during the interwar years to recast birth as a passive act and in the process appropriated from women the reproductive role that they longed for. Once racial identity was released from its biological moorings, men could arbitrate racial belonging in the public arena and make it a central part of a masculine identity freed from women's influence. Any influence that women were thought to have enjoyed when blood had been an important part of French Canadian identity faded with this new definition of "race."

4
War and Manhood

THE CONCERNS ABOUT a supposed racial degeneration during the late nineteenth century prompted a growing number of English-speaking Canadians to begin to think about ways of building closer political, economic, and cultural ties with Britain. Such ties were to be based on a presumed shared sense of Anglo-Saxon racial identity that would also serve to shore up manhood. For many English-speaking Canadians, a larger role for Canada in the British Empire offered an opportunity to share in the civilizing process in which England was engaged and to participate in an increasingly martial culture that would permit them to showcase their manhood. Imperialism would thus produce a much more aggressive form of manhood that encouraged young men to prove themselves on the battlefield fighting in imperial wars. As many English Canadians, and especially those living in Ontario, came to measure manhood through martial displays and by one's loyalty to the British Empire, French Canadians who resisted a greater role for Canada within the empire, as well as any imperial wars that would arise from this enhanced role, inevitably found themselves accused of cowardice and weakness – that is, unmanliness.

But if many English Canadians tended to view the South African War and then the Great War – the two major military conflicts during this period – as opportunities to exhibit their manhood, many French Canadians came to view these wars as challenges to the type of manhood that they were constructing at home. French Canadian leaders who opposed these wars very often characterized their opposition to war as evidence of their own superior manhood, describing English Canadian support for these wars as unmanly because it rested on an irrational and emotional – that is, feminine – attachment to the empire. In the end, French Canadian leaders deflected accusations of cowardice by invoking an alternate model of manhood that highlighted a desire to abstain from military conflict as evidence of a superior type of manhood. Canada's participation in these wars also accelerated efforts to bind manhood more closely to French Canadian national identity.

IN OCTOBER 1899 Joseph Chamberlain, the British colonial secretary, announced his intention to send troops to South Africa to support British settlers there who had been deprived of their political rights in the South African Republic. These settlers had arrived in the region following the discovery of gold there some years earlier, a situation that produced considerable resentment among the Boers, who were descendants of Dutch settlers and struggling to maintain their independence from Britain. Fearing that they would become overwhelmed by this influx of outsiders, the Boers limited British rights, including the right to vote, in an effort to preserve their political control of the territory. This affront to the British sense of liberty, coupled with Britain's growing economic interests in the region, prompted Chamberlain to support the British settlers in their claims for political rights. Chamberlain also used this crisis as an opportunity to promote greater imperial integration by requesting support from the dominions, including Canada.

At first, Prime Minister Sir Wilfrid Laurier did not feel that the conflict had much to do with Canada. Perhaps he thought that the Boer War might play out like the Sudan incident had in 1885, when Britain had requested Canadian support for its Egyptian expedition only to have Prime Minister Sir John A. Macdonald refuse to "pay for the incoherence of Gladstone's foreign policy."[1] But Laurier, Canada's first French Canadian prime minister, was much more vulnerable than Macdonald had been to attacks from English-speaking Protestants who might question his loyalty to the Crown. It would matter little to those who favoured Canadian participation in this war that Laurier was a great admirer of the English parliamentary system and a firm believer in maintaining Canada's British ties.

Much had changed in Canada since Macdonald uttered those words. Imperial sentiment had grown in English-speaking Canada in the last two decades of the century. At the same time, Britain was signalling a greater interest in pursuing closer ties with the dominions as part of its desire to create greater imperial unity. This attitude marked a shift for British authorities. During the middle decades of the nineteenth century, Britain became less interested in its colonial possessions as it pursued a policy of free trade. British disengagement from Canada had contributed to the push in 1867 for Confederation, by which Canadian leaders sought to produce their own economic space in North America to make up for the loss of the protected British market. Although it would be wrong to suggest that men like Macdonald were seeking to create a new nationality in Canada, they were pursuing an increasingly independent political path that was in part necessitated by England's shifting economic priorities. By the closing decades of the century, however, and especially with the arrival of Joseph Chamberlain in the Colonial Office in 1895, British officials displayed a renewed interest in empire as part of an effort to expand their economic and political influence in the world.

Chamberlain's request for support in South Africa came at the very moment when the prospect of a more integrated empire was capturing the imaginations of many English Canadians. For those Canadians who welcomed this renewed attention from England, the strengthening of the imperial connection would serve both to preserve Canada's independence from the United States and to enlarge the country's international influence by positioning Canada as an important actor within the empire.[2] The war would also, not incidentally, provide English Canadians with the opportunity to test their manhood. It broke out, of course, during a period of heightened anxiety about manhood arising from the industrial transformation of the country.[3] Influential observers like G. Stanley Hall and George Beard in the United States had suggested that industrial life may have brought about great advances, but it had ultimately estranged men from their more primitive instincts and thrust them into the effeminizing grip of modern civilization. Pointing to Victorian cultural expectations of male behaviour that stressed self-restraint and emotional reserve as a particular threat to proper manhood, many critics suggested that boys should be encouraged to act out their supposedly more natural primitive instincts during their adolescent years so that they could avoid slipping into a state of "overcivilization" later in life. Parents and teachers were thus encouraged to nurture boys' rough instincts by allowing them to fight and to take part in competitive activities.[4] Adolescents should be encouraged to explore their emotional (i.e., instinctual) side, develop their physical courage, and experience a more primitive existence in nature before they moved on to respectable adulthood.

For some people, the physical courage and roughness that men like Hall promoted could be nurtured most effectively on the sporting field. It was said that competitive sports would rejuvenate the body, encourage male camaraderie, and serve as an antidote to a seemingly feminized world.[5] Others believed that boys could best explore what was described as their savage personalities through outdoor activities and by reading books about nature. The naturalist Ernest Thompson Seton subscribed to Hall's theories of adolescence, writing that "the boy from ten to sixteen years is ontogenetically and essentially a savage."[6] With such works as *Wild Animals I Have Known* (1898) and *Two Little Savages* (1903), which chronicled the adventures of two boys who "played" Indian, Seton inspired a generation of boys to reconnect with their supposedly natural environment by embracing the outdoors.[7] For still others, manhood could be expressed most effectively by turning to militarism. According to the historian Carman Miller, the Montreal militia, "with its emphasis on competitive, combative activities," provided men with "a clear affirmation of manliness."[8] Another historian, Carl Berger, describing the appeal of military activities, observed that "just as warfare was seen as a rather strenuous sport and an expression of self-assertiveness and fitness, so too the martial spirit appeared to be synonymous with a masterful and upright manhood, order and stability, a necessary aspect of vital national feeling, and an antidote to the follies of the age."[9] As war came to be seen as an extension of the playing field, military conflict became the ultimate expression of one's manhood.[10] "To be a man," the historian Mark Moss has pointed out, "meant to engage in action and competition and to strive for physical prowess." By the late nineteenth century, many English Canadians came to regard war as the "definitive test of manhood."[11]

French Canadians were just as worried as English Canadians about the effects of modern industrial society on traditional gender relations and male identity. They had also shown their readiness to take up arms when the cause appeared just. In 1868, for example, many French Canadians responded to Bishop Ignace Bourget's call for volunteers to travel overseas to defend Rome from Italian troops fighting for peninsular unification. Over the next two years, just over 500 French Canadian Zouaves volunteered to defend Rome.[12] And French Canadian boys also learned about the exploits of such military heroes as Dollard des Ormeaux and read books about nature and wild animals, like Philippe Aubert de Gaspé's *Le chercheur de trésor* (1837), Patrice Lacombe's *La terre paternelle* (1846), and Joseph-Charles Taché's *Forestiers et voyageurs* (1863).[13] Although these books had been intended for an adult audience – and it would not be until 1920 and the appearance of the children's magazine *L'Oiseau bleu* that children's literature truly appeared in French Canada – they were distributed to the province's schools for children to read.

Even so, French Canadian boys had not been, as one observer at the time noted, reading books by the likes of Rudyard Kipling, whose tales of imperial adventure influenced a generation of English Canadian boys.[14] Nor had they been taught to embrace the virtues of British imperialism in the same way that English Canadian boys had been. And it was this imperialism, especially the connection between manhood and imperialism, which they suggested had a "distinctly racial" character, that made some French Canadians uncomfortable.[15] When English Canadian boys learned of the superiority of Anglo-Saxon civilization in school, for example, and participated in organized sports that instilled in them the belief that their own healthy and virile bodies represented the pinnacle of civilized manhood, French Canadians understood that they were not included. According to many French Canadians, manhood could not be strengthened with emotional appeals to imperial unity or by unleashing passions on the sports field. Rather, the emotions and "savagery" that men like G. Stanley Hall promoted for adolescents were the surest means of undermining a truly confident manhood based on self-restraint and order.

These long simmering differences burst out into the open with the outbreak of the South African War. To many English Canadians, the war represented a splendid opportunity to put their manhood to the test by showing that they were ready to move from the playing field to the battlefield. French Canadians, in contrast, generally did not view the war as a noble or manly venture. They tended to oppose Canadian participation in the war and even to sympathize with the Boers as a kindred people suffering under the yoke of British imperialism.[16] As English Canadians promoted a militarized and imperial version of manhood and French Canadians defended one based on the land and Canadian autonomy within the empire, the Boer War became a contest to determine which side represented a more authentic version of Canadian manhood. Caught in the middle of this increasingly contentious argument was Sir Wilfrid Laurier.

Laurier's initial reaction to the war was not well received in many of the country's English-language newspapers. The conservative *Montreal Gazette* expressed dismay at Laurier's suggestion that he could do very little to support Britain in the war because his hands were tied by the militia law forbidding the dispatch of troops for overseas service. The *Gazette* responded that "it is not the law that is lacking, it is the heart."[17] The paper worried, moreover, that Laurier's hesitation to act had meant that Canada had "missed her chance" to help the mother country and to shine on the world stage.[18]

Acknowledging that he had underestimated the imperial sentiment in many parts of English-speaking Canada, Laurier was forced to retreat from his initial refusal to contribute to the war effort.[19] Laurier agreed to send a contingent of 1,150 volunteers in October 1899, to be followed by a second contingent the following January.[20] Describing his decision as an honourable compromise that reflected the will of the people,[21] he proceeded to construct the war as an opportunity to deliver liberty and civilization to Africa and as a test of Canadian honour and manhood.[22] In March he told the House of Commons, "Today there are men in South Africa representing the two branches of the Canadian family, fighting side by side for the honor of Canada."[23]

This compromise, of course, pleased nobody and precipitated a crisis within his government. The Catholic Church in Quebec, Montreal mayor Raymond Préfontaine, and some of the province's major dailies like Quebec City's *Le Soleil*, a Liberal Party organ, and Montreal's *La Presse* supported Laurier's decision. But many others argued that the prime minister and his English Canadian supporters were displaying anything but honour in their support for what they called an imperial war. Henri Bourassa, the rising Liberal star and member of Parliament for Labelle, resigned from the party in protest to sit as an independent. In a letter to Laurier, Bourassa expressed his anger and disappointment with his leader's decision. "I will always regret what I consider to be an act of feebleness on your part," he wrote, accusing the prime minister of weakness and of capitulating to English Canadian pressure.[24]

Bourassa framed the war as the product of Anglo-Saxon values that were steeped in a misguided ideal of manhood. In a speech in Montreal at the start of the war, he observed,

> In British youths, brutal instincts are being developed by the invasion of sportic [*sic*] games. There is, now-a-days, in the higher ranks of English society a large class of young men who have become masters in such acts as managing a stud, organising a stable, supervising a dog-kennel. Thirsting as they are for glorious adventures, these hardy young men are very ill-prepared to shine in the councils of the nation. From the ascendancy which this class of athletes are daily gaining, the debasement of the moral and intellectual standards of the British Parliament, and the growing power of fiery appeals to a spirit of pride and aggressiveness, are easily accounted for.[25]

He also noted that "the lust of abnormal expansion and Imperial pride have ever been the marked features of all nations on the verge of decadence."[26] And in the House of Commons, he complained that the British Empire had become bloated with complacency and arrogance, which reminded him of the "decadence of the Roman Empire."[27]

Like many other French Canadians, Bourassa was concerned that Canadian participation in the war threatened to disrupt the country's economic prosperity as well as its political stability. He predicted, "If before we are fully grown up, we put on our shoulders the yoke of militarism, which is proving too heavy for nations enjoying the plenitude of their manhood, we put a stop to our progress."[28] Many other French Canadians framed the war as a humiliating reminder of Canada's weakness and dependence within the empire. The anti-clerical newspaper *Les Débats* described Canada's participation in the war as "emasculating" and "humiliating." It also took aim at those newspapers that supported the war, suggesting that they were merely "preaching servility under the guise of loyalty, accepting events with a sickening passivity."[29] It could not understand Canadian imperialism and wondered, "We are at the age of manhood; why do we wish to remain children?"[30] In a plea for greater Canadian autonomy within the empire, it argued, "The colonial state is but a transitional one ... It represents a state of childhood that must culminate with the attainment of full manhood."[31]

The war also appeared to many people as an unmanly act of bullying on the part of the British. Jules-Paul Tardivel's ultramontane newspaper *La Vérité*, for example, pointed out, "In the name of an imbecilic loyalism, we are calling on Canadians to eviscerate Boer women and children under cries of Long Live the Queen! Long Live Freedom!"[32] And Montreal's *Le monde canadien,* which provided extensive coverage of the war, sympathized with the Boers: "We see a small people of 200,000 men defending their land and their independence against an empire of three or four hundred thousand subjects."[33] Many French Canadians wondered how a powerful empire could, in good conscience, attempt to crush a much smaller people.[34] Some newspapers wondered what had happened to the traditional British sense of "fair play."[35]

At the same time, many French Canadians were concerned that they were being asked to support an imperial adventure designed to crush a small nationality that they had come to respect and with whom they identified. *La Vérité* praised the Boers for their patriotism and claimed that "love of freedom was so strong that they would never submit to the English yoke." It predicted that the Boers "would prefer to lose their lives than to lose their national independence."[36] Describing the Boers as a "peaceful people, hard-working and honest," it praised them for having created a society that operated "along patriarchal lines."[37] The editors at *Les Débats,* too, sympathized with the Boers. Although its circulation was limited to a nationalist elite, the paper provides insight into nationalist opposition to imperialism. In declaring its sympathy for the Boers, as one might sympathize with the weak against the strong, it praised their "brave warriors" for resisting what it called the "brutal invasion" by the British.[38] The newspaper *Le monde canadien* agreed, declaring its support for French Canadians' "Boer brothers."[39]

In addition to concern about Canada's subservient place within the empire and doubts about the fairness of such an uneven fight, French Canadians wondered how the war would affect manhood at home. Henri Bourassa warned that the economic demands of war would compromise a man's ability to support his family and would thus undermine his honour as the head of his household. He also argued that the war would drain the country of able-bodied men and plunge it into economic and social instability. Speaking in the House of Commons, Bourassa warned that those men who volunteered to fight in South Africa were not simply risking their own lives but also undermining the families that they left behind, especially if their death were to deprive their family of the economic means to survive.[40] In Bourassa's mind, British imperialism was little more than "a lust for land-grabbing and military dominion," which involved "military contributions from the colonies to Great Britain, in men and treasure, but mainly in men."[41]

French Canadian nationalists directed some of their harshest words at those French Canadians who volunteered for military service overseas. *Les Débats* believed that English Canadians were free to go and fight in South Africa, saying, "we will not stand in their way if they wish to go off to be beaten up in Africa." But, the paper went on, "we will not offer our best wishes to those French Canadians who have enrolled to fight because we consider their participation in the war to be a national disgrace."[42] It added, "French Canadians have no kind words to offer to those who have abandoned Canada to go off to play Chamberlain's games."[43] And *La Vérité* bristled at the sight of soldiers returning to a heroes' welcome in November 1900 because it felt that Canadian soldiers had taken part in the "atrocities" committed by the British in Africa.[44]

French Canadian opposition to the war left them vulnerable to attacks on their loyalty and honour. But French Canadians resented attempts to measure loyalty according one's support for imperialism. According to *Les Débats*, the idea of loyalty itself had lost much of its meaning and appeal since it had come to be seen as "servility" to Britain.[45] It then challenged the historian Benjamin Sulte's insinuation that French Canadians were somehow being disloyal to the Crown by attacking *his* manhood: "The province of Quebec has remained as loyal to the Crown as Mr. Sulte, but has done so in a more manly fashion."[46] And it ridiculed the mayor of Montreal, Raymond Préfontaine, for his support of the war by mocking his effeminate fashion sense, describing him at one point as "magnificent in his large hat and ermine-lined cape."[47] These French Canadian critics, in the end, were convinced that their opposition to war demonstrated their own superior manhood. *Les Débats*, which pointed out that the war was being waged by a country that had produced the likes of Oscar Wilde,[48] noted that French Canadians opposed Canadian participation in the war less because they were afraid to fight and more because they were disgusted by the "stupid zeal" with which some English Canadians supported the war. It then declared that it was "as men, and especially as British subjects," that it opposed sending Canadian soldiers off to a foreign land to be "massacred."[49]

Emotions came to a head on March 1, 1900, when a group of McGill University students took to the streets of Montreal to celebrate British victories at Paardeberg and Ladysmith. The students marched toward the Montreal offices of *La Patrie* and the Montreal campus of Laval University to protest what they said was these institutions' insufficient enthusiasm for the war. The march quickly degenerated into a riot as the McGill students attempted to raise the Union Jack above the offices of the newspaper.[50] Many English-speaking Canadians, including those at the *Montreal Star* who supplied the students with free beer, either praised the riot as an act of loyalty and patriotism or downplayed its importance, as the member of Parliament for North Bruce did when he declared the riot to be nothing more than some college boys "having fun."[51] Sensing that the episode would further inflame the already volatile situation, Laurier downplayed the significance of the riot itself by describing it in the House of Commons as a "boyish prank" and by lamenting that "boys will be boys." He directed his anger at the *Montreal Star*, however, for sensationalizing the whole affair. "We can always forgive boys for this sort of thing," he said, "but when men who ought to be respectable, instead of putting down, with a firm, but gentle hand, such proceedings, rather characterized them as something to be commended, as a lesson in loyalty ... there was occasion to be alarmed."[52]

The riot confirmed in the minds of many French Canadians their suspicions that English Canadian support for the war had been guided by irrational emotions rather than by reason. The minister of public works, Israël Tarte, whose sons published *La Patrie*, stood up in the House of Commons to denounce the riot as an act of aggression "against civilization."[53] The French-language press also used the riot to prove the dangers of imperialism and to chide English Canadians for their lack of manhood. *Le monde canadien*, for example, criticized the McGill students because "instead of proving their loyalty to the British flag by going off to fight alongside those men who have fallen in Africa," they chose to provoke a riot from the safety of home.[54] In other words, they chose to be cowards and bullies. Those McGill students offered these French Canadians all the evidence they needed to reaffirm their suspicions about imperialism and proved to them that English Canadians were lacking in self-restraint. Just a few months earlier, Bourassa had complained to the prime minister, "Mr. Laurier, when do you take account of opinion in the province of Quebec?" In response, the nation's leader told him, "My dear Henri, the province of Quebec does not have opinions, it has only sentiments."[55] Following the Montreal riot, it appeared that it was English Canadians who were being guided by their sentiments.

In the end, the war drove English and French Canadians further apart, revealing deep tensions that reflected conflicting ideas about nationality as well as manhood. Both sides framed their position using gendered language, each hailing its own stance as evidence of its superior manhood. The war made Henri Bourassa famous and persuaded him to continue his pursuit of Canadian autonomy within the empire. In early 1903 a number of people who had been associated with *Les Débats* and who were inspired by Bourassa's vision founded the Ligue nationaliste to push for greater Canadian autonomy within the empire. English Canadians also dug in to defend their position. The war, it turned out, only increased their imperialist fervour because it revealed that Anglo-Saxon men were not as prepared for war as many people might have anticipated. The unexpected military setbacks only reinforced suspicions that the nation's men had grown soft and convinced people that more needed to be done to strengthen the male body and to improve men's military preparedness.

The British campaign to renew manhood and to ensure that boys were better prepared to answer future calls to defend imperial values would be led by Robert Baden-Powell. Baden-Powell, a British hero of the South African War, was determined to train boys to become better citizens and better men. His book *Scouting for Boys* (1908), which would become the basis for the Boy Scout Movement, reflected late-nineteenth- and early-twentieth-century fears of British decline and the absence of national efficiency.[56] Baden-Powell denied that his movement was a training ground for war, but the uniforms, discipline, and physical training it offered inevitably aroused such suspicions. Ernest Thompson Seton, for example, grew disillusioned with the Boy Scouts because of what he claimed was the movement's emphasis on militarism. But many English Canadians embraced the Boy Scouts, seeing in the movement a useful training ground for proper manhood. French Canadians, for their part, were at first suspicious of the Boy Scouts, viewing the movement as a militaristic and Protestant instrument to promote imperialism.[57] Not much would change, then, in the years following the end of the South African War as both sides consolidated their prewar views of manhood.

When war broke out in Europe in August 1914, many English Canadians once again cheered. Many French Canadians, in contrast, were caught off guard and were not entirely sure how to react. Henri Bourassa, for one, was in Europe at the time and thus could not publish a position in *Le Devoir* until the following week. And when he did return, he appeared to endorse the war. Indeed, over the next few months, he maintained that Canada had "a vital interest in the preservation of France and Britain ... It is therefore the national duty of Canada to contribute in the measure of her resources and by such means of action as she may command."[58]

Many French Canadians understood that, unlike the South African War, this war was not a small imperial skirmish. Criticism of the war was at first muted, and nationalists found themselves in a difficult position because a case could be made, and was made, that Britain and now France were directly threatened, making Canada more vulnerable. Many French Canadians even supported the war, calling on the province's young men to enlist. Lieutenant-Colonel L.G. Desjardins, for example, a former member of Parliament and a member of Quebec's Legislative Assembly, reminded young French Canadian men of their heroic French forebears who had settled Canada, and he asked them to "rally around the English and French flags, united in a heroic effort to save civilization from the peril that threatens it." He went on, "thousands have preceded you on the battle fields in France, where they have found glory. Follow their noble example by going off to replace those who have fallen in the fields of honour."[59] Many French Canadians answered these calls and would look back on their service in the war with pride. One volunteer, writing after he returned from the front, suggested that one day the war would be seen as "the most beautiful page in the history of the French Canadian race." He noted, "Our ancestors fought for themselves, for their country, their belongings. Our boys fought for an idea, for peace in the civilized world, for the triumph of justice."[60]

French Canadian loyalty to France also turned out to be greater than many people had anticipated. French Canadians had had little contact with France since the Conquest, and the church had never forgiven the French for their Revolution. But some people, like Arthur Lapointe of the 22nd Battalion, believed that it was their duty to pay a "debt of gratitude to Ancient France." The war, Lapointe would later write, allowed him to fulfil his boyhood dream "of visiting the faraway country whence my ancestors had come."[61] Others like Frank Maheux, a thirty-one-year-old French Canadian from Quebec City, enlisted in 1914 to take advantage of the army salary, which would improve his family's economic stability.[62] French Canadian opinion of the war was thus divided, and even nationalists appeared to be taking a wait-and-see attitude. But as the war continued past Christmas and into the spring, French Canadian enthusiasm began to wane.

French Canadian support for the war diminished for a number of reasons. The passage in 1912 of Regulation 17 in Ontario, which restricted French-language instruction in the province's schools, remained fresh in many people's minds, prompting some nationalist leaders to wonder why French Canadians were being asked to fight and risk their lives for a country that refused to protect their basic rights at home. Armand Lavergne, for example, a rising young nationalist leader, also claimed that the fight for liberty had to begin at home. Telling French Canadians that "it is not in the trenches of Flanders that we shall win the right to speak French in Ontario," Lavergne wondered whether "the German regime might not be favorably compared to the Boches of Ontario."[63] Bourassa, too, began to question English Canadians' motives in fighting a European war in the name of liberty when liberty was threatened at home. "To speak of fighting for the preservation of French Civilisation in Europe while endeavouring to destroy it in America," he noted, "appears to us as an absurd piece of inconsistency. To preach Holy War for the liberties of the peoples overseas, and to oppress the national minorities in Canada, is, in our opinion, nothing but odious hypocrisy."[64] French Canadians wondered whether English Canada's attitude and response to the war had less to do with protecting freedom and liberty and more to do with fulfilling an image of manhood steeped in militarism. Many feared, moreover, that English Canadians' emotional attachment to the empire blinded them to injustices at home and was setting the nation on a path toward economic and political ruin.

Many English Canadians, it was true, had retained a healthy appetite for war. Military adventurism reinforced the warrior ideal that they had read about in adventure stories and learned in school, and it was widely perceived to be the ideal testing ground for a male culture that emphasized physical strength and courage.[65] So great was the belief that war offered a positive rite of male passage that one English Canadian observer was moved to lament that those French Canadians who refused to enlist would miss out on a useful opportunity: "The greatest loss which the French Canadians will suffer by reason of their abstention from the war is the loss of self-respect. They will also lose the broadening of character which comes of association in a great enterprise, and finally they will miss the deepening and ennobling of character which follows from a great sacrifice. I am sorry – sorry."[66]

But if this ideal had shaped English Canadians' reaction to the war, mounting casualties reminded them that many of these men would not be returning home. The reality of mutilated soldiers also challenged the image of physical perfection that had taken shape before the war, forcing English Canadians to adjust their idea of manhood in order to accommodate the broken and dead bodies on the battlefield.[67] A soldier's death or mutilation, therefore, came to represent courage and sacrifice to a grateful nation, as well as to embody the manly ideal as much as his virile and functioning body had before the war. Death on the battlefield represented the ultimate sacrifice one could make for his country and thus became a powerful image of selfless manhood. Death and mutilation also became potent symbols to soldiers and civilians alike of the righteousness of the cause and provided the justification to continue the fight. Suffering on the battlefield thus became a heroic act of nation building.[68]

Many French Canadians understood these new rules of manhood. Talbot Papineau, the great-grandson of the rebel Louis-Joseph Papineau and cousin of Henri Bourassa, joined the Princess Patricia's Canadian Light Infantry at the outbreak of the war. His biculturalism and famous name had moved some people to comment that he would enjoy a bright political future. Like many Canadians of his generation, he welcomed the war as an adventure and the battlefield as a stage upon which to receive honours that would catapult him into national prominence when he returned home.[69]

Papineau became famous during the war for an open letter he addressed to Henri Bourassa expressing his views on honour, courage, and manhood, which was reprinted in a number of Canadian newspapers as well as in the *Times* of London.[70] In the letter, he attacked his cousin's position on the war, which he argued would merely fan the flames of national disunity, and forwarded a vision for Canada that, in its call for an independent Canadian foreign policy and nationality, did not differ fundamentally from Bourassa's own. But Papineau's vision of the Canadian nation was shaped in battle and built upon a manhood that could be achieved only in war. He wrote, "You would have felt that in the agony of her losses in Belgium and France, Canada was suffering the birth pangs of her national life. There, even more than in Canada herself, her citizens are being knit together into a new existence, because when men stand side by side and endure a soldier's life and face together a soldier's death, they are united in bonds almost as strong as the closest of blood ties."[71] All true Canadian nationalists, he suggested, should view the war as a "great opportunity" and as "the great sacrifice which should have appealed equally to all true citizens of Canada and should have served to cement them with indissoluble strength."[72] Papineau praised war for creating the indissoluble male bonds required for true nationhood. He wrote of "the heroic and able manner in which French Canadian battalions have distinguished themselves here," and he criticized his cousin for his role in bringing "dishonour upon our race." He told Bourassa, "Could you have been here yourself to witness in all its horrible detail the cruelty of the war – to have seen your comrades suddenly struck down in death and lie mangled at your side, even you could not have failed to wish to visit punishment on those responsible. You too would now wish to see every ounce of our united strength instantly and relentlessly directed to that end."[73]

Papineau expanded on these themes in an address to the Canadian Corps School at Pernes. He told the audience that "in the trial and pain and bloody sacrifice of war the national life of Canada has taken birth," and he praised the soldiers for their willingness to "pay the extreme price for national honour." This national honour could be fortified following the war, he suggested, with "compulsory military training" that would become a "means of improving the physique of a nation" and serve as "an admirable disciplinary measure."[74] Papineau reminded his listeners that they were "making the foundation stone of Canadian greatness" and warned them of the dangers of slipping into complacency following the war: "We have lived and fought like men out there. Are we going to become mollicoddles when we return to Canada?"[75]

Although Papineau recognized the ennobling effect of military training and its utility in moulding the proper male body and character, he also recognized that some soldiers would not be returning home. Death became such a powerful symbol of heroism, and such a mark of bravery, that some soldiers were overwhelmed with the guilt of having survived or avoided dangerous assignments. In a letter home, Papineau wondered, "More friends have gone. By what strange law am I still here? What right have I to selfish pleasure any longer? Should my living life not be consecrated just as their dead lives have been?"[76] It was this guilt, and this desire to participate in the fraternity of warfare, that persuaded Papineau to leave his safe desk job in 1917 to return to the fighting, knowing, according to an old friend, that "he was going into a place from which he was likely enough not to return."[77] Two weeks later, Papineau died in the battle of Passchendaele. In this ultimate act of bravery, Papineau's promising life came to an end, but he would be remembered for embodying the best in manhood. In this manly culture of courage and sacrifice, heroism came to be so closely defined with injury or death that soldiers knew that being wounded in battle would only enhance their manly honour. Being wounded or killed became a sign of courage and evidence that one had not evaded the harsh realities of modern warfare.[78] Talbot Papineau had performed his role as a man brilliantly.

Most French Canadian leaders, however, did not share Papineau's code of manhood and were more interested in keeping men alive so that they could contribute to domestic prosperity. Bourassa claimed that draining the country of the very men it needed to maintain economic stability and patriarchal order was no way to defend manhood. Canada's troop commitments, he warned, would paralyze agricultural production and precipitate the collapse of many farms that had lost their male workers.[79] He was also concerned that families that were already stretched too thin faced the prospect of paying higher taxes to finance the war.[80] Others worried that French Canadians' traditionally higher birthrates would hurt them disproportionately if conscription was introduced.[81] One cartoon from the period depicted a muscular French Canadian worker being replaced by an effeminate looking English Canadian man on the job. The caption warned, "When we are gone their *blokes* will come to take our place, to take our homes, and to take our women."[82] Displays of courage on the European battlefield, this cartoon appeared to suggest, would dilute manhood at home and leave women vulnerable to the advances of English Canadian men.

Despite his restraint at the outbreak of war, Bourassa would come to describe the war as an imperial conflict, even suggesting that it did not matter which side prevailed in the end.[83] He argued that the war would compromise national manhood by highlighting Canada's "state of willing subservience"[84] within the empire and referred to Canadian politicians as "slaves to imperialism."[85] Bourassa argued that Britain treated the empire as a reserve of able-bodied men to draw upon in times of war and insisted, "To any re-arrangement that would not give them [the British] the full benefit of the manhood and material resources of the Dominions, in all wars, the British would most likely prefer secession pure and simple."[86] For Bourassa, therefore, the war drained the country of its able-bodied men, which compromised patriarchal authority at home and validated the oratory of "weak-kneed politicians" who had degraded "national dignity and pride."[87]

French Canadian nationalists did not see much that was honourable in a war that forced men to serve against their will for a country that refused to treat them with the dignity and respect that the war was supposedly meant to secure for others overseas. Armand Lavergne reminded French Canadians that it was their duty to refuse to serve overseas, calling on them to resist appeals from English Canada to enlist in order to defend liberty abroad as long as their liberty at home was threatened. "Every cent that is spent in Quebec to aid enlistment of men is money stolen from the minority in Ontario," he wrote, adding that "every French Canadian who enlists fails to do his duty."[88]

Nor did French Canadian nationalists see anything particularly honourable about military life itself. Bourassa was disgusted, for example, by the behaviour of Canadian troops stationed in Quebec City. He observed,

> The peaceful inhabitants of Quebec had come to the point of doubting whether they should not take means to protect themselves as well as their wives and daughters against the enterprises of the defenders of the Empire ... In two hours' time I have met, in the streets of Quebec, a larger number of inebriated soldiers, calling loudly at all by-passers, men or women, than in two weeks' time in Germany, Belgium and France.[89]

Such behaviour convinced many French Canadians that the army would do little to mould honourable and upstanding examples of manhood.

But what particularly offended French Canadian nationalists was the war fever that appeared to have overtaken English Canadians. Bourassa was disturbed by the emotional irrationality that appeared to him to be at the heart of Canadian war policy, and he feared the consequences of Canada's "run towards extreme militarism."[90] Prime Minister Robert Borden's commitment to send 500,000 men overseas appeared to be just the type of irrational policy that he feared would destroy the country. Nationalists argued that they had maintained their rationality and kept cool heads throughout the crisis, whereas English Canadians had succumbed to their passions. Bourassa proclaimed that in the face of English Canada's "demagogic and sterile clamouring," French Canadians would offer "fertile and disciplined action."[91] By reminding English Canadians that "opposition to conscription and war-madness in Canada is not antipatriotic: it is essentially patriotic and clear-sighted," Bourassa and other nationalists framed their opposition to the war as evidence of their own superior manhood based in rational self-control.[92] But in the end, suggestions that Canadian politicians were unmanly because they had plunged Canada into war could not prevent the introduction of conscription. Some leaders advised French Canadians to ignore the conscription law, but most were resigned to the inevitable even as they clung to the belief that they had defended their manly honour throughout the debate.

In many ways, the conscription crisis represented the peak of disunity between English and French visions of manhood in Canada. Cracks within nationalist circles had already emerged to divide the leadership. The fiery journalist Olivar Asselin, for example, surprised many of his nationalist friends and colleagues when he announced that he would be enrolling in order to fulfil his duty to defend France.[93] He worried that French Canadians were failing to perform their duty, and he called on young men to follow him in this great fight for freedom against tyranny.[94] Bourassa continued to oppose the war, but his energy seemed to wane with the introduction of conscription. Besides, the pressure on French Canadians to enrol was so great that Bourassa thought that conscription might even be preferable to what he called coercive voluntarism.[95] He wrote, "regular military service would be much preferable to the present system of 'free' enlistment kept up by blackmail and intimidation, and the degrading 'oratory' of *slacker* politicians, who have betrayed all their past pledges, under the broad pretense of 'saving the liberties of the world' ... by proxy."[96] But he also warned that "the adoption of conscription would not only result in an economic collapse of the country: it would also shake their [French Canadians'] faith in the honour and truthfulness of their public men."[97] By the end of the war, French Canadians appeared ready to celebrate the return of the soldiers, giving them heroes' welcomes that seemed to overshadow some of the divisions surrounding the debate over conscription.[98]

In the two decades following the end of the Great War, English and French Canadians each moved closer to the other's vision of manhood. The bitter divisions that had arisen between English and French Canadians during the war prompted a number of people to work to achieve greater unity. Even before the end of the war, Arthur Hawkes, a Toronto journalist and publicist, criticized the country's war policy. In *Canadian Nationalism and the War* (1916), Hawkes denounced Canada because it had "supinely abdicated all the true functions of a nation at war." He argued that Canada had become "a mere puppet among the nations, accepting, apparently with grateful servility, the promise of being 'consulted' about her own destiny." Hawkes wrote that full partnership in the empire would be preferable to the present state of colonialism, suggesting that "it would help Canada to attain the full stature of a man in the world."[99]

After the war, Hawkes called on Canadians to establish their manhood at home with a more manly approach to English-French relations. In *The Birthright* (1919), he argued,

> Individual emergence from adolescence to full manhood means marriage and fatherhood – no bachelor enters his ordained kingdom. No diversified people can emerge from international adolescence except through certain of the disciplining processes of marriage between their component bodies. They must partake of a common fatherhood and common motherhood of the future. From this point of view the relations of French and English Canada have sadly failed of the goodly content without which prosperity cannot be. They have kept apart. They must learn to enjoy the larger communion of the birthright whose crown of rejoicing must finally be discovered in a full national manhood.[100]

Observing that "many of us are as afraid of the French as a gawky youth is afraid of a girl," he attacked English Canadians' feelings of superiority over French Canadians:

> We vow that we will never enter into full national manhood on level terms with them. We are like the honest, but marvellously incomplete young man who says, "I'm always going to stay with you, mother." We can never attain full national manhood if we refuse to arrive. Nobody can grow up nationally in Canada who forgets two millions of his fellow-countrymen.[101]

In challenging English Canadians to reconcile their differences with French Canadians by acting like a real nation and like real men, Hawkes contributed to a reorientation in the perception of manhood by linking it more closely to the attainment of Canadian autonomy.

By the 1920s English Canadians were also beginning to turn away from the militarism that so many people had embraced before the war. Although the cadet movement remained strong after the war, some people began to question the values it promoted. In 1924, for example, the Reverend Dr. M.F.M. McCutcheon told the First Baptist Church in Montreal that the cadet system "is putting the germ of militarism in these boys who have not yet come to their teens. The wearing of uniform and going through military drill is one of the most effective means of keeping alive the spirit of militarism in the young lads of the Dominion."[102] At the same time, Canadians elected a new prime minister, William Lyon Mackenzie King, a man who, according to the historian James Eayrs, "had a marked aversion to the military life and the military mind[,] whose workings he failed to understand and whose virtues he ignored."[103]

Because King was primarily interested in preserving national unity, he worked to discourage the militarism that he claimed had divided the country prior to the Great War. In 1922, in a letter to J.R. Boyle, the leader of the Alberta Liberal Party and former minister of education, who had angered many French-speaking Albertans by insisting that all instruction in the province's schools be delivered in English, King wrote,

> In matters of real fundamental concern our interest is a common one, and that unity of action is essential to secure our common end in the face of our common foe, the jingo-tory-militarist. I believe we have found the basis on which the Progressives of Western Canada may be brought into real accord with the Liberals of the province of Quebec and other parts of the Dominion.[104]

As prime minister, King also relied on Oscar Douglas Skelton, a professor of political science and economics at Queen's University in Kingston, who had written an admiring biography of Wilfrid Laurier, for advice on imperial matters. Skelton advocated greater Canadian control over the nation's foreign affairs because, as he explained in a speech to the Canadian Club in Ottawa in January 1922, foreign policy was "simply a projection of domestic policy."[105] Five years earlier, Skelton had predicted "matters will hereafter be put on a self-respecting national basis whereby we'll act as a nation, not as an echo, and can find room for every national element in our action."[106] King was so impressed with Professor Skelton's ideas that he took him on as an adviser and then, in 1925, appointed him undersecretary of state for external affairs.[107] It would not be long before King demonstrated that he would be taking Canadian foreign policy in a more autonomous direction. In 1922, for example, he rejected a British request for troops to support London's position in Turkey.[108] In praising the decision, Skelton wrote, "Never again will a Canadian government be stampeded against its better judgement into giving blank cheques to British diplomacy, now that your government has set this example of firm and self-respecting deliberation."[109]

As King tilted Canadian policy away from militarism and imperial entanglements and toward autonomy, he relied heavily on the advice of his trusted Quebec lieutenant, Ernest Lapointe. His close relationship with Lapointe prompted some critics to complain that he was aligning Canadian policy too closely with the French Canadian nationalist program.[110] Although it was true that King was incorporating certain nationalist ideas into his foreign policy, it was also true that these nationalist ideas were more acceptable to English Canadians. By the time that Henri Bourassa returned to the House of Commons in 1925, not all that long after the divisive debate over Conscription during the

First World War, his denunciations of what he called the "servile worship of everything English" and his view that Canada needed to "stand up in the face of Great Britain, not in defiant attitude, but an attitude of self-respect and virile admiration," no longer appeared radical to many Canadians.[111] King was friendly with Bourassa, and he shared many of the old nationalist's views on Canada's place in the empire. But he also understood that not all Canadians were yet ready to loosen their ties with the empire and that being too closely associated with Bourassa could cause problems for him. Following a dinner with Bourassa at the end of the summer of 1926, for example, King noted in his diary that Bourassa would attend the upcoming Imperial Conference, "for which I am sorry, as his name and mine will be linked up by the Tory press."[112]

Nevertheless, King's affection for the old nationalist leader grew over the next few years, and he expressed satisfaction when he received Bourassa's approval. In March 1936, following lunch with Bourassa, Skelton, and Lapointe at Laurier House, King noted in his diary that Bourassa was "exceedingly pleasant" and also that Bourassa "deplores the nationalistic movevement in Quebec (as against rest of Canada) and the priests siding with it." King also wrote that he had told Bourassa during lunch that he "stood for full national rights etc. as the best thing for the British community of nations." But he also informed Bourassa that he "would do more to preserve a united or common front in a time of crisis such as the present [German remilitarization of the Rhineland], than I might be prepared to at conferences of the empire and other times." King was thus pleased when Bourassa responded "with great affection and admiration" toward him and when he described him as one of "the strongest men in Canada today."[113] And although Skelton never let go of the his belief that Bourassa was a radical and a troublemaker, his position did resemble the old nationalist's position, and as the historian Barry Ferguson suggests, "He sounds more like a prophet of bicultural nationalism in the mould of Henri Bourassa than a critic of it."[114]

It was clear by 1939 that the public mood had shifted as well. English Canadians, it turned out, showed little enthusiasm for another European war. Memories of the loss of life from the Great War meant that there would be no cheering crowds to greet news of the Second World War.[115] King also knew that Canadians did not expect their government to follow Britain automatically into war. So he waited a week after Britain declared war on Germany before doing the same. King told the House of Commons,

> Such action as this government is taking today it is taking in the name of Canada as a nation possessing in its own right all the powers and authority of a nation in the fullest sense. The actions we are taking today ... are being and will be taken

> by this country voluntarily, not because of any colonial or inferior status vis-à-vis Great Britain, but because of an equality of status.[116]

But as English Canadians appeared ready to link manhood to Canadian autonomy, and as King worked to limit the influence of those people he called "jingo-tory-militarists," many French Canadian leaders were moving toward a more aggressive posture that linked manhood more closely to militarism. As it turned out, the Great War had dealt a serious blow to Henri Bourassa's pan-Canadian vision for the country in French-speaking Quebec. He was supplanted by a new generation of nationalists who promoted a more aggressive agenda. Lionel Groulx replaced Bourassa as the province's leading nationalist, and he used his position to promote a narrower allegiance to the Province of Quebec.[117] Groulx was concerned that French Canadians had acquiesced too easily in the face of English Canadian attacks on their rights. He denounced French Canadian complacency and called for a more aggressive nationalism that would be bolstered by a more rigorous "national education" in the province's schools designed to "give back to the sons of conquerors of old the desire to become once again masters in their own house."[118] Groulx's ideas resonated among a generation of French Canadians who had witnessed the setbacks of the Great War and experienced the disappointing returns of industrial capitalism.[119]

One of the rising stars within this radicalized and energized movement was André Laurendeau, who emerged on the scene with impeccable nationalist credentials. His father, Arthur Laurendeau, was editor of *L'Action nationale*, and one of his teachers at the University of Montreal was none other than Lionel Groulx, who also happened to be a friend of his father's. In 1932 the young Laurendeau helped to organize Jeune Canada, a movement composed primarily of students from the University of Montreal, in order to protest the federal government's tendency to appoint unilingual anglophones to the Ministry of National Revenue and Customs in Montreal. With Groulx's encouragement, Laurendeau delivered a rousing speech in Montreal in which he called on the crowd to provide a "vigorous" response to this affront. He appealed to young people and hoped that "an ardent desire will be awakened to recover lost ground and build a better future."[120] Three years later, in *Notre nationalisme* (1935), Laurendeau asked members of his generation to break with the conservative attitudes of their fathers and to adopt a vigorous defence of French Canadians' national aspirations.[121]

The members of Jeune Canada became preoccupied with reinvigorating nationalism.[122] Pierre Dansereau, for example, acknowledged, "We had very little in the way of precise doctrine except the general principles laid out in our manifesto ... But, perhaps more than perfect homogeneity; we sought vitality in our association."[123] This search for vitality also meant that Jeune Canada sometimes pointed its finger at French Canadians themselves for being complicit in the perpetuation of their marginal position in the industrial order. Jeune Canada feared that French Canadians had left themselves unprepared to face the challenges presented by industrial capitalism. In *Nos déficiences, conséquences, remèdes* (1935), for example, Thuribe Belzile accused French Canadian elites of intellectual laziness and of failing to provide adequate leadership. He also chided French Canadian workers for what he felt was their failure to take on positions of responsibility and for becoming too enamoured with the luxuries of the age. Belzile argued that French Canadians lacked the self-discipline and drive needed to succeed in the modern world.[124] Once French Canadians came to terms with their "character flaws," they could overcome their limitations and become, in André Laurendeau's words, "masters in our own house."[125]

The new generation of nationalists had grown disillusioned with traditional democratic institutions as well, which they viewed as the stage from which corrupt politicians bartered away Quebec's wealth. The Great War, too, had exposed the limits of parliamentary institutions when it came to defending their rights. Younger nationalists now rejected the seemingly endless discussions and fruitless political debates, which in the end did very little to improve people's lives in any meaningful way. Arthur Laurendeau argued that democracy had hindered Quebec's national development, and he called French Canadians "disputatious babblers, vain and sterile."[126] Lionel Groulx also attacked party politics as a game that merely distracted French Canadians from the job of finding real solutions to their national malaise. This new generation hoped to replace the disorder and unpredictability of parliamentary democracy and party politics with an ordered and hierarchical society.

This search for order led many French Canadians to corporatism.[127] Corporatists argued that industrial capitalism had institutionalized social tensions by pitting workers against employers and business against government. They proposed a social reorganization that would see business, labour, and government working together to reach solutions that served the interests of the entire society. Nationalists argued that some form of corporatism could rationalize society by eliminating the inefficient and confrontational nature of industrial capitalism. Many Catholic authorities, meanwhile, embraced corporatism in the hopes that it could reorganize the industrial world along patriarchal lines. Just as family members were expected to subordinate their individual interests to the good of the whole (i.e., father), they claimed, so too would corporatism force individual segments of society to curb their individual interests in favour of the general (i.e., national) good.[128]

This flirtation with corporatism was part of a larger infatuation with strong leadership and authoritarianism. Many French Canadians in the 1920s were impressed with the way that Benito Mussolini had seemingly reinvigorated Italian society and dreamed that Quebec might one day find a leader, or *chef,* of its own.[129] Mussolini's strong leadership over his ordered society provided an alluring example to French Canadians yearning for their own *chef* who might deliver hope to a population marginalized by industrial capitalism. André Laurendeau dreamed of the coming of a national leader and saviour to restore the order and self-confidence that Quebec sorely lacked. But he suspected that his search for such a leader would end in disappointment because, he noted, "I have scanned the horizon and could not find this national saviour ... the great man who would embody our aspirations."[130]

The search for order and strong leadership, as well as the growing frustration with democratic institutions, set the stage for the rise of such radical figures as Paul Bouchard.[131] Bouchard founded the newspaper *La Nation* in 1936 in Quebec City to promote the creation of an independent Quebec state modelled on the Fascist regime in Italy. At the heart of Bouchard's campaign was a push to revitalize French Canadian manhood. *La Nation* promoted the idea that Quebec was plagued by unmanly decadence and a democratic culture corrupted by party politics. "One hundred and seventy five years of English parliamentary democracy [in Canada]" has resulted, it suggested, only in failure.[132] Bouchard had also grown weary of the older generation of nationalists, whom he referred to as "word-mongers," and he called on young men to reject the values of "the petty bourgeois who prefer slavery and even death" and to live instead "audaciously and dangerously, as free men and a masculine people."[133]

This appeal for renewed manhood was evident in the inaugural issue of *La Nation,* which declared, "We want to make of the French Canadian a man who is worthy of freedom, conscious of the value of his Latin and French civilization." This "dynamic, energetic, and progressive man," it went on, "would be the antithesis of the type of man who exists now after 175 years of foreign domination." Worried that French Canadians had "lost their taste for audacity and war," its editors announced that the newspaper had been launched with the intent of encouraging those men "who still had the fight in them" to fight for their nation. In a nod to Mussolini, *La Nation* declared, "war is to man what motherhood is to women: a completion of his being."[134] Bouchard used his newspaper to promote his vision of a militarized, ordered, and totalitarian society that would finally "make men" of French Canadians.[135]

Although Bouchard's separatism and overt call to reorganize Quebec society along totalitarian lines set him apart from more moderate voices of the time, many nationalists were attracted to his muscular approach and ideas about manhood. Dostaler O'Leary of Jeune Canada, for example, was a regular contributor to *La Nation* and shared Bouchard's attraction to Fascism.[136] Lionel Groulx, too, supported the paper, although he distanced himself from Bouchard's overt support for Quebec separatism. But Bouchard described Groulx as his primary intellectual influence and considered him to be "the first man since Papineau who has sought to offer direction to the nation."[137] Bouchard also claimed that his own radical agenda was simply an extension of Groulx's disillusionment with democratic institutions, as well as Groulx's calls for a new social order and national vitality. Bouchard's attraction to militarism was also in tune with André Laurendeau's view that French Canada suffered from "a lack of discipline." What French Canadians needed, according to Laurendeau, was "martial training, even military training."[138] Bouchard's call for a martial society along with Laurendeau's appeal for strong national leadership and Groulx's distrust of messy democracy were motivated by a shared desire to reinvigorate French Canadian manhood.

As French Canadians came to embrace a more aggressive and even a martial idea of manhood, they also took another look at the Boy Scouts. Prior to the Great War, nationalists had dismissed the Boy Scouts as a bastion of Anglo-Saxon and Protestant values. But by the 1920s the Boy Scout Movement had become more international in its appeal and gained in popularity throughout Europe, shedding some of its associations with British imperialism in the process. Moreover, the Boy Scouts' emphasis on personal discipline, physical fitness, and outdoor activity fitted more easily into the muscular French Canadian manhood that nationalists were promoting in the 1920s and 1930s.

The Boy Scouts grew modestly in French Canada from approximately 2,000 members in 1921 to 5,000 by 1944.[139] But more than these numbers, it is the fact that French Canadian nationalists dropped their reservations about the group and began promoting it as a useful tool to promote manhood that is significant.[140] Abbé Paul Grondin, for example, recognized that scouting offered the type of physical activities that excited young people and encouraged French Canadians to support the movement.[141] Others, like Adélard Dugré, embraced scouting because it offered a means of "producing the complete man and citizen,"[142] and the journalist Omer Héroux praised scouting in *Le Devoir* for its role in building character, teaching responsibility, and sculpting boys' bodies.[143] Lionel Groulx, too, recalled being converted to the cause of scouting when he witnessed a group of English Canadian Boy Scouts in action: "What could be a better means of teaching resourcefulness, initiative, and observation! These proud boys, who are so calm, so sure of themselves miles from their camp, struck me as different from our own boys ... who have been for too long tied to their mothers' skirts. Scouting has conquered me."[144]

The Boy Scouts' appeal grew in the 1920s as French Canadian nationalist leaders became increasingly preoccupied with producing men capable of grappling with modern society.[145] The historian Maurice Séguin spent much of his time looking for ways to reconcile French Canadian ideals of rationality and morality with English Canadian ideals of pragmatism and utilitarianism in an effort to revive the French Canadian spirit.[146] In the Boy Scouts, Séguin found a useful organization that could reconcile these two poles. He championed the Boy Scouts as an institution ideally positioned to produce the vigorous men he believed French Canada was lacking. Séguin's view that boys should make full use of the winter months to develop their hardiness and strength led him to embrace the Boy Scouts as a means of instilling the values of outdoor activity and physical discipline.[147] Scouting, he observed, "strengthens a boy's body, develops his senses and his manual dexterity and makes him ready to serve."[148] The Boy Scouts also "help the boy take charge of his personal development by encouraging him to flourish. In this sense, the Scouts complete the education that a boy would normally receive from his parents, his school, and his church." In words reminiscent of G. Stanley Hall, Séguin spoke of boys going through training in the "primitive" arts.[149]

By 1939 French Canadians had been exposed for almost two decades to a more aggressive and militant nationalist movement and had come to recognize the virtues of order and discipline that were said to accompany military life. So when war broke out that September, French Canadians appeared much more receptive to the prospect of Canadian participation. They supported the war in part out of a sense of revulsion for Nazism. They also trusted King, aware of his stand on Canadian autonomy and his promises not to impose conscription. When Maurice Duplessis called a Quebec election in September 1939, expecting to capitalize on what he believed would be anti-war sentiment and hoping to position himself to resist the expected assault on provincial powers from the federal government, the provincial Liberal leader, Adélard Godbout, defeated him handily at the polls. To be sure, Godbout won because federal Liberals threw the full weight of their party machine behind their provincial cousins and because prominent federal Cabinet ministers such as Ernest Lapointe threatened to resign if Duplessis was re-elected. Both the federal and provincial Liberals were also convinced that French Canadian rights would be defended more effectively from within the government and that a Union Nationale victory would only isolate Quebec and make the introduction of conscription more likely.

But French Canadians also appeared more willing to follow Godbout's Liberals into the war because their attitudes about manhood were evolving. For two decades they had been exposed to a revitalized nationalist movement and embraced the order, discipline, and strong leadership that militarism promised. Their attitude about war had changed, as well, signalled by the fact that enlistment rates were much higher than they had been at the outbreak of the Great War.[150] Two regiments, the Fusiliers Mont Royal and the Régiment de Maisonneuve, had filled their ranks even before the country declared war. Moreover, according to C.P. Stacey, "Military District No. 4 (Montreal) reported on 10 September that French-speaking units had had more applications for enlistment than English-speaking ones."[151] It is true that many men enlisted to escape the decade-long economic depression, but the increased enlistment also occurred against the backdrop of changing attitudes about manhood.

It was also clear that many French Canadians were more attracted to the values associated with war and to an aggressive and martial idea of manhood than they were to the Allied cause. This was evident with the fall of France in June 1940, when a number of prominent French Canadians signalled their support for the Vichy regime. André Laurendeau wrote that French Canadians supported France's chief of state, Philippe Pétain, because he had succeeded in taking France out of the war.[152] But they were also attracted to Pétain's promise to lead a national revolution aimed at restoring the values of family, work, and nation. Many French Canadians blamed the fall of France on the presumed decadence and anti-clericalism of the Third Republic.[153] Pétain appealed to those people hoping that the values of pre-revolutionary France might be restored. Vichy also represented order and discipline and a return to patriarchal values, things that many French Canadians had been searching for since the end of the Great War.[154] Most French Canadians were not sympathetic to the Nazis, nor were they collaborationists. Those who supported Vichy did so, instead, because they were attracted to the ordered version of society that the regime appeared to represent.

Between the end of the Great War and the beginning of the Second World War, then, English and French Canadians each renegotiated what it meant to be a man. English Canadian leaders retreated from the militarism and imperialism that characterized their identities as men prior to the First World War and became more likely to associate manhood with greater Canadian autonomy. French Canadian leaders, in contrast, turned toward a more vigorous nationalist program aimed at restoring the order and discipline that they claimed they were lacking. They focused on creating a greater emotional attachment and loyalty to the nation by emphasizing militaristic fraternity. That is, they embraced a version of manhood that many English Canadians had promoted prior to the Great War. Canadian ideas about manhood converged by the late 1930s, as English Canadians showed little enthusiasm for another war and French Canadians appeared more receptive to the order and discipline that a war could provide. As English Canadian men abandoned militarism and imperialism as the key parts in their manhood, instead linking their identities as men to the country's progress toward greater autonomy, and as more French Canadian men focused on introducing greater order, discipline, and a degree of militarism into their lives, they reached a temporary consensus that allowed for a smooth entry into the Second World War. This consensus was in part achieved with King's promise to avoid conscription.[155] But it had also been made possible by a momentary convergence of attitudes about manhood.

5

The Revitalization of National History

French Canadian nationalists knew that their embrace of a more aggressive and virile type of manhood depended to a large degree on their ability to transform the prevailing historical consciousness in Quebec. For much of the nineteenth century, the Catholic Church had taught French Canadians to accept their fate as a conquered people and to remain on the land while others, namely English-speaking Canadians, indulged in business and industry. In the twentieth century, however, some nationalists complained that this narrative was out of step with their newly invigorated and muscular culture. They charged that it portrayed French Canadians as passive spectators of their own history and that it clashed with their attempts to integrate the province more fully into the modern industrial landscape. So they called on teachers and historians to reimagine the historical narrative in ways that emphasized French Canada's martial past and that highlighted its virile heroes. By rehabilitating previously neglected figures like the *patriotes* of the 1837 Rebellions and *coureurs de bois,* French Canadian leaders sought to recentre strong and assertive men in the province's historical narrative and to position their own nationalist ambitions within a heroic and virile narrative that they now imagined could be traced to the earliest days of New France.

During the late nineteenth century, English Canadians tended to portray French Canadians as a quaint and slightly backward people.[1] Influential writers like William Douw Lighthall, for example, an Anglo-Montreal imperialist and poet who admired the simplicity that he imagined characterized the French Canadian experience, celebrated French Canadians in his books as a romantic and chivalrous people.[2] Others like William Parker Greenough in *Canadian Folk-Life and Folk-Lore* (1897) described the *habitants* as "patient and frugal," as well as "content with results that did not satisfy the more restless and ambitious Americans."[3] And another English Canadian observer wrote, "The French Canadian is naturally, almost instinctively, conservative in his notions; and consequently he is very shy of trying new methods in any department of life, even the simplest."[4] It was the Montreal doctor William Henry Drummond, however, who probably did the most to entrench this image of French Canada as a quaint and somewhat backward society with his popular poetry. In the poem "De Habitant," for example, from his first collection *The Habitant: And Other French Canadian Poems* (1897), Drummond captured what he said were authentic French Canadian attitudes and speech:

De fader of me, he was habitant farmer,
  Ma gran'fader too, an'hees fader also,
De don't mak' no monee, but dat is n't fonny
  For it's not easy get ev'ryt'ing, you mus' know

All de sam' dere is somet'ing dey got ev'ryboddy
  Dat's plaintee good healt', wat de monee
    can't geev,
So I'm workin' away dere, an'happy for stay dere
  On farm by de reever, so long I was leev.

...

But I tole you – dat's true – I don't go on de city
  If you geev de fine house an' beaucoup d'argent –
I rader be stay me, an' spen' de las' day me
  On farm by de rapide dat's call Cheval Blanc.[5]

In addition to drawing enthusiastic crowds to his readings, Drummond attracted critical praise. Louis Fréchette, one of French Canada's leading poets, for one, hailed Drummond as the "pathfinder of a new land of song" and praised him for his sensitive portrayal of the *habitants*.[6]

English Canadians embraced Drummond's poetry in part because it affirmed their assumptions about French Canadian society. The nostalgic picture Drummond painted of a French Canada left untouched by modernity and happy in its backwardness also reinforced English Canadians' feelings of cultural superiority.[7] The invention of this simple French Canadian past also provided, in the words of the historian Donald Wright, a "psychological retreat" from a modern world that many English Canadians perceived as a threat to their own traditional social and gender conventions.[8] Although Drummond claimed that his verse was a faithful reflection of the spoken language he had heard while living among French Canadians and denied that he was motivated by "any thought of ridicule," his work reinforced English Canadians' view of French Canadians as happy, simple, and backward people who were content to let the modern world pass them by.[9]

French Canadians' presumed distinctiveness aroused considerable interest during these years from a number of American scholars who were drawn to Quebec's supposed folk character. In *St. Denis: A French Canadian Parish* (1939), for example, the anthropologist Horace Miner set out to understand "the old rural French Canadian folk culture in its least-altered existent form" before it disappeared.[10] And in *French Canada in Transition* (1943), the sociologist Everett Hughes noted that Quebec was home to "great modern industries and restless urban masses" but that it was also "the seat of North America's most stable and archaic rural society."[11] Even as these works described Quebec as an urbanizing and modern society, they also reinforced stereotypes that French Canadians were only just beginning to emerge from their rusticity and backwardness.[12]

Some French Canadians also contributed to perceptions that Quebec had been left behind by the modern world. It was during these years, for example, that the folklorist Marius Barbeau began collecting songs and stories in his project to document and preserve French Canada's cultural heritage. But his efforts tended to reinforce English Canadian perceptions of the province as a quaint throwback to an earlier era. In 1936, for example, Barbeau worked with Canada Steamship Lines to produce *The Kingdom of the Saguenay,* a book intended to bolster tourism in Quebec. In the book, Barbeau depicted French Canadians as "leisurely and old-fashioned," and he noted that "these rustic folk were not rich; yet they lacked nothing essential, and they were certainly happier than town people."[13]

The Quebec government, too, seized upon these stereotypes in its effort to attract tourists to the province. Beginning in the 1920s, for example, the provincial tourism bureau produced a number of pamphlets and books depicting French Canada as a folk society that had resisted the corrupting influences of modern life.[14] One pamphlet, describing the province as a "land of romantic allure" that, "though of the New World, remains part of the old," claimed that "the whole population of the Old Province lives on the past ... Everything conjures up by-gone days: manners, customs, language, quaint dwellings, narrow fields, antiquated wind-mills, old churches," and it portrayed the habitant as "temperate, law-abiding, traditionally prudent in social matters and, having never tasted the hard life of European workers, he is not a ready listener to the labour agitator or socialist propagandist."[15] Another pamphlet promised that in Quebec "one finds life exactly as it was lived years ago. Its villages are old-fashioned and its inhabitants simple and unaffected as in old France. It is as though time stopped centuries ago so that the visitor might step back into the past and view the manners that prevailed then."[16] Ironically, much of the tourist literature was published by the Provincial Roads Department, which promised readers that Quebec's quaint Old World charms were easily accessible because of the province's network of modern roadways.[17]

French Canadian historians also tended to reinforce such perceptions by presenting the province as a rural and slightly backward place. Even François-Xavier Garneau, who presented his work as a response to Lord Durham's famous declaration that French Canada lacked a distinctive history, portrayed French Canadians as a simple and static people.[18] In the closing lines of his monumental *Histoire du Canada,* which appeared in three volumes between 1845 and 1848 and remained influential into the twentieth century, Garneau called on French Canadians to be true to themselves and to be proud that their greatest achievement had been their survival on the continent. He warned French Canadians to resist the seductions of grand political and social theories, and he reminded them that French Canadians were a small people without the strength to compete in the world of big ideas and should thus leave those dreams to others. Garneau concluded that French Canadians should be satisfied with their history and their fate.[19]

At first, religious authorities attacked Garneau for what they described as the anti-clerical tone of his work. They were rankled, in particular, by Garneau's suggestion that the church had exercised too much power in the past, by his characterization of Bishop François de Laval as an authoritarian figure, as well as by his criticism of the policy to restrict Huguenot emigration to the colony. But they could not ignore the work, especially its toned-down later editions, because it complemented their teachings in a number of ways.[20] They were pleased with Garneau's criticism of the French Revolution, for example, and with his emphasis on French Canadian survival, which became one of the main tenets of nineteenth-century conservative Catholic ideology in French Canada.

For much of the rest of the nineteenth century, most French Canadian Catholic historians incorporated Garneau's theme of survival into their own works, but they dropped his pessimistic assessment of the Conquest as a defeat for Canada as well as his portrayal of New France as a lost cause. The historian Abbé J.B.A. Ferland, for example, offered a more conciliatory interpretation of the Conquest. In his two-volume *Cours d'histoire du Canada* (1861–65), he praised the British conquerors for their benevolence and for their decision to allow religious freedom. Since France had been too preoccupied to pay much attention to the colony, Ferland argued, French Canadians were better off under their new rulers following the Conquest.[21] The liberal historian Benjamin Sulte also refused to see the Conquest as a tragedy for French Canada. In his multi-volume *Histoire des Canadiens français* (1882), Sulte emphasized Britain's "fair and generous treatment" of its new Canadian subjects.[22] Thomas Chapais, too, credited the British Conquest for providentially sheltering Canadians from the French Revolution. In a series of lectures also entitled *Cours d'histoire du Canada* (1919), he stressed that the British had not been interested in oppressing

Canadians and insisted that they had fought to defend the rights of the French Canadian population.[23]

This conciliatory interpretation of English-French relations following the Conquest suited English Canadian sensibilities at the time. In a speech to the Canadian Club in Hamilton in April 1908, the former premier of Ontario George William Ross claimed that the Battle of the Plains of Abraham had left a legacy of reconciliation, partnership, and brotherhood and that with the fall of Quebec, "the brave men who defended her were permitted to march out of the city in all the 'pomp and panoply of war' without any reflection upon their honour or their courage as soldiers of France." He praised New France as well, saying "history is romance in concrete form – romance in which adventure and chivalry and heroism and tragedy are unmistakeably blended." The battle, he said, produced two heroes – Louis-Joseph de Montcalm and James Wolfe – whose deaths on the battlefield inaugurated a partnership between the two great races. Purging from his speech any hint of loss, difference, or competition, he argued, "a partnership was formed on the Plains of Abraham between two great world races," and he referred to the peace treaty as "the articles of partnership."[24] Ross thus constructed the Conquest – supposedly the site of French Canada's greatest defeat – as the central unifying force in Canadian history.

The idea that Canadian history was characterized by mutual respect and partnership was expressed most dramatically later that summer at the tercentennial celebrations in Quebec City. Originally conceived to celebrate Samuel de Champlain's founding of Quebec, the event was transformed by English Canadian imperialists into a commemoration of the British Conquest. The governor general, Lord Grey, hoped the celebration would produce a series of founding myths that could form the basis for national unity. He thus reimagined the Battle of the Plains of Abraham as a unifying event. Like Ross, Lord Grey described the Conquest as an event that forged a partnership between the two great "races."[25] The governor general attempted to rewrite the story of the Conquest by emphasizing the "Second Battle of the Plains of Abraham," which took place at Ste-Foy and which the Canadians won, in his effort to redeem Montcalm's loss and to allow French Canadians to share in the victory of 1759.[26] By purging conflict from the battlefield and replacing it with the idea of partnership, Grey hoped to demonstrate that French Canada had not, in fact, been conquered at all.

A conspicuous visual legacy of this particular view of history can still be seen on the façade of Quebec's Parliament Building in Quebec City. Completed in 1886, the building's façade had space for a number of small statues depicting significant figures in Quebec's history. Two of the first statues to take their place on the building were of Montcalm and Wolfe, which were placed directly above the front entrance on May 25, 1894. Honouring both men was a way to be, according to one observer, "sympathetic to the feelings of the English who had to help put the monument up." But the decision was also in keeping with the government's desire to be "careful not to disparage either of the two peoples whose destinies they directed."[27]

By the first decades of the twentieth century, however, the accommodation and consensus that these sculptures represented appeared increasingly out of step with the times. The debate over Canadian participation in the Boer War had exposed deep differences on the question of Canada's role within the British Empire, and the restrictions placed on French-language education in Manitoba and Ontario reminded French Canadians of the precariousness of their language and culture outside Quebec. The Great War, too, pitted English and French Canadians against one another in a debate over conscription for overseas service. French Canadians also continued to negotiate the difficult transition into an urban and industrial economy, only to find that they remained marginal players in an economy controlled by English Canadians. The first two decades of the twentieth century, in other words, appeared to be marked more by disappointment and confrontation than by accommodation.

In an attempt to understand why French Canadians appeared to be suffering so much disappointment and to be sliding into a state of inferiority, one priest, Father Louis Lalande, suggested that they appeared far too willing to submit to English Canadian domination. He claimed that French Canadians wasted too much time arguing with one another rather than finding solutions to their economic and political problems. He wrote, "We talk too much when it is not necessary or useful to do so; *speechomanie* is exhausting us." If only French Canadians talked a little less and displayed greater initiative, he lamented, "our nationality would not have been reduced to the pale state of womanhood."[28] According to Dostaler O'Leary, a leading member of the youth movement Jeune Canada, French Canadians had become pushovers because they had lost confidence in themselves and now suffered from an inferiority complex. Writing in 1935, he observed, "Ever since their arrival the English have considered us to be an indigenous people that needed to be introduced to civilization ... In the face of such an attitude, we came to rely upon ourselves and little by little we came to believe that we could do very little except serve the English who claimed to be civilizing us."[29]

Lionel Groulx also noticed that French Canadians were suffering from "an incredible lethargy, and an almost complete lack of national sentiment, collective solidarity, a morbid resignation to their own servitude."[30] He wondered how "a supposedly proud people" could have turned into a people "stripped of all sense of its own destiny and content to serve others."[31] French Canadians, he suggested, had come to believe the stereotypes that portrayed them as simple and obedient people content with their inferior place in society. They had accepted the caricatures of themselves that historians like Francis Parkman had produced.[32] They were squandering their virile heritage, in other words, because they had become too detached from that heritage.[33]

In an article for *Le Jour* titled "Our Ancestors Were Not '*Fifis*,'" Édouard Le Doret blamed school teachers for French Canadians' feelings of inferiority. Arguing that teachers tended to distort the past by leaving out its heroic figures, he wrote, "We see the first settlers as lay missionaries rather than as soldiers, or merchants, or *habitants*. One would think that they had come to Canada to save Indian souls rather than to create a new nation where whites might live in comfort." He lamented, "They depict the first Canadians as being thin, with pale faces and white hands." "Would it not be preferable," he wondered, "to see them as they really were – as stocky jawbreakers, loud, beefy, poorly dressed men?" He called for a new version of the past that "could serve our needs today ... in the interest of creating a greater rapport between ourselves and our ancestors," one that emphasized French Canadians' hardiness: "It was us, not them, who explored the continent all the way to the Rockies in the West and all the way to the Gulf of Mexico in the South. It was us, not them, who built and then defended forts in the Ohio and Mississippi Valleys." Proposing a more muscular narrative, he wrote, "it is now the time for our history to be rewritten to include all of its brutal and raw colours; it is time for us to relearn the lessons that we too quickly forgot after 1759."[34]

In an illustration of this renewed interest in history, the Quebec government in 1906 made Canadian history compulsory during the first eight years of a child's education.[35] But it was the way that history was taught that mattered, and by the early twentieth century, it was said that history should teach boys about manhood. It was often said that if only French Canadian boys became acquainted with their past, and saw that their ancestors had played a leading role in determining their destinies, they might exhibit greater manhood themselves and assume positions of leadership when they graduated. In an address to the Societé d'histoire du Canada in 1926, Father Georges Courchesne claimed that the surest way to turn boys into men was to ensure that they understood "that our men had been at the head of governments, negotiations, and armies."[36]

Lionel Groulx was at the forefront of the campaign to have schools do a better job of teaching students about the heroic past. He implored teachers to use their classrooms in order to challenge their students to see themselves as masters rather than servants and as conquerors rather than a conquered people.[37] He also believed that students should be taught to project a level of confidence and strength in their interactions with other people. His fervent hope was that when he came across a man walking on the street who lacked assertiveness and whose arms were dangling beside him with his shoulders hunched forward, he would not automatically think that this was a French Canadian. In the end, he noted, "In a world where wolves are king, there is not much of a future for sheep."[38]

Teachers had long known, of course, that they were expected to use their history lessons to emphasize "the virile courage of the French Canadian race."[39] In his popular school text *Abrégé d'histoire du Canada* (1874), for example, F.X. Toussaint understood that French Canada's heroic past could serve as an inspiration and "a guarantee for future glories."[40] In 1900 he blurred the line dividing the past and the present when he wrote that "a history lesson is a lesson in patriotism."[41] Toussaint was also keen to show that French colonists had been manlier than their English counterparts, describing them as being "more vigorous in body, more energetic in spirit, and more ingenious than their neighbours." He went on to suggest that they were "more enterprising and more intelligent; their society was more manly."[42] And in 1901 the Quebec government's official education journal, *L'Enseignement primaire,* promoted pride in the classroom when it wrote, "If the schoolboy does not carry with him the memory of our national glories; if he does not know that our ancestors fought in a thousand battlefields for noble causes; if he does not become a citizen aware of his duties, the teacher will have wasted his time."[43] The history classroom was thus to be a place where boys learned about leadership and where they would learn to create their own "nation of men."[44]

As teachers were being reminded to emphasize virility in the classroom, professional historians began rewriting the historical narrative in an effort to reinvigorate French Canadian society in their own time.[45] French Canadians, they said, had been depicted as passive spectators of their own history, and they were determined to write French Canadians back into the history books. In his memoirs, Lionel Groulx suggested French Canadians had been in the process of "forgetting their history" when he started out as a historian and thus felt he could best contribute to the cultural and spiritual reawakening that he sought by writing history.[46] In 1926 Groulx described history as "a genealogy of a people," adding that history plays a role in ensuring racial survival by preserving the stories and describing the traits that make that race distinct.[47] The teaching of national history, then, became a matter of national survival.[48]

Ever since François-Xavier Garneau set out in the 1840s to write his *Histoire du Canada* in response to Lord Durham's famous declaration that French

Canadians had no history and no literature, the writing of history in the province had been a political act.[49] In 1897 Thomas Chapais wrote that history "teaches us about the past, explains to us the present, and prophesies for us the future."[50] Meanwhile, Groulx's *Notre maître, le passé,* which one writer has described as "a re-synthesis of ancestral vigour," provided but one indication of the reverence with which the past was held.[51] Guy Frégault also recognized the importance of the past when he wrote, "If history were only a game, it would be easy to revel in learned research without relating past facts to the present. But then one would have to create a science that could measure the pressure of the past on the present and determine the nature of that pressure." He argued that the purpose of history was "to explain the present by showing how it came into being" and that history "is a means of organizing the past so that it may not be too heavy a burden for the shoulders of men."[52] Michel Brunet was more blunt in his observation that "men change the interpretation of their past when they realize that they can give a new orientation to their collective action." Brunet pointed out that when historians wrote, they revealed at least as much about their own society as they did about the past. He observed, "The interpretation which each society gives to its past reveals much on its ways of living and thinking. Written history is a document for the social scientist."[53]

Lionel Groulx was one of the first historians to rewrite Canadian history in a manner that would make French Canadians appear more assertive. As a young teacher in 1905 at the Collège de Valleyfield west of Montreal, he set out to upend the two pillars of nineteenth-century French Canadian history – providentialism and survivalism – because he claimed that they tended to portray French Canadians as passive historical actors. But these themes were so entrenched that Groulx was unable to find a suitable text with which to advance his interpretation of the past.[54] So he produced a series of lectures for his classes that attacked French Canadians' placid acceptance of their fate following the British Conquest and that challenged historians' tendency to attribute French Canadians' survival to the benevolent policies of their British conquerors. He wrote of the need to challenge the widely held assumption that French Canadians had achieved their rights largely due to the generosity of the English. Groulx offered a different interpretation, which stated that French Canadians had lost most of their rights following the Conquest and had only "won them back as a result of the battles waged by our ancestors."[55]

Groulx was determined to use his historical writing as well as his teaching to make French Canadians more self-reliant and aggressive in their struggle to defend their rights. In 1916 he asked that French Canadians abandon the idea that "our freedoms were a gift from a liberal England," reminding them that "our freedom was not a gift but a conquest."[56] Although he agreed that the Conquest had shielded French Canadians from the effects of the French Revolution, he also claimed that historians had gone too far when they attributed French Canadian survival to British goodwill. In 1920 his frustration was evident when he wondered, "Is it really necessary to treat the English Conquest as a blessing? The lessons of history do not support this view. Submission to a foreign people is, for an adult race, always a calamity."[57]

Groulx found the providential thesis to be so unpalatable because it portrayed French Canadians as too passive in the struggle for survival on the continent and because it was at odds with his conviction that men created history and controlled their own fate.[58] He critiqued the ideology of *survivance* for the same reasons. In a speech in Quebec City in 1933, he pleaded, "Deliver us finally from this nightmare of *survivance* that has for too long monopolized and paralyzed all of our energies." "Is it not time," he wondered, "that we became an adult race, a race strong enough and sure enough of itself and of its future, that we could abandon once and for all a childish state of mind that has us constantly worried about our future?"[59] Mere survival was no longer a desirable option, he had noted elsewhere, stating, "we are aiming, thank goodness, for something more positive and more elevated than that. What we want is to live normally and powerfully."[60]

Maurice Séguin, one of Groulx's disciples, also assailed those narratives that portrayed English and French Canadians as equal partners. He suggested that this narrative tended to promote the idea that French Canadians controlled their own destinies and were thus responsible for their economic and political inferiority. This interpretation of history, he suggested, had led to French Canadian feelings of inadequacy and failure.[61] Michel Brunet went even further by accusing church authorities of seeking to present the past as a series of accommodations in order to consolidate their own power and influence. He argued that the church and its historians perpetuated a series of myths that idealized agrarianism, French Canada's spiritual mission on the continent, and an aversion to the state in order to justify French Canada's "backwardness" and to create a compliant population that would be unable to take part in the modern secular world or to challenge its authority.[62]

The political cleavages of the early twentieth century convinced Groulx that Garneau's narrative of racial conflict had come closer to the truth than those narratives celebrating racial reconciliation. So like Garneau, who had described New France as a warrior society characterized by almost constant war,[63] Groulx began to emphasize French Canada's violent and militaristic heritage. In 1918 he noted, "it is perhaps one of the novelties of this population that it should have such a military temperament," reminding French Canadians that

New France had never enjoyed a period of peace that lasted longer than thirty years.[64] He hoped that a renewed emphasis on war and conflict would present French Canadians as strong, assertive, and virile figures who had been active participants in their own history.

This new and assertive version of the past also reflected French Canadian historians' reading of English Canadian history during these years. Narratives of French Canadian defeatism and complacence, they discovered, contrasted with English Canadian narratives of the past that were brimming with confidence, determination, and stories of nation building.[65] While French Canadian leaders had been extolling the virtues of humility and survival, English Canadian historians had been producing a steady stream of works detailing the country's progress toward liberty and constitutional independence. Writers like W.P.M. Kennedy and Chester Martin in the 1920s, for example, wrote about Canada's march toward responsible government within a heroic narrative of nation building. By the 1930s Harold Innis and Donald Creighton were proposing that Canada's economic and political development had depended upon its ability to extract staples, such as fur and timber, which it could then sell to metropolitan centres in Europe. Their work served as the foundation for a nationalist historical narrative suggesting that Canada's emergence as a nation followed its patterns of economic development.

This nationalist reading of history exerted considerable influence over the Montreal School of historians.[66] Innis and Creighton, it turned out, were paving the way for Maurice Séguin and Guy Frégault to argue that the Conquest represented a devastating break in French Canadian history because it had cut off commercial ties between the colony and France. Following the nation-building narrative being forwarded by English Canadian historians during these years, Lionel Groulx began to emphasize that French-speaking Canadians had enjoyed, prior to the Conquest, "a homeland, a common ethnicity, language, history and set of traditions." The inhabitants of New France were thus the "founders of a country and the founders of a race."[67] Frégault, too, conceptualized French Canadian history within the nation-building narrative by suggesting that the *habitants* in New France "were laying the foundations for a new country."[68]

As this version of the past that portrayed French Canadians as virile participants in a narrative of heroic nation building gained momentum during the 1930s, some historians wondered whether its emphasis on conflict and division had become a bit too divisive. Abbé Arthur Maheux, the head of the History Department at Laval University, for example, was unimpressed with Groulx's interpretation of the past and declared that any divisions that existed between English and French Canadians were simply temporary setbacks that could be overcome with a show of goodwill from both sides.[69] He dismissed the new history as a litany of complaints, stating that French Canada's "vigorous history of conquest has given way to a tearful history." Although Maheux shared Groulx's belief that French Canadians may have at times exhibited a bit too much timidity, he worried that historical narratives that emphasized conflict and tension between English and French Canadians would inevitably fail to provide the inspirational history that Groulx claimed to be looking for.[70]

But Groulx and others continued to highlight conflict and division in the past in order to bolster French Canada's vigour and manhood in his own day. For too long, he claimed, French Canadians had been depicted as a people blindly accepting the fate imposed on them first by the British and then by English-speaking Canadians. This version of the past had only fed existing ideas that French Canadians were simple *habitants* unconcerned about such worldly events as conquests or about who their political masters happened to be at any given time. Groulx argued that French Canadians needed to rediscover a sense of pride that had been lost as a result of "an ignorance of our past."[71] He thus called for the writing of a virile history that would help to liberate French Canadians from their defeatist attitudes and nudge them out of their docility.[72] In the 1920s and 1930s, a growing number of people would take up this call.

As teachers and a new generation of professional historians were working to reinvigorate the historical narrative, amateur historians were busy transforming the public's encounters with history on Montreal's streets and in its public squares. During the late nineteenth and early twentieth centuries, a number of historical societies evolved from sleepy discussion groups into assertive promoters of a more muscular and manly past. The Société historique de Montréal (SHM), for example, was founded in 1858 and had spent much of its first decades highlighting the missionary and religious character of the French Canadian past. Its low-key approach to the past was evident in its decision to commemorate the 250th anniversary of the founding of Montreal in 1892 with a modest Pioneers' Obelisk engraved with the names of the city's original forty-seven settlers. The unassuming monument reflected the SHM's desire to portray Ville Marie as a religious settlement and to celebrate, according to the historian Alan Gordon, "devout French settlers, not the great man."[73]

The SHM's decision to mark the city's anniversary with such a humble monument celebrating those original settlers was in marked contrast to the Antiquarian and Numismatic Society of Montreal's (ANSM) plan to erect a monument to the city's founder, Paul Chomedey de Maisonneuve, in Place d'Armes. Established in 1862 by a group of English- and French-speaking Montrealers, the ANSM had played an active role in promoting the city's heritage by sponsoring a number of commemorative plaques. It had also been instrumental in the fight to preserve the city's built heritage, including the Château Ramezay in Montreal. Unveiled on July 1, 1895, the monument depicts Maisonneuve standing tall and triumphant on a pedestal, surrounded by figures representing the colony's martial past. The monument overshadowed the SHM's obelisk, which had been unveiled farther west at Place d'Youville and which now appeared unable to reflect the hopes and expectations of a French Canadian population in search of virile heroes.

As public tastes evolved, and more and more people expressed an interest in French Canada's heroes and great men, the SHM adjusted its approach to the past. When Victor Morin assumed the leadership of the SHM in 1916, he shifted its emphasis away from French Canada's Catholic beginnings and toward its great men and events. One of his first acts as president, for example, was to move the Pioneers' Obelisk to a more prominent location at Place Royale. He also began planning for the city's 275th anniversary, to take place in 1917, which he hoped to mark by erecting a number of plaques honouring the builders of Montreal and by placing a greater emphasis on the role that Maisonneuve had played in the city's history.[74]

In 1915 Morin had also assumed the presidency of the Société-Saint-Jean-Baptiste de Montréal (SSJBM). During his ten years as president, he transformed the organization founded in 1834 to celebrate Saint-Jean-Baptiste into one that would use the past to pursue a more aggressive agenda. At a meeting of the SSJBM congress in 1916, for example, Morin reminded French Canadians of their "determination to fight to preserve their national rights and to resist the powerful forces of assimilation." Morin thus positioned the SSJBM to assume a leading role in "directing the life of the race."[75]

As the SHM and the SSJBM began to turn their attention to the great men of the past, they also tended to focus more heavily on events and figures from New France.[76] This emphasis on an earlier period in their history reflected the anxieties of a population that had become increasingly uneasy about its place in Confederation. New France represented a time when French Canadians were thought to be in control of their own lives and destinies. By 1760 they had lost control of their territory and political institutions and then, in the late nineteenth and early twentieth centuries, of their economy and natural resources. In an industrial and urban environment believed to be controlled by English Canadian capital and managers, this preindustrial and pre-Conquest past provided evidence of French Canadian assertiveness, vigour, and heroism.[77] At the same time, many people imagined the period before the Conquest to be French Canada's golden age, one defined by heroes and not yet complicated by its defeat. One figure from this period – Dollard des Ormeaux – emerged during these years as the model of French Canadian manhood.

Interest in Dollard des Ormeaux grew as the 250th anniversary of his death in 1660 at the Battle of Long Sault approached. The story of how Dollard organized sixteen men and some Native allies and led them into the forest in an effort to pre-empt what he believed was an imminent attack on the fledgling settlement of Ville Marie, and the subsequent battle against a much larger group of Iroquois fighters that ended in his death, was well known. The earliest accounts of his excursion highlighted Dollard's courage, but it would not be until the French historian and priest Étienne-Michel Faillon wrote about his exploits in 1865 that the Dollard myth really began to take shape.[78] Faillon characterized Dollard's death as an act of providence and declared that it had spared the colony from certain destruction. Moreover, he claimed that Dollard had entered the forest knowing that he would never return alive. Faillon thus described Dollard as a martyr and positioned him within the providential story of French Canada.[79]

But it was Lionel Groulx who transformed Dollard into the leading figure of a narrative of the past marked by violence and into a virile specimen of manhood for public consumption.[80] In a speech at the Monument-National in 1919 titled "Si Dollard revenait," Groulx mused about what Dollard would think of French Canada if he were alive: "What a scandal, what a startling anachronism the man would be, a knight of holy courage and sacrifice, in our age of fear and pragmatism!" He told the audience that French Canadians were once again in need of a "leader of men" like Dollard, and then he spoke pleadingly, as though addressing the spirit of Dollard:

> Arise, Dollard, and live on your granite pedestal. Summon us with virile charm, with a hero's accents. We lift toward you our hands quivering like palm leaves, ardent with ambition to serve. Together we shall work for the reconstruction of our family's house. And should you command it, O Dollard, O powerful leader, we are ready to follow you to the supreme holocaust for the defence of our French tongue and our Catholic faith.[81]

The Dollard cult developed at a time when French Canadians were on the defensive over their response to the Great War and their refusal to support compulsory military service. Some English Canadians accused them of cowardice, and recruitment posters attempted to convince French Canadians to follow in Dollard's footsteps by signing up to fight in Europe. But anti-conscription forces also turned to Dollard's image to demonstrate that they were just as manly and courageous as English Canadians and did not need to support the war to prove it. In this sense, according to the historian Patrice Groulx, French Canadians turned to Dollard to prove "both to themselves as well as to their detractors that they were just as capable as anybody else of patriotic sacrifice."[82]

Although the image of Dollard was used to deflect charges of cowardice during the Great War, it was also deployed to remasculinize the narratives of the past. Dollard's revival as the embodiment of French Canadian manhood coincided with the decline of Madeleine de Verchères' fortunes. Like Dollard, Verchères had become a mythic figure in French Canada because of the bravery she displayed in 1692 while defending her family fort east of Montreal. Verchères was only fourteen years old when she held off a surprise Iroquois invasion for seven days until French troops could arrive to rescue the occupants of the fort. Her actions secured her a place in the popular imagination as the "Canadian Joan of Arc." But by the late nineteenth century, Verchères' status as a female icon was increasingly out of step with the sensibilities of a province experiencing, as the historians Colin Coates and Cecilia Morgan have put it, "gender anxiety."[83] Because she wore male clothing and engaged in traditionally male activities while defending the fort, Verchères was seen to have transgressed acceptable gender boundaries.[84] In fact, Groulx was so horrified that Verchères' exploits might be compared to Dollard's heroism that he reminded people that the hero of Long Sault was superior in every way. He pointed out, for example, that Dollard had not been surprised by his enemies and had instead taken the initiative by seeking them out. For her part, Verchères had acted in a manner consistent with her sex because her actions were primarily defensive and thus less heroic. Groulx, therefore, proclaimed Dollard to be "the real hero of our history."[85]

The revival of Dollard and decline of Verchères suggested that true heroism in the province's historical narrative would be reserved for men.[86] As historians rewrote the past in an effort to remind boys of their virile and active heritage, passive figures such as Verchères served only to remind French Canadians of their "feminine" past.[87] Only men, moreover, could become leading characters in a historical narrative increasingly defined by the theme of nation building. Dollard, therefore, emerged as the ideal male figure in this new narrative because he had "given birth" to the French Canadian nation on the battlefield.[88]

The transformation of Dollard into a heroic and manly nation builder set the stage for a reconsideration of the *patriotes* of 1837. The approaching 90th anniversary of the Rebellions provided an opportunity to remember another male-induced rebirth of French Canada. The Rebellion in Lower Canada was in part an act of frustration by French Canadian leaders determined to challenge the power of the British merchant classes as well as the social hierarchies that the church supported. Louis-Joseph Papineau's flirtation with republicanism, as well as his apparent challenge to constituted authority and ecclesiastical power, disturbed the Catholic establishment, which had come to rely upon popular obedience and social peace for its authority. The church had thus condemned the rebels' decision to take up arms.

Before the 1920s, most French Canadian leaders tended to downplay the significance of the Rebellions in Canadian history.[89] In 1884 Laurent-Olivier David wrote a series of articles that heralded the *patriotes* for their courage and attempts to defend French Canadian culture. But he remained an exception among writers who tended to blame the rebels for poisoning the peaceful atmosphere of accommodation that they imagined had characterized relations between English and French Canadians since the Conquest.[90] Even François-Xavier Garneau, who compared the events of 1837 to those of 1759, criticized the rebel leaders for their adherence to individual rights and their flirtation with republicanism, which, he believed, threatened French Canada's collective survival.[91] Thomas Chapais, too, portrayed the Rebellions as an attack on the Catholic Church and chastised its leaders for what he claimed was their demagoguery. He described the French Canadian population as generally happy people who were not interested in disrupting their peaceful existence through rebellion.[92] Even traditional ideological foes found common ground on the question of the Rebellions. Benjamin Sulte, the liberal-leaning historian with imperialist sympathies, for example, downplayed their importance in his work, and Jules-Paul Tardivel, the radical ultramontane journalist and anti-imperialist, refused to treat the rebels as heroes, preferring to see them as a threat to the church.[93] It was widely assumed that the swift retribution from the British authorities following the defeat of the Rebellions proved that the uprising had done more harm than good and had made French Canadian survival even more precarious than it might otherwise have been.[94]

The public's ambivalence about the Rebellions was also evident at the unveiling of a monument honouring Dr. Jean-Oliver Chénier, the leader of the Battle of Saint-Eustache, in 1895. The discovery two years earlier in a Saint-Eustache cemetery of what were thought to be Chénier's remains provided the impetus for the memorial. The former mayor of Saint-Eustache as well as other prominent citizens had hoped to raise a monument to Chénier in their town but encountered resistance from the church there. They then proposed transferring Chénier's remains to the Catholic Notre-Dame-des-Neiges Cemetery on the slopes of Mount Royal, next to an obelisk that had been built there in 1858 to commemorate those who had died during the Rebellions. But Édouard-Charles Fabre, the archbishop of Montreal, objected to that plan, refusing to consider the idea that a man who had taken up arms against the wishes of Bishop Jean-Jacques Lartigue should be permitted to rest in consecrated ground.[95] So supporters of the Chénier monument raised the funds to build the statue in Viger Square, without his remains. But for all of these efforts to raise the monument, few Montrealers appeared all that interested in celebrating the rebel. Fewer than 1,000 people attended the ceremony dedicating the statue, a disappointing crowd for a city that would draw as many as 50,000 people to the unveiling of a statue to Bishop Ignace Bourget in 1903.[96]

By the 1920s attitudes about the rebels were changing, and the *patriotes* were emerging as key figures within the remasculinized French Canadian historical narrative, which showcased assertiveness, vigour, and violent struggle. The divisive debates over wars and language rights that characterized the years following the unveiling of the Chénier monument, it turned out, were transforming the public perceptions of the Rebellions. By this time, too, the church's presumed complicity with the British authorities during the Rebellions was becoming an inconvenience for the clergy, whose members were attempting to position themselves as the champions of French Canadian nationalism and liberty. But before the *patriotes* could be reintegrated into the historical narrative, a number of obstacles needed to be overcome. Unlike Dollard, who had proved his manhood and his patriotism by defending Ville Marie against a suspected Iroquois attack, the *patriotes* had risen in part to protest the power of the church.

Lionel Groulx sidestepped this inconvenience by suggesting that the church may not have been as opposed to the *patriotes* as had been assumed. In a series of articles that appeared in *L'Action française* in 1926, Groulx argued that Bishop Lartigue of Montreal did not speak out against the rebels until after the fighting had begun. In a pastoral letter of October 24, 1837, Lartigue reminded the population of its duty to respect the civil authority. But this call for order was not, Groulx suggested, directed toward the rebels. It was, instead, simply a general statement of Catholic doctrine.[97] Only on December 4, 1837, after the Battle of Saint-Denis, the first major clash of the Rebellions, and after the Battle of Saint-Charles, Groulx pointed out, did Lartigue, in a letter to Jérôme Demers, a priest in Saint-Denis, for the first time speak directly against the *patriotes* by agreeing that rebels should not receive Catholic burials.[98] According to this timeline, Groulx suggested, the *patriotes* could not be deemed to have acted against the wishes of the church. Although he conceded that some priests might have been overzealous in their desire to maintain order, he insisted that the church did not support British authorities against the French Canadian rebels. To respond to those who had claimed otherwise, Groulx quoted approvingly from an 1840 issue of *Le Canadiens:* "If the Catholic clergy had been the blind instruments of the oppressors, the last vestiges of our nationality would have long ago disappeared."[99] Groulx argued that any clerical appeals to end the Rebellions had been guided more by a desire to limit violence than by any desire to promote a sense of loyalty to the government. Groulx therefore disentangled the church from any presumed collaboration with British authorities during the Rebellions and positioned it firmly on the side of the French Canadian people.

Groulx's new reading of the Rebellions built upon his earlier reassessment of Louis-Joseph Papineau. The *patriote* leader remained a divisive figure because of his support for republicanism, his call for annexation to the United States, and his anti-clericalism. But in 1921 Groulx described Papineau as a great man and a strong leader of his people. He wrote, "It is natural for people, in times of difficulty, to turn to the great names of their past." And there were few men, he continued, greater than Papineau, who had "contributed to the glory of our past" and had served as "the conscience of his nationality." It was Papineau's qualities as a *chef* that Groulx found most attractive, explaining, "If one day our country, and perhaps even our people, gravitates toward its destiny, we will once again embrace the ideas and the men who, long ago, prepared the way for this magnificent dawn ... On that day, Louis-Joseph Papineau will stand even higher on his pedestal."[100] By the 1930s Groulx would look past Papineau's perceived shortcomings because of what Papineau had accomplished for his race, identifying him as "our first national leader, the first to become the true voice of our people, the potent incarnation of an ideal."[101]

By producing a strong leader and showcasing French Canadians taking the initiative in defending their rights, the Rebellions emerged in the 1920s as a useful episode in French Canada's virile historical narrative. The rehabilitation of the Rebellions was also significant because it represented an important moment for French Canadian manhood in the 1830s. Historian Allan Greer has referred to the *patriote* uprising as "a fundamentally masculine phenomenon," whose emphasis on "independence, honour and manly valour" appealed primarily to men.[102] It should be remembered, too, that Louis-Joseph Papineau had been vocal in his call for women to refrain from participating in the public sphere, a move that entrenched public life, and by extension the Rebellions, as an exclusively male domain.[103] As the exercise of political power became increasingly defined as a male prerogative, the Rebellions played out as a male struggle and emerged in the historical narrative as an important moment when French Canadian men took control of their own destinies.[104]

By 1926 it was evident that the *patriotes* had been reintegrated into the historical narrative as full heroes when 250,000 people attended the unveiling of a monument honouring the twelve men executed for their involvement in the Rebellions on the site where they had been put to death. That the twelve men being honoured had fought in a movement that at times called for the separation of church and state no longer seemed to matter to the church. By recasting the *patriotes* as nationalists acting to secure French Canadian liberty, men like Lionel Groulx and Victor Morin transformed the Rebellions into an expression of male vigour on the very political stage that had so recently been carved out as a male sphere. In the 1920s, therefore, criticism of the Rebellions evaporated as more people recognized that those events fitted nicely into their revivified version of a past characterized by French Canadian action, initiative, and nation building.[105] The church and its liberal opponents thus gravitated toward a united interpretation of the *patriotes* as freedom fighters that would have been inconceivable only a few years before.[106]

As the new historical narratives about the heroic and manly nation-building acts of Dollard and the *patriotes* were taking shape, another figure was undergoing an image makeover. The *coureur de bois,* once deemed a troublesome outlaw who had undermined the viability and mission of New France, emerged in the 1930s as a model of manhood. Historians recast the *coureurs de bois* as independent figures who had exhibited the rugged and active manhood that they claimed had characterized the past. The *coureurs de bois'* reputations as explorers and adventurers, moreover, could be used to inspire French Canadians in desperate need of male role models.

The *coureurs de bois* transported furs from the Canadian interior to Montreal and served as intermediaries between the Native populations in the West and their merchant masters back in the East. Along with the *voyageurs,* who had acquired more formal recognition from authorities in the colony, the *coureurs de bois* had developed a reputation as rugged and independent types and as being slightly wild.[107] The myths surrounding their exploits in the wilderness captured the imagination of the colonists and continue to dominate our perceptions of the *coureur de bois.*[108] Part of the appeal of the *coureurs de bois* derived from the fact that they lived for extended periods of time in the wilderness beyond the reach of church and political control. These long absences fed the stories about their drinking, gambling, and licentiousness, a reputation that they only encouraged with tales of their exploits when they returned home. And these stories reinforced the image of this group of men, whose activities in the Northwest reinforced the paternalistic and commercial structures back home, as romantic and independent-minded adventurers.[109]

English-speaking historians were among the first to be drawn to the image of the *coureurs de bois.* The American historian Francis Parkman, for example, understood them in the context of late-nineteenth-century attitudes about individualism and liberty. The *coureurs de bois* redeemed New France in Parkman's eyes because they infused the story of religious domination and political tyranny with a streak of manly adventure and romance.[110] Others, like the McGill University professor and historian Charles Colby, celebrated the *coureurs de bois* precisely because they "stood outside the pale of respectable society." Colby wrote, "Though profane and disreputable, [the *coureur de bois*] was interesting. His recklessness kindled a spark of admiration." He claimed that the *coureur de bois* was driven by much more than mere profits and that he was drawn to the "excitement of the game" and "the chance to test his powers in wrestling with the obstacles he encountered ... to escape from the stifling restrictions of state control, to indulge in the liberty and license of the forest – there lay the temptation." Colby thus solidified the myth that the *coureur de bois* "liked the woods because they emancipated him from restraint."[111] It was this very otherness that made the *coureur de bois* a figure of such glamour to an English Canadian population weary of the growing conformity and monotony of industrial life.

French-speaking historians, in contrast, had found it difficult to incorporate this troublesome group of supposed freethinkers into their narratives that portrayed French Canadians as deferential to authority and attached to the land.[112] The French historian and Jesuit priest Pierre François-Xavier de Charlevoix, for example, worried about the impact of the *coureur de bois* on the colonists. In 1743 he warned of "the attraction which the young men feel to this savage way of life which consists of doing nothing, in being restrained by nothing, in pursuing all one's urges, and placing oneself beyond the possibility of correction."[113] Charlevoix portrayed the *coureur de bois* as a nuisance, who was "ruining and depopulating the country and annihilating commerce."[114]

François-Xavier Garneau, too, pointed out that the real heroes of the wilderness were the missionaries who attempted to convert the Native populations in the West, not the *coureurs de bois* or *voyageurs*. Garneau argued that the fur trade promoted licentiousness and encouraged too many men who were looking for "deceptive wages" to turn away from settlements and an agricultural lifestyle. He compared the situation in New France with the American experience, stating that rather than "stray too far from their homes," the English chose to "cultivate their land and build factories." He called on French Canadians to follow the American lead so that they might create a "more profitable and more lasting" trade. The fur trade hindered Canada's development as a settlement colony, he wrote, because it pulled men away from the settlements and into the forest in search of adventure.[115] Abbé J.B.A. Ferland also emphasized the problems that the *coureurs de bois* created between Natives and French colonists. He suggested that the licentious and heavy-drinking *coureurs de bois* had interfered with the efforts of the missionaries to assimilate the Natives to European ways.[116] By relying on official correspondence in New France, which depicted the *coureur de bois* as a nuisance, these historians were very often simply echoing the views expressed by seventeenth-century officials like Governor General Louis de Buade de Frontenac and Intendant Jean Talon.[117]

In the mid-nineteenth century, some writers attempted to integrate the *voyageur* into the French Canadian historical narrative. In *Forestiers et voyageurs* (1863), Joseph-Charles Taché offered a fictionalized account of a figure who represented the best qualities of both the *voyageur* and the clergy and whose excursions into the forest served the needs of the church and the colony.[118] Taché stressed the *voyageur*'s Catholicism, praising him for his "adventurous spirit" and for his ability to be, all at once, "a discoverer, interpreter, lumberjack, settler, hunter, fisherman, sailor, and warrior." Taché thus fused the sacred and secular stories of New France in the figure of the *voyageur*.[119]

Other writers had attempted to integrate the *coureur de bois* into the narrative of the past. In 1879 the historian Benjamin Sulte, for example, described the *coureur de bois* as a family man who spent long periods of time in the wilderness but who always returned home to settle down and raise a family. Sulte praised the *coureurs de bois*, moreover, for promoting colonization and for contributing to the spread of French civilization throughout the continent. He wrote that the *coureurs de bois* had taken "up the cause of Champlain, Richelieu, Colbert, Talon, La Vérendrye, Vaudreuil, Beauharnois, and others, who wished to introduce the French fact to all of North America."[120] Sulte singled out the bravery of the *coureurs de bois:* "One had to be strong and brave to face the perils of these long journeys, where many left their skin, because of the difficulties of the journey, attacks from savages, or illnesses caused by famine." Describing them as strong, fearless, and confident, and hoping they might inspire French Canadians in his own day, he wrote, "At the point where European courage falters under the effects of snow, cold, and solitude, French Canadians feel perfectly at ease." He concluded that with such men, French Canadians could accomplish whatever they wanted.[121]

Sulte, however, was regarded as something of an imperialist and was seen to be slightly anti-clerical, so it took some time for his views to become fashionable.[122] It would not be until the 1930s that the *coureur de bois* would fully emerge as a manly hero in French Canadian historical writing. The release of a fifth edition of Garneau's *Histoire du Canada* in 1920 turned out to be an important step in the *coureur de bois*' rehabilitation. Edited by his grandson, Hector Garneau, this new edition of that famous work of history emphasized the exploits of the *coureurs de bois* to a greater extent than earlier editions had done, thereby integrating them more fully into the province's historical narrative. Hector Garneau identified the *coureurs de bois* and explorers by name and placed them right at the centre of his story of French Canada's past. He also emphasized the discovery of the Mississippi River and described the exploits of Pierre-Esprit Radisson and Médard des Groseilliers to a greater degree than his grandfather had, stressing the fact that the French were the first to explore the continent's interior.[123] In his preface to the new edition, Gabriel Hanotaux of the Académie française captured the tone of the book when he stressed that French Canadian history had been characterized by exploration, suggesting the discovery and exploration of the interior of the continent were among the greatest achievements of early French Canadians. He also noted, in a manner that further distinguished this edition from earlier ones, "a great people cannot turn inward unless it wished to perish."[124]

This emphasis on individual explorers represented an important departure for French Canadian historians. Clerical historians had portrayed the exploration of the West in their narratives as part of the religious mission of the colony but had usually downplayed the specific exploits of the *coureurs de bois* because they claimed that their participation in the commercial trade undermined this mission. But the appearance of more secular-minded historians on the scene in the 1920s and 1930s, who were less concerned with describing the religious nature of the past, and the influence of economic historians writing in English Canada cleared the way for the *coureur de bois'* reintegration into the historical narrative. By the 1940s Guy Frégault, who reimagined New France as a North American colony full of vitality, described the *coureurs de bois* as an important part of the French Canadian experience. He wrote that they "contributed to the transformation of the French colonists in Canada into a typically North American people." Referring to them as "Caesars of solitude," he remarked that they represented "one of the most original social types" found in New France.[125] Frégault suggested that it would be wrong to downplay or lament that there were so many such adventurers in French Canada's past. It would be better, he said, "to emphasize the balance that was struck between the colonists' dynamic and more sedentary tendencies."[126]

Lionel Groulx was also eager to integrate the *coureurs de bois* into his narrative of the past. He had described the *coureurs de bois* as "a disease" and "a chancre," dismissed them as a "waste of virile youth," and characterized them as "our first proletarians" because they were "men without a home, often without a family, and without any money" and because they were "exploited by government officials and the *seigneurs*."[127] He also had referred to Radisson as "an ignoble traitor to the French nation, a debauched adventurer,"[128] and pointed out derisively that the *coureurs de bois* often worked for the English.[129] But he also recognized the need to prepare French Canadian boys for their future roles as "masters and conquerors," as well as the need to instill in these boys a strong work ethic, discipline, and most especially a "taste for liberty."[130] Thus he insisted that students be made aware that "their ancestors were discoverers, the first explorers, and the first civilizers of this country." He also hoped that students would understand "that their race had not been created to become a race of servants."[131] As a result, he recognized that the exploits of the *coureurs de bois* fitted easily into his narrative of a past characterized by proactive and adventurous men.

To reinforce this point, Groulx stressed that the *coureurs de bois* were motivated by loftier ideals than crude commercial interests. Like some English Canadian historians, he argued that they were drawn to the forest primarily as men and patriots in search of adventure. "It was not simply trade that drew so many young men into the forest," Groulx wrote. "There was the promise of freedom, to be sure," but once these men arrived in the wilderness, "patriotism and their love of their religion would be re-awakened," as would their love of God and his representatives on earth, namely the governor and the king.[132]

In spite of his lingering doubts about the *coureurs de bois*, Groulx welcomed them into the historical narrative as "empire-builders,"[133] elevating them into the pantheon of heroes from New France alongside the *habitant* and the Catholic missionary.[134] He abandoned some of his reservations about the *coureurs de bois* because he recognized that these figures fitted into his nation-building narrative, which emphasized evidence of courage and manhood. Describing the colonists in general as a "race of steel,"[135] he singled out the *coureurs de bois* for being among the most "virile" and "robust" specimens of youth.[136]

Those same qualities – independence and freedom – that had kept the *coureurs de bois* on the margins of the historical narrative for much of the nineteenth century had become by the twentieth century the very same ones that led to their reintegration into the story of French Canada's past.[137] This once maligned figure, who had been thought to represent libertinism, freedom of thought, and liberty, was transformed into a virile hero to serve the needs of a modern French Canadian male audience still coming to terms with the changes associated with industrialism and urbanization and struggling to reaffirm its manhood.[138]

THIS NEW HISTORICAL NARRATIVE, which highlighted men's muscular and heroic acts rather than their religiosity or attachment to the land, reflected a larger shift in the public's attitudes about manhood. By placing greater emphasis on the exploits of men like Dollard des Ormeaux, the *patriotes*, and the *coureurs de bois*, historians were directing attention away from the role that the church had played in the history of French Canada. The priests and missionaries, who had dominated previous histories, appear in this new narrative as much more passive actors. In this new history, as well as in the larger cultural consciousness, there was a shift away from a passive, celibate, and clerical model of manhood and toward one that was much more active, heterosexual, and secular. Such narratives, then, contributed to the erosion of clerical influence in the province during the interwar years because they downplayed the role that clerical leaders had been thought to have played in the story of French Canadian survival.

In addition, using history to tell the story of heroic and manly acts further marginalized women in the historical narrative as well as in their own time. By transforming nation building into an exclusively male endeavour, emphasizing the ways that French Canadian men fought to secure their rights and their survival, and downplaying the ideology of *survivance* and its implicit reliance on women's bodies, this narrative eliminated many vestiges of supposed feminine passivity from the story. To be sure, women never occupied a major place in the historical consciousness. But whatever role they had played would be downplayed in this new historical narrative, which was intended to contribute to the remasculinization of French Canadian culture. As women's contributions to French Canada's historical development were downplayed in order to make room for the exploits of virile, ambitious, and political men, women were removed from the historical narrative of survival, just as they had been denied any role in the perpetuation of the race. By the middle of the twentieth century, then, women as well as priests would become increasingly marginal in a nationalist project that was becoming much more masculine in character and much less tied to the church.

6
The Critique of National Manhood

As many nationalists promoted a closer integration of the individual and the nation as a means of bolstering French Canadian manhood, some critics began to wonder whether nationalism itself might be the problem with the state of manhood in the province. By the 1930s a number of journalists and writers were suggesting that some nationalists were focusing so heavily on nurturing a man's national character that they were paying too little attention to nurturing that man's masculine identity. Emboldened by the Great Depression and influenced by French personalist thinking, which rejected the ideological extremes that characterized interwar political thinking, these critics sought to disentangle manhood from national identity and to renegotiate man's relationship with his society and with the nation. By privileging a person's identity as a man above his national and racial identities, these critics challenged the authority of the Catholic Church and offered a version of manhood that was an alternative to the one promoted by some nationalists.

In January 1938, following almost a decade of economic depression, the poet Hector de Saint-Denys Garneau wrote in his journal, "A worthy intention – to make men more themselves by making them French Canadians." But, he went on to note, "It is by human measures that the ills of our compatriots can be remedied, not their human ills by nationalist measures. For man's ills go beyond the idea of the national, they are human, and only human measures can overcome them."[1] It was perhaps fitting that Garneau would come to symbolize his generation's growing disillusion with nationalist assumptions about French Canadian manhood. He was a member of one of French Canada's oldest and most distinguished literary families. His grandfather was the poet Alfred Garneau, and his great-grandfather was François-Xavier Garneau, the historian whose writing had played a significant role in shaping French Canadian nationalist sentiment. F.-X. Garneau had written his histories to celebrate French Canadians' resilience and survival on the continent and to encourage them to remain loyal to their nationality. But this version of history would have struck Saint-Denys Garneau as overly passive because, as he often pointed out, French Canadians "want not only to survive, but to live."[2] He was, in fact, deeply troubled by the nationalism that his great-grandfather's words had helped to shape, insisting that French Canadians required more than a sense of nationality to achieve personal fulfilment and to confront the challenges they faced in the modern world. What they needed was a degree of spiritual and personal fulfilment that moved beyond their sense of national identity and that could be achieved only when they renegotiated their personal relationship with the nation. Garneau's life and writing were part of a larger cultural shift taking place during the 1930s, one that challenged traditional nationalist claims that a person's manhood and his nationality were intimately connected.

Saint-Denys Garneau was suspicious of any ideology that restricted a man's individual actions and thoughts or that burdened him with a set of conditions in the name of collective and national ambitions. In his attempt to understand the motivations behind some French Canadians' determination to introduce a type of nationalist education, for example, he wondered, "An education designed to create a nation in a French Canadian mould? And then the holding up to the people of certain moulds, certain formulas, a national myth? Would that give our people the consciousness of nationhood? And then what? Can such an education even exist without a sense of restrictiveness?" In rejecting the establishment of a program of national education, he wrote, "Any method not properly directed towards the essentially human is likely to be restrictive and short-sighted. And so is all education founded on historiography and nationalism." He warned, too, that nationalism stifled individual thought because it promoted simplistic solutions to what he suggested were complex social and spiritual dilemmas. "Only those who pursue the answer to a question are alive," he wrote, adding, "a man is dead when everything appears to him as solved." Any ideology that ignored individual needs and aspirations or asked men to elevate their national or racial identities above all others, he argued, was necessarily oppressive. For this reason, Garneau focused on solutions that were devoted to "freeing the human spirit" rather than to "freeing French Canadians," and he wrote that the plight of the French Canadian worker should be addressed "not insofar as he is a French Canadian but insofar as he is a worker." French Canadian nationalism, Garneau argued, required man's submission to the nation and to the collective and thus merely distracted society from its primary obligation, which he claimed was to "form men, not French Canadians."[3]

Garneau's skepticism about French Canadian nationalism as well as his determination to rework men's relationship to the state was rooted in his aesthetic sensibilities. As a painter and a writer, he had been particularly eager to define his own relationship with his subjects by overcoming those obstacles and filters that he claimed separated him from his perceived reality. "Between ourselves and the object," he wrote in his journal, "there may be some intermediary region which is accounted for and understood, but ultimately or initially there is a mystery. And it is faith alone which is able, not to understand the mystery, but to grasp it somehow, to communicate through it with reason." Garneau suggested that "it is through faith that all connection with reality is affected" and that any other means of defining reality resulted from the arrogant attempt to displace God.[4] Art, he claimed, "should be a transparency for beauty" and should "not impose conditions on it."[5] Garneau was ultimately searching for the authenticity that he suspected his society had denied him.[6]

Garneau likened nationalist rhetoric to a painter's brush that imposed too many demands on the audience, obstructing its perceptions of reality with a set of ideological obfuscations and filters. In addition, he suggested, nationalists had placed all their hopes and expectations for the nation on the province's youth. The result was an entire generation of young men overwhelmed with crushing responsibilities even before they reached adulthood. Boys learned of their responsibilities at an early age at school, where nationalist teachers relentlessly reminded them of their duty to fulfil the heroic legacy left to them by their brave and virile forefathers and where they were told that the survival of the race and the nation depended on their ability to contribute in a manly way to the national project. The expectation that boys and men would acquiesce to a nationalist ideal only intensified in the years following the Great War and then again during the Great Depression, when boys were reminded that the future of the race rested on their shoulders.[7]

Although Garneau's privilege and social standing shielded him from the economic crisis of the 1930s, he was not immune from the nationalist pressures that he was describing. He had grown increasingly alienated from his surroundings, spending much of his life on his family's estate at Ste-Catherine-de-Fossambault, near Quebec City. He claimed to feel particularly detached from the world, confiding to his journal, "More and more I feel out of my element in this society."[8] He characterized his own estrangement in this way:

> It is they who killed me
> Fell on my back with their weapons, killed me
> Fell on my heart with their hate, killed me
> Fell on my nerves with their shouts, killed me
>
> ...
>
> They trod everything underfoot without seeming to
> Without knowing it, wanting it, without being able to
> Without thinking, without heeding

> by their one terrible strange mystery
> Because they did not come forward to embrace me.[9]

The imagery of death and murder reflected larger cultural anxieties over the manner in which a closed society had insisted on social conformity. Garneau resented this demand for conformity, which forced him to make "base concessions to their habits, thinking, manners, ways of seeing and feeling" because it became evident to him that "they only tolerate him when he is crushed, humiliated and worthy of their contempt. They look on him always as a sick man and only put up with him when he has been made harmless."[10] Searching for an escape from such oppression, Garneau appeared to look forward to his own death, writing in his journal, "It has never repelled me. I have always looked on it as liberation."[11]

In 1943 at the age of thirty-two, Garneau suffered a heart attack while paddling alone in his canoe.[12] He found his way to an island and died there, alone and physically removed from the society he felt had rejected him. Almost immediately following his death, Garneau emerged as a symbol of his generation's alienation. His friend Jean Le Moyne was perhaps most responsible for transforming Garneau into a tragic and heroic victim of the stifling conditions of French Canadian society, opening his famous tribute to the poet the following year by writing, "I cannot speak of Saint-Denys Garneau without anger. Because they killed him. His death was an assassination prepared over a long time."[13] His tribute to Garneau was in fact an indictment of his society and an attack on priests who carried out a process of "disembraining" congregants every Sunday and who had created a society in which "it is forbidden to love and be happy because – guess why – because it is a sin." He also condemned society's inability to accommodate Garneau's individuality and creativity, concluding that his

> analytical drive led him to undervalue the worth of his own talent and work, led him to accuse himself of being an imposter, to sentence himself morally and spiritually with extreme severity, even to deny the presence of desire in himself and, the supreme error, led him to the conclusion that he lacked existence, that his own identity was too weak to justify his external reality.

He warned, "We cannot tolerate that a single person, in the name of anyone or anything whatsoever, should be cast out into the desert like Saint-Denys Garneau in order to fulfil and surpass himself," and he concluded, "A society whose internal dynamics are so warped that it is led to make such extreme demands deserves nothing better than to be evacuated."[14]

Garneau was part of a new generation of French Canadian thinkers who had grown increasingly alienated from their society and had begun to look for ways out of the crisis that they said was confronting the province. The Depression demonstrated quite clearly the failures of the market as well as just how unprepared Quebec's institutions appeared to be to respond to the crisis. But to many young French Canadians like Garneau, the economic collapse appeared more as a symptom of a much larger predicament confronting the province than as the actual cause of the crisis. According to these young thinkers, Quebec was experiencing a much larger spiritual crisis, which was hampering French Canadians' ability to respond to the economic collapse as well as alienating them from their society and their political institutions. As part of this effort to encourage French Canadians to reimagine their place in society, Garneau would join with a group of like-minded individuals and launch *La Relève*, a periodical that very quickly became one of the most influential publications of the era as well as an important conduit for European ideas in Canada. Founded in Montreal in 1934 by Robert Charbonneau, Paul Beaulieu, and Jean Le Moyne, who had all graduated from Collège Sainte-Marie in Montreal, *La Relève* sought an alternative to what it called the sterile debates that it claimed had characterized French Canadian politics for too long. The editors called on young French Canadian Catholics to rehabilitate the province's long-dormant intellectual and cultural life, and they presented *La Relève* as "the first journal for the youth of today ... that does not simply promote the ideas of a particular organization."[15] Charbonneau, for his part, framed the issue in generational terms, expressing dismay that the province's boys "reached the age of manhood in a closed world that offers them nothing ... and that leaves them without any hope for the future."[16] Over the next decade, *La Relève* would provide a forum for the growing disenchantment with traditional nationalist assumptions in the province as well as with the apparent triumph of materialism, individualism, and secularism, which the editors suggested were stifling French Canadian spiritual development and manhood.[17]

The editors of *La Relève* were particularly interested in removing those obstacles said to be standing in the way of man's relationship with God. Dismayed by the tendency on the part of some thinkers during the interwar years to elevate economic and political reform above considerations of spirituality, they pointed out in their inaugural issue, "To live fully as a Catholic does not mean that one ceases to be a Canadian. Rather it means to be more adequately Canadian."[18] Two years later, in a special issue entitled "Préliminaire à un manifeste pour la patrie," *La Relève* spelled out its reasons for wishing to disentangle men from the national community. Charbonneau and Beaulieu, along with Robert Élie, another Saint-Marie graduate who joined the review in 1935, and Claude Hurtubise, went further, declaring, "A doctrine that states 'Let us first be masters of the economic and political worlds of Quebec and then we will firmly establish our spiritual and cultural values' is a doctrine that negates the spiritual and threatens to plunge us into a world of materialism." Patriotism, they stated, "cannot be considered outside of the person" and "only takes on its true meaning and its real value when it is subordinated to a Christian order."[19] They objected to economic and political programs that did not take into account cultural and spiritual values, and they argued that a man derived his freedom from his ability to reconcile his spiritual and his temporal concerns rather than, as certain conservative nationalists would have it, from his nationality or racial identities, insisting, "It is as members of a society, and not as members of a nationality, that men have the right to determine the form of government that suits them."[20] *La Relève,* therefore, called on French Canadians to renegotiate their relationship with the nation by peeling away the ideological layers that had slowed their movement toward spiritual fulfilment.

La Relève was modelled on the French periodical *Esprit,* which was founded in Paris in 1932 by Emmanuel Mounier and which attracted young intellectuals who were growing increasingly disillusioned with the failure of the political classes to offer citizens anything except ideological responses to the social and spiritual challenges of the era. Mounier had become alarmed over the ways that political leaders had succeeded in dividing the civic body by pitting citizens against one another through demands for ideological purity and loyalty to particular parties or movements. Claiming to be neither on the right nor on the left of the political spectrum, Mounier was critical of liberalism, which he felt placed too much emphasis on the individual, as well as communism, which appeared to him to be preoccupied with the group, because such movements tended to isolate small parts of the person and thus necessarily failed to address the full spectrum of the person's material, social, and spiritual needs.[21] Both capitalism and socialism were viewed as dangerous ideological constructs because they denied men's full selves and displaced the centrality of God in the process.[22] Refusing to believe that nationalism, individualism, collectivism, faith, and reason were discrete and incompatible elements in the manner that certain ideologues were appearing to suggest at the time, Mounier and the figures associated with *Esprit* set out to restore the balance between a person's individual and his social impulses in order to produce "un homme équilibré" who could balance his spiritual and material desires while at the same time recognizing that God remained at the centre of his existence.[23] This personalist equilibrium would permit men to overcome the oppressive ideologies that had thrived during the interwar years primarily by exploiting their fractured selves.

Associated with the new Catholic left during the interwar years, Mounier appeared especially determined to incorporate social justice into his Catholicism so as to make the church relevant once again in the lives of working-class people.[24] He had grown increasingly frustrated with the church because it appeared to be in the process of squandering what he claimed was its best opportunity to ensure its relevance in a rapidly modernizing world since it had decided to ignore the encyclical *Rerum novarum* and Pope Leo XIII's appeal that Catholics demonstrate greater compassion for those who were suffering as a result of modern industrial society. Instead of embracing this challenge, Mounier argued, the church had become decadent and increasingly disengaged from ordinary people's lives because it had grown preoccupied with defending its own power within the bourgeois social structure. As a result, the masses were increasingly turning away from the church, which they viewed as increasingly irrelevant to their lives, and were embracing those ideological and political movements, such as communism and fascism, that claimed to be addressing their concerns. The movement away from God and the growing irrelevance of the church among the working classes had brought on the present condition whereby men had become, in the words of one scholar, "mortally endangered" by their "own political, social, economic, and ideological creations."[25]

If personalist thinkers clearly identified the dilemmas that they suggested were confronting the modern man, they had a less easy time coming up with a coherent way out of those dilemmas.[26] This failure is perhaps to be expected of individuals who had, after all, objected so strenuously to the ideological certitude that characterized much of the era's political discourse. That personalists appeared to be promoting abstract principles in response to the threats that they identified can also be regarded as consistent with their contention that the primary threat that they identified, namely ideological dogma presented using divisive rhetoric, was itself an abstraction. Their call to rehabilitate the full person is best understood as an assertion of principle rather than as a fully developed program for achieving that ideal.[27] The absence of a coherent philosophy can thus be explained in part by the fact that personalists were interested primarily in finding a release from the overwhelming ideological constraints of their time.

This desire to escape the oppressive political and cultural landscape as a means of restoring the integrity of the full person was also sufficiently abstract as a principle to attract a diverse range of individuals to personalism. The young intellectuals associated with *La Relève* were drawn in particular to the ideas of Jacques Maritain, one of the leading French Catholic philosophers and Thomist thinkers during the interwar years and a key figure in the founding of

Esprit. Like many others at that time who were associated with personalism, Maritain was suspicious of any movement that privileged political ideology or material gratification above the spiritual concerns of the person. He rejected modern ideological constructs because they threatened to supplant God and to alienate men from what he suggested were transcendent human values. Western culture's retreat from universal truths and its apparent embrace of individualism beginning with the Renaissance, he argued, had created the conditions that had led to the rise of such pernicious ideologies as communism and fascism. And he feared that such ideologies encouraged men to position themselves at the centre of their existence and to diminish the importance of spirituality. In its inaugural issue, the editors of *La Relève* acknowledged their considerable debt to Maritain's ideas, quoting his writing directly as they presented their intentions for the journal: "We are not fighting to defend and maintain the present political and social order. We are fighting to defend the principles of truth and justice, the remains of our living heritage, and the remnants of the divine on earth, as well as to prepare and bring about a new order [*ordre nouveau*] that must replace the present disorder."[28]

The idea that society had become disordered was, of course, hardly limited to personalist thinking. Concern about the effects of modernity on the individual had become, in fact, especially widespread by the 1930s, particularly among intellectuals who were watching with increasing alarm the rise of Fascism and Nazism in Europe. And this concern could be found on both the left and the right of the political spectrum. The generation that had come of age during the Great War had become disillusioned with modernism. With its promise of rationality and especially its notion of human progress, which had been tied so closely to a deep faith in the power of technological innovation, modernity had been regarded as an unambiguous improvement over the medieval era. But this notion that one could create a utopian, rational, and technologically sophisticated world that permitted individuals to pursue their independent paths unencumbered by the religious burdens associated with the premodern era was shattered in the aftermath of the war when the entire modernist project appeared to have simply offered men one more way of killing more people. The scale of the destruction of the Great War, as well as the seeming futility of the entire conflict, seriously challenged men's faith in human rationality.

In the minds of some critics, the emergence in the 1920s of an individualistic consumer economy seemingly steeped in the pursuit of hedonistic pleasures was the outgrowth of the disillusion of a generation of young men who had lost faith in their institutions and their leaders. But in the minds of others, the roots of the social crisis of the interwar years could be located in an earlier era. For these critics, the problem could be traced to the Enlightenment, which had ushered in the modern era by liberating individuals from the supposed darkness of the Middle Ages and by promoting rationalism, individualism, and secularism above all other values. But modernity had failed utterly, according to these critics, to liberate the individual in a manner that would permit him to assume greater control over his own life. Instead, the Enlightenment had privileged individualism and rationality in a manner that ensured people would be capable of developing only narrow aspects of their personality, which would in turn render them vulnerable to their surroundings because they had been left without a moral or spiritual compass. The triumph of rationality and secularism, therefore, did little to liberate individuals from the burdens that were said to have held them back during the medieval period. Instead, modernity had encouraged individuals to turn their back on their moral and spiritual values in favour of a false liberty supposedly found in temporal pleasures, leaving them fractured and vulnerable to exploitation by the church and by the political and ideological movements of the moment. The focus on rationality and individualism that is associated with post-Enlightenment life had untethered men from any moral grounding, producing a deep distrust of concepts such as universal truths or natural rights, which had done less to liberate individuals than to place them on a path toward cultural and moral relativism, as well as nihilism, which had also left them vulnerable to the cynical appeals from authoritarian regimes in places like Nazi Germany.[29]

The distinctions between the left and right are problematic, of course, and are much more useful in retrospect as a means of categorizing particular thinkers or ideas than in capturing the dynamic intellectual ferment of the period. The case of Maritain is instructive in this regard. Prior to his association with Emmanuel Mounier and *Esprit*, Maritain had been drawn to the reactionary and monarchist ideas of Charles Maurras and the Action française movement. Maurras was a leading critic of the secular French Third Republic, which had been established in 1870 following the reign of Napoleon III and which promoted such notions as parliamentary supremacy as well as a professional civil service. Although Maurras endorsed the secularism that had come to define the Third Republic, he remained opposed to the individualism that democratic institutions appeared to promote and called for the restoration of the monarchy and for a renewal of French nationalism as a means of restoring the country's greatness.

Maritain had gravitated toward Maurras' ideas in part out of a shared concern about the effects that modern secular ideas were having on the individual. But he did not share Maurras' emphasis on *politique d'abord* (political action) to address the nation's problems. Thus, when Pope Pius XI condemned the Action française movement in 1926 for privileging political concerns over religious ones, Maritain distanced himself from the group. Although some observers were disappointed that the pope had come out so strongly against a movement that was, after all, critical of the secularism of the Third Republic and although they resented the prospect of being forced to choose between their religious faith and their patriotism, Maritain defended the pope's right to intervene in temporal matters, especially when political movements or ideologues used the teachings of the church to promote a particular agenda.[30] Maritain defended religion and papal activism because of the important role he thought that they could play as a buffer between the individual and the state. Maritain would also break from Emmanuel Mounier not long after the founding of *Esprit*, claiming that the new journal had become too preoccupied with political questions at the expense of spiritual concerns.

If the editors of *La Relève* were drawn to Maritain's emphasis on spirituality as well as to Mounier's interest in social justice, other contributors were attracted to the ideas of thinkers like Alexandre Marc, who was associated with the right.[31] Marc founded the journal *Ordre nouveau* in 1931 in Paris to announce his unwillingness to conform to the prevailing intellectual currents of the time. He suggested that man would remain trapped by modernity, unable to participate fully as a complete person in his community until such time that he could reconnect with those values that he said had prevailed in the period before the Enlightenment. Marc differed from many of the personalists who followed him in his disavowal of democracy and his embrace of an authoritarian order that would permit individuals to rekindle their ethnic and national identities within the framework of a federated Europe. Once individuals were freed from the tyranny of modernity, they could replace it with a New Middle Ages, which would permit individuals to reconnect with the historical, ethnic, and spiritual traditions that had been interrupted by the modern era. Believing that a decisive break with the present, or a revolution, was needed if individuals were to be released from the ideological burdens of their own time, some people would come to regard the rise of communism, Fascism, and Nazism as the beginnings of a crisis that might precipitate the necessary rupture from modernity that would permit individuals to restore the values associated with this New Middle Ages.[32]

Marc's ideas about a New Middle Ages pointed a young Guy Frégault toward a new reading of the history of New France that permitted him to rethink the challenges French Canadians were encountering in his own time. Frégault, who would in the postwar years become one of Quebec's most prominent historians and also serve as the province's deputy minister of cultural affairs during the Quiet Revolution, was drawn to Marc's concept of a New Middle Ages in part because it offered him a framework for understanding why French

Canadians appeared to be suffering much more under the conditions of industrial modernity than English-speaking Canadians appeared to be.[33] Drawing on Marc's ideas, Frégault explained the supposed failures of French Canadians in his own day by pointing to the British Conquest, which he described as the central trauma in the collective experience of French Canadians. According to Frégault, the Conquest represented the moment when the French Canadian nation was diverted from its prescribed historical destiny. The Conquest put an end to the progress of a dynamic nation, condemned French-speaking Canadians to live under the authority of a foreign political power, and taught them to submit to an authoritarian and inward-looking Catholic Church. By the twentieth century, French Canadians had been so completely drained of any sense of self-worth and individual initiative, and had become so accustomed to submitting to authority figures, that they had become stagnant and unable to advance beyond their low-level positions within industrial modernity. The damage caused by these developments could be arrested only by reversing the effects of the Conquest and by restoring the values associated with New France, which Frégault suggested embodied those spiritual, communitarian, and national values that had been absent since the middle of the eighteenth century.

Historians had long presented New France as an agrarian ideal worthy of emulation and had viewed the Conquest as a decisive and disruptive moment in French Canada's life. But few had actually described the colony as a dynamic and entrepreneurial society that saw its development as a modern society stifled. Writing in the context of economic dislocation and war, when historians were asking why French Canadians appeared so unprepared for industrialism, Frégault suggested that it was in part because the Conquest had cut them off from their spiritual, cultural, and ultimately entrepreneurial destiny, placing the population at the mercy of a traditional church that would maintain and perpetuate its power by encouraging the newly conquered people to demonstrate loyalty to the new English leadership and by promoting a simple and narrow interpretation of French Canadian culture and of New France as an agrarian ideal. According to Frégault, however, New France should not to be so narrowly defined. It was, in fact, a near-perfect society representing the fully formed person, whose destiny had been violently interrupted first by the Conquest and then by an ideological church hierarchy as well as the English ideologues promoting industrial modernity and rationality. This idea would be echoed by other historians, like Michel Brunet, who pointed to "agriculturalism, anti-statism, and messianism" as the three dominant themes in French Canadian thought.[34]

This interpretation of New France placed these historians at odds with Lionel Groulx, who agreed that the Conquest was a calamitous event but presented a much narrower portrait of the French colony as an agrarian and religious society. According to Frégault, New France was a normal society, and in the context of the period, this meant that it was one largely untouched by the ideological problems of the modern era and one that permitted the French-speaking Canadians to live fully. It was this version of New France that would serve much less as a model worthy of emulation – the colony was, after all, an authoritarian society – and more as the basis for critiquing the problems associated the modern French Canadian man.

Frégault found a way out of the period's ideological and political impasse by calling for the restoration of the pristine world that was thought to have existed prior to 1760. The purity of the person would be restored only by casting off the reality of his own time, which represented a catastrophic deviation from the values of the past. It was in this way that Frégault embraced nationalism without embracing the narrowness or authoritarianism with which it was sometimes associated.[35] Marc's ideas resonated among young French Canadians who had grown weary of the effects of modernity but who were not prepared to turn away from nationalism.

The individual who is perhaps most associated with the effort to incorporate French Canadian nationalist aspirations into a personalist philosophy, and who did the most to popularize these ideas to the reading public, was Abbé Rodolphe Dubé, an instructor of philosophy and history at the elite Jean-de-Brébeuf College in Montreal during the 1930s. Although Dubé was at times conflicted over French Canadian nationalism and in some instances supported aspects of Lionel Groulx's teachings, he challenged nationalist claims that the French Canadian man was intertwined with the nation and that a person's manhood was the product of his feelings of national belonging. As a teacher at Brébeuf, Dubé taught some of Quebec's most privileged young men, leaving an indelible impression on many of these future leaders.[36] But after only a few years at the college, his superiors grew concerned that he was straying too far from the established curriculum and exposing his students to unorthodox ideas and books. By the summer of 1941, concerned that Dubé might be encouraging his students to develop their own thoughts and ideas, his superiors transferred him to a college in Sudbury, Ontario. In 1949 Dubé would leave the church and Quebec to settle in France for a prolonged period of self-imposed exile because he claimed he could no longer tolerate the intellectually stifling confines of the province.[37] Although his influence as a teacher was considerable, it would be outside the classroom, and under the pseudonym François Hertel, that Dubé would have the greatest impact.

Hertel devoted much of his writing to questions of adolescence and young manhood.[38] In his first major work, *Leur inquiétude* (1936), he exhibited empathy with French Canadian boys in particular because he claimed that they were being asked to endure pressures that others their age in other provinces did not face. He complained that in addition to the challenges of finding their own role in society, the province's boys were also expected to take on the responsibility for ensuring French Canadian survival on the continent.[39] Such expectations placed young men under considerable pressures that they could not be expected to meet, Hertel suggested, and produced mediocre men who were unable to serve their society or God.[40]

These pressures had also produced what Hertel described as a crisis because men had lost their sense of direction in life as well as their ability to find personal fulfilment. In *Pour un ordre personnaliste* (1942), he argued, "Our great flaw is apathy in all of its forms, it is laziness and numbness." "Our primary duty," he wrote, "is to live," by which he meant "to be a man, a living person."[41] He was suspicious of a purely political expression of nationalism because it would "do violence to the person in the name of an abstraction" and because "it would divide up one's being."[42] Like the editors of *La Relève,* Hertel attempted to fuse the temporal and the spiritual worlds and rejected appeals to ideologies that served only to divide the French Canadian man against himself. He suggested that men could achieve greater personal balance by reversing nationalist priorities: "We must place the emphasis on the person more than on the nation, act more within the social and cultural realm than in the political realm."[43]

Hertel thus challenged the nationalist contention that manhood flowed from national and racial identities. Whereas Groulx had noted, "Like the past, like history, the country is our master. One is the son of his native land, as one is the son of his race, of his time," and appeared to imply that men were the sons of everything but their mothers,[44] Hertel rearranged Groulx's order of things, reminding his readers, "before being the sons of a country, we are the sons of a woman,"[45] and "every individual is a person before being a member of a family, of a social class, or of a state."[46] This reordering of things marked an important dissent from nationalist thinking at the time, and it offered an alternate reading of manhood. By focusing on the development of the individual man before concentrating on his integration into the national community, Hertel reprioritized French Canadians' duties, reminding them, "Before being French Canadian we must be men."[47]

If Hertel took issue with certain aspects of nationalist thought, he also approved of others. He agreed with those individuals, for example, who believed that the province lacked a national mystique, describing French Canadians as "an arrested people, an ossified people, a people more oriented toward the past than toward the future."[48] One of the causes of this situation, he noted, was the province's educational system, which had failed, in his mind, to transform boys into proper men. "Rather than forming men, beings of body and spirit," Hertel continued, our schools appear "intent upon producing machines for reasoning."[49] Like the nationalists, then, he supported the introduction of a rigorous program of national education that would produce French Canadian men capable of dealing with their current malaise and prepared to face their future with confidence. He wrote, "Making men, that's the formula: the only sound and only effective form of a national education," noting, "this complete man that we're waiting for, it is up to the teachers to give him to us."[50]

Hertel also differed from the editors at *La Relève* by showing greater interest in finding solutions to French Canada's economic problems. The writers associated with *La Relève* were largely isolated from the effects of the Depression and showed little interest in the actual economic problems associated with the crisis. They were also wary of any proposal that focused on economic or material solutions to the Depression because they preferred to interpret it as a symptom of a larger spiritual crisis.[51] In contrast, Hertel was determined to reconcile material and spiritual concerns by emphasizing the role economic reform could have in rehabilitating French Canadian manhood. One of the major challenges confronting French Canadian men, he noted, was that they had very little toward which to aspire in an economy dominated by English Canadian capitalists. French Canadians, he argued, reached the age of manhood only to find themselves shut out of positions of power. The realization that they were unlikely to advance in the industrial world and that they were merely working to advance the economic interests of their English-speaking bosses contributed to French Canadians' feelings of inferiority and plunged them into what he described as a state of forced idleness. He complained that French Canadians behaved as though they were members of a minority group and that they had failed to become "the undisputed masters of a province that should be fully ours."[52] So he called on French Canadians to adapt to their surroundings[53] and to become "maîtres chez nous."[54] French Canadians, he would also write, needed to "show signs of life," and "one of the sure signs of life would undoubtedly be this economic revitalization."[55]

With his practical assessment of the problems facing French Canadian society, and his ability to synthesize his ideas in an accessible manner, Hertel appealed to a wide audience. He incorporated the spiritual priorities of *La Relève* with the more politically active European model of personalism and even accommodated certain features of Groulx's nationalism by endorsing a form of nationalist curriculum for the province's schools. In the process, he tapped into the increasingly materialistic ambitions of some new scholars who were rethinking French Canadian manhood at the same time that they searched for ways to reverse the province's economic stagnation. Hertel and Frégault's nationalism was neither reactionary nor based on a nostalgic yearning for an imagined simpler past. Rather, it served a larger personalist commitment to restoring individuals to their rightful place within a balanced social order that did not force men to choose which portion of their identity should be elevated above the others.

But even those personalists who were more critical of nationalism were not necessarily completely opposed to nationalist thinking. Personalists may have differed in their approach to the problems that they identified, but they also shared a desire to remove those obstacles that they identified as standing in the way of the individual's realization of full personhood. In Quebec personalists were determined to escape the stultifying ideologies of their time, and for many people this objective meant a rejection of traditional forms of nationalism. Their priority was to reduce the burdens being imposed on young men and to ensure that the individual could live fully as a person within a national community. Although they attacked nationalism when it threatened to overwhelm the person, they could not be anti-nationalist because to abjure nationalism completely would simply further alienate individuals from their community and precipitate a further descent into the materialist and secular values associated with modernity.

The personalist message was particularly attractive to many French Canadians during the interwar years because the population was being pulled between, on the one hand, a traditional form of nationalism espoused by some church leaders and, on the other hand, the materialism and capitalism of the provincial Liberal Party of Lomer Gouin and Louis-Alexandre Taschereau. Quebec proved to be a fertile ground for personalist ideas because it was going through a period of change, led by the Catholic Action Movement, which was transforming the social and religious character of the province. A growing number of working-class and middle-class French Canadians would be drawn to Catholic Action groups. Organized and led by lay Catholic figures, these groups altered people's relationship with their church and their faith. In bringing Catholicism closer to the public, these groups appeared to be fulfilling the long-held desire of many Catholics to modernize the structure and the outlook of the church. Through initiatives such as the marriage-preparation movement, greater openness to birth control methods, and more liberal attitudes about gender relations, these groups would bring vitality to the religion and provide a material change that reflected the needs of the people rather than serve an abstract ideological purity. The Catholic Action Movement thus permitted individuals to believe that they exercised greater control over their spiritual lives as well as over the church itself. Moreover, in spite of the not insignificant reality that these groups operated under the direction of the church hierarchy, Catholic Action permitted the more liberal ideas of social justice to permeate an otherwise closed and conservative province.[56]

It was this desire for change rather than any particular program of reform that characterized the youth movements of the era, including the more liberal-minded members of Catholic Action groups as well as the more conservative and reactionary Jeune Canada, which placed a much greater emphasis on nationalism. Looking back on his involvement with Jeune Canada, Pierre Dansereau acknowledged that he, along with other young reformers, was less interested in proposing new ideas than in challenging older ones. "We had very little in the way of precise doctrine," he said but went on to note that "more than perfect homogeneity, we sought vitality in our association."[57] It was a desire on the part of a new generation of people to move beyond the tired and static dogmas of the time and to take control of their political, economic, social, and spiritual lives. These young intellectuals were, in the end, largely reacting to the circumstances of their time rather than presenting a program of reform.

The personalist movement was thus made up of people who shared an aversion to the ideological rigidity of the interwar years. What the personalists did offer was a critique of a society that appeared to be unable to break free of the stale political rhetoric of the era, which was propping up increasingly discredited ideological assumptions. Whether one privileged the *politique d'abord* of Maurras or the *primauté spirituel* (spiritual primacy) of Mounier, the personalists were attempting to break from the accepted ways of doing things. Above all else, personalism offered individuals the hope that change was, in fact, possible. Thus the personalist philosophy was embraced so fully by such seemingly disparate figures precisely because it offered a new way of thinking about politics, society, and religion, as well as the individual. It offered, in short, a means of breaking free of the conventional wisdom of society, and it encouraged individuals to take greater control of their own material, social, and spiritual lives. Whether one was sympathetic to nationalist thinking or critical of it, there was a general sense that French Canadian men should be given the opportunity to live fully as persons. The degree to which one turned to nationalism in order to accomplish this objective would be entirely up to the individual. The individual man became, in the end, the key to both personal spiritual fulfilment as well as national renewal.

According to a growing number of people in Quebec, the surest way to ensure the emancipation of the individual and the fulfilment of the person was to pursue substantial educational reform. The church continued to control education in the province, which meant that students were being exposed to a classical education rather than being taught the skills said to be necessary to participate in an industrialized and increasingly secular society. The solution appeared to be to encourage the state, which until that time had exhibited very little interest in increasing its role in education, to assume a larger role in the administration of the province's schools and in shaping the curriculum. For some reformers, this objective meant reducing, or even ending, the role played by the church in the province's schools. Only a reformed educational system would permit the student to think more freely and then to break free of the society's rigid ideological assumptions. Once individuals acquired the necessary skills to compete in the new economy and to think independently, they would be free to renegotiate their relationship with their community on their own terms.

During the interwar years, a group of professional economists and sociologists working at the École des hautes études commerciales (HEC) in Montreal was determined to renegotiate the boundaries of the industrial economy in an effort to rehabilitate French Canadians' identities as men. Esdras Minville, a leading member of this group, had been at the HEC since 1924 and would lead the school from 1938 until 1962. In many ways an unlikely reformer, he was a traditional conservative nationalist who remained loyal to small-scale industry and agrarian values. But he also recognized that French Canadians needed to adapt to the province's industrial reality if they were to survive as a group, and he worked to ensure that French Canadians received their fair share of the benefits. Minville argued that Quebec's rapid industrialization had unfairly benefited Montreal, which had the effect of subordinating the province's regions to that city's economic power and in turn subordinating French-speaking Montreal workers to English Canadian capital. He called for a program of economic decentralization whereby rural inhabitants would modernize their techniques and equipment so that they could improve their ability to compete with Montreal's power. This would break the city's hold on the province and help rural Quebecers to modernize and catch up with English Canadians.[58] In this way, Minville hoped to reconcile his traditional nationalism with the industrial realities of his time.[59]

Minville also linked spiritual and national fulfilment to economic and material achievement. He embraced economic reform because he recognized that the church "could no longer be the bulwark of the French Canadian nation" and realized that French Canadian men had to be prepared to succeed in the industrial world, and to succeed as men, if the nation were to prosper.[60] "What we need, above all else," he wrote, "are virile and conquering personalities," arguing that "building French Canada requires, first and foremost, the formation of French Canadians, which is to say men and women who will live, instinctively, in accordance with the values of the national culture."[61] Although he remained committed to the idea that men would uphold the "national culture," his hope that they would "instinctively" live as French Canadians marked a shift from nationalist priorities. Whereas nationalists usually claimed that a person's manhood was derived from his immersion in the national and racial community, Minville implied that the French Canadian man shaped his own identity and environment. Minville thus tentatively recognized the autonomy of the French Canadian man within the nation.

Many of these ideas were developed in Victor Barbeau's *Pour nous grandir: Essai d'explication des misères de notre temps* (1937), a book that highlighted the connections between French Canada's supposed economic backwardness and the state of its men. Based at the HEC during the 1930s, Barbeau was determined to uncover the reasons for French Canadians' apparent inability to compete with English Canadians. He could be blunt in his assessment of French Canadians' condition and did not hesitate to blame them for contributing to their own difficulties. He characterized French Canadians as a dispirited and submissive population that was in the process of squandering its proud heritage with its defeatist attitude and its lack of drive and ambition. But he also blamed the province's schools for their irrelevance in the industrial age and for their failure to prepare students to deal with the challenges that awaited them after graduation. Schools that offered a classical education and taught Latin and Greek, he argued, merely perpetuated French Canadians' economic marginality by condemning boys to lives of economic and industrial servitude, whereby they remained content with their economic oppression at the hands of English Canadian and American industrialists. Schools, he wrote, were failing the province's boys because, "Far from liberating us from our constraints, they have increased them instead."[62]

Any solution to French Canadians' economic inferiority and any plan to reintegrate them into the existing industrial framework, Barbeau argued, had to begin with the education system. He claimed that the province's schools, which he said "suffocate and destroy all personality," were destroying French

Canadian manhood with an "emasculating" curriculum that "proletarianized" and "devirilized" students.[63] If only schools would provide students with the tools they needed to demonstrate their business and management skills, he argued, French Canadians would reclaim their rightful place in their society and put an end to the "infantilization" that they were suffering at the hands of their English-speaking "masters." They would then regain their confidence and join the industrial order as full and equal participants – and as full men. French Canadians would reassert their primacy within the province, Barbeau asserted, only by "rehabilitating the individual to his state of manhood."[64]

But before French Canadians could become real men, Barbeau suggested, they needed to discard their "colonial" outlook. He complained, "Like the Negroes of Africa, like all the primitive peoples from the four corners of the world who have served as stepping stones for megalomaniacal Anglo-Saxons, we have been enslaved by the merchants and the industrialists. We have become lumberjacks and day labourers."[65] And he reserved some of his harshest words for those "smooth-talking" leaders, whom he blamed for promoting an "emasculating" program that condemned French Canadians to a perpetual state of submissiveness.[66] Turning to the past and to those men whose character and independence of spirit had made them real men,[67] Barbeau concluded that there were no longer French Canadians in this mould and that such a French Canadian man in his own time remained "a stranger."[68] In the place of real men, he could find only "spineless" men submitting to their "colonial" masters.[69] So he appealed to French Canadian men to throw off the shackles of their "colonial" oppression by reasserting their strength, pride, and independence as men.[70]

Barbeau was clearly positioning his appeal for renewed French Canadian manhood within the gendered language of decolonization. The literary critic Katherine A. Roberts has pointed out that "the colonization process can clearly be seen as one of 'devirilization,' emasculation and reduction to the status of women."[71] Although she is describing the nationalist discourses of the 1950s and 1960s, a time when the rhetoric of decolonization reached the peak of its popularity among Quebec intellectuals, her assessment can be applied to the situation in the 1930s. During the Depression, English Canadians continued to dominate economic power in the province, whereas French Canadians found that they could do little except submit to their English-speaking bosses, who controlled their livelihood in much the same way that French Canadian women were expected to submit to their husbands. As a result, some French Canadian men had come to associate industrialization with their emasculation and humiliation as men and to see it as a threat to the patriarchal system upon which they had depended for their power. These men grew eager to escape the supposedly feminine roles that they had been assigned within the industrial order and to re-establish their patriarchal authority.

Concern about the effects of industrialization ran deep in French Canadian society. For some people, it represented such a threat to traditional gender roles that they claimed manhood could be preserved only if men escaped industrial urban centres altogether. The colonization movement and the back-to-the-land campaigns of the late nineteenth and early twentieth centuries, for example, promised to deliver French Canadians from the emasculating drudgery of industrial work and into the countryside, where they would rediscover their virile heritage and rugged manhood by working the land.[72] These new spaces would provide French Canadian men with the opportunity to reassert their power as leaders and to rediscover their pride and manhood.[73] Although Barbeau's discourse of decolonization tapped into such anxieties over Quebec's rapid industrialization and urbanization, he never went so far as to reject industrialization. Rather, he promoted French Canadian integration into the industrial landscape through technical training that would provide the means by which men could reclaim their manhood and become, once again, *maîtres chez nous*. Groulx agreed that something needed to be done to prevent French Canadians from becoming a race of proletarians. He argued that it was time for them to become "an adult race,"[74] by which he meant "a race of men."[75] Each of these expressions of decolonization shared a common desire for, to use Roberts's formulation, "full masculinity and the concomitant destruction of one's femininity."[76] After all, Mary Jean Green has reminded us, decolonization was a decidedly male project that associated "the image of the newly decolonised subject as a virile, heterosexual man."[77]

By linking French Canada's economic backwardness and failure to achieve full manhood to its supposed colonial condition, Barbeau also shifted the debate into the political realm in a manner that permitted him to continue to align himself with some of Lionel Groulx's nationalist assumptions.[78] Groulx had begun his career as a teacher and historian at a time when French Canadians had been portrayed as an embattled but largely contented minority struggling to survive and to preserve its language and religion on an Anglo-Saxon continent. Groulx rejected this version of the past, reconceiving French Canadians as a frustrated majority searching for ways to reclaim the political and economic power and influence that they had lost following the British Conquest. So he reimagined the people of New France as nation builders, referring to the *habitants* as "founders of the country and founders of the race" whose national ambitions had been frustrated by an external and occupying power.[79] Nationalist historians based at the University of Montreal during the 1930s and 1940s elaborated on Groulx's analysis by suggesting that the British had excluded French

Canadians from the fields of commerce and industry. Maurice Séguin, for example, who had studied under François Hertel at Jean-de-Brébeuf College, attributed French Canada's economic backwardness to structural factors arising from the Conquest and grew determined to remove those obstacles that were standing in the way of a man's full development.[80] And Guy Frégault was eager to portray New France as a normal society composed of strong and "balanced" men who were "artisans d'une patrie" before their progress and civilization were interrupted by the Conquest.[81]

Emphasizing the political roots of French Canada's economic problems during the 1930s meant that Barbeau avoided blaming the ills of society entirely on the church. In fact, although he indicted the church for its role in "emasculating" boys at school and for instilling them with "colonial" attitudes, it had never been his intention to blame it entirely for French Canada's economic inferiority. He was always careful to include the church in his plans to reintegrate French Canadians into their industrial surroundings, reminding people that more than simply economic solutions were necessary to solve the province's problems.[82] And although the church was stung by Barbeau's claim that their schools had played a role in "devirilizing" the province's young men, it found much in his program with which it could agree. Since it found *La Relève*'s version of Catholicism and its anti-nationalism troubling, the church was relieved that Barbeau supported traditional social and gender hierarchies and agreed that nationalism should be integrated into a boy's education at school.[83]

By presenting his reforms in a language that conservative nationalists might accept, Barbeau avoided a full confrontation with the church. But in politicizing the question of French Canadian economic inferiority, he also rendered the church more vulnerable to attacks. *La Relève,* after all, reminded its readers that the church played an important role in propping up the very political structures that oppressed the population and that it had cooperated with the "conquerors" for much of the preceding century. The church's slow response to the Depression, moreover, offered working-class men tangible evidence of its indifference to their plight and led to the rise of populist figures such as Jean-Charles Harvey. Whereas Garneau and his friends at *La Relève* wrote for a small circle of intellectuals in Montreal, and Minville and Barbeau were part of a new class of university-trained professors, men like Harvey, a journalist and popular novelist who would emerge as one of the most vocal and virulent critics of the church hierarchy during the interwar years, appeared less interested in accommodating traditional elite concerns and more willing to exploit the vulnerabilities of the church that had become evident during the Depression.

Harvey had been a journalist at a number of newspapers before becoming editor-in-chief of Quebec City's liberal daily *Le Soleil* in 1927. His campaigns for educational reform and individual freedom challenged much of the conventional wisdom of the time, prompting some recent observers to refer to him as a pioneer of the Quiet Revolution in the 1960s.[84] His support for bilingualism, internationalism, individualism, and freedom of thought, however, along with his iconoclastic nature and combative style, made him a controversial figure during his own time. Following the collapse of France during the Second World War, Harvey exhibited a level of moral and intellectual clarity when he spoke out against the Vichy regime and embraced Charles DeGaulle's resistance movement before many other French-language publications in the province would.[85] He also angered many nationalists when he encouraged French Canadians to discard their traditional isolationism and fear of the outside world and to support the plebiscite on conscription in 1942. And he flouted conventions in his personal life by living with a woman he would not marry until later in life and with whom he would become a father.

Harvey would praise Jacques Maritain's call on youth to live fully and to take greater control of their spiritual and social lives.[86] But he was too much of an individualist and materialist to be thought of as a personalist. As well, his belief that the surest means of ensuring individual liberty was to empower the state in a manner that would limit the power of the church differed from Maritain's emphasis on spiritual matters. The fullness of the person that the personalists were talking about could be achieved by escaping the power of an oppressive church and handing authority over the province's institutions to the state – that is, to the people. Harvey was seeking a form of liberty that could best be achieved through society's secular institutions. Unlike Frégault, who equated liberty with a revival of an idealized image of New France that made considerable room for nationalist sentiment, Harvey promoted the individual above all else. As a result, he was much more focused on political action than were the personalists in Quebec, who were preoccupied with spiritual renewal. This focus on the political realm placed him closer to the reform-minded individuals working at the HEC, although he did not share their nationalist inclinations. Despite his differences with the personalists at *La Relève* as well as with the nationalists at the HEC, Harvey's relentless attacks on the church would significantly weaken the authority of the church hierarchy, ultimately clearing a path that would permit personalist and nationalist ideas to triumph in the postwar years.

Harvey accused the church hierarchy of using its control over the province's social and educational institutions to promote a type of nationalism that condemned French Canadians to a state of subservience. Harvey loathed nationalism for what he said was its tendency to privilege "national values" above "human values," and he loathed French Canadian nationalism in particular for turning the province of Quebec into what he called a backward and amusing tourist attraction for curious outsiders. Describing it as a distraction from more important matters, Harvey called on French Canadians to move on from their obsession with nationalism.[87] In 1937 he launched the newspaper *Le Jour* to promote his anti-nationalist message, using it to reach a younger generation that he claimed was being held hostage by its elders' preoccupation with nationalism.[88] In an early issue of the paper, he wrote, "They have wasted too much of your time attempting to cultivate our national pride. Nations, like men, have been stunted in their development by their pride. Vain men have become so convinced of their own superiority that they no longer feel the need to progress. These men have become trapped in a state of childishness."[89] Week after week, he encouraged his readers to assert their real manhood and to become "des simples hommes normaux."[90] This normal manhood, it became abundantly clear, would be incompatible with nationalism.

Central to Harvey's critique of nationalism was his conviction that it was destroying French Canadian manhood. In 1938 *Le Jour* reported with great satisfaction, for example, on the findings of an American psychiatrist who had described nationalism as a form of homosexuality. Referring to the doctor's report, the article noted, "Nationalism is the result of an individual's extreme proclivity toward an individual of the same sex. Nationalism is, quite simply, cultural homosexuality."[91] Although the story was intended to be light-hearted and whimsical, it reflected Harvey's general belief that nationalism stood in the way of French Canadians' development into heterosexual men.

Harvey worked to disentangle manhood from national identity because he claimed that such a link was burdening the province's boys with a set of expectations that threatened to undermine their development into men. He suggested that nationalists were effectively telling French Canadians that they were inferior to, and unable to compete with, English Canadians so that they could then secure the population's allegiance to the nation and to the race. In the process, he claimed, French Canadians internalized these feelings of inferiority and failed to develop into strong and productive men. He pointed to the Saint-Jean-Baptiste Parade in Montreal in 1938 to illustrate the problems he saw with nationalism, suggesting that the floats in the parade projected to the crowd an image of weakness and appeared to be telling French Canadians, "Be poor! Be soft! Be weak! Be submissive!"[92] Two years later, he would attack that year's parade, this time setting his sights on the crowd, which he described as a sea of "anemic faces ... with blank stares, narrow shoulders, sunken chests, and deformed legs."[93] It was as though the crowd had internalized the lessons of weakness, resignation, and submission from the earlier procession.

These lessons in submission and servitude, Harvey contended, were learned at school. The primary function of the educational system, he said, should be to facilitate a boy's passage into manhood and to equip him with the tools he might need to confront the challenges that awaited him after graduation. What he found instead was a school system that he claimed was churning out boys who were woefully unprepared to succeed in the capitalist and industrial economy and who would become trapped in society's lowest-paying jobs. Instead of producing confident men ready to take on the world, the province's schools had stifled youthful ambition and condemned their graduates to a "sterilizing" life of mediocrity. Harvey accused church-run schools of leading students toward "a host of physical ailments such as neurosis, tuberculosis, and chronic dyspepsia that will diminish their minds and compromise their future careers,"[94] and he warned that they were producing a generation of timid and physically diminished young men who would be unable to function in the modern world.[95] He complained that following their graduation from the province's schools, French Canadian students did not yet realize that they had just gone through a decade-long "castration." "Only much later," he continued, when these men came face to face with their own powerlessness in the workplace, "will they realize just how emasculating their education had been."[96]

In addition to his objections about school curriculum, Harvey expressed growing concern about the prominent role that priests were playing in boys' lives. He wondered, for example, how an educational system that was managed by celibate priests, whose cloistered existence had done little to expose them to the challenges of the "real world" or to the experiences they would need to teach boys about manhood, could be expected to produce the strong and virile men that the province so desperately needed. He suggested that men like Groulx, whom he had labelled the "apostle of separatism"[97] and had accused of using the classroom and his historical works to steer the province into an "isolating and sterilizing nationalism," were incapable of providing masculine leadership to students desperate for male role models.[98] When Groulx declared that French Canadians had little need to learn the English language, for example, Harvey retorted that Groulx was in fact in no position to know what French Canadians needed, pointing out that he never had to support himself and never had to look for a job. He mused, "I would like to see Abbé Groulx with a family on his arm," suggesting that Groulx would change his tune because he would find that he could not support a family just by talking about nationalism.[99] By highlighting Groulx's celibate and cloistered life, Harvey challenged a priest's right to speak for a manhood he could never know, much less impart to a generation of boys. In the process, he showed that a priest's vow of celibacy was increasingly at odds with a society that venerated heterosexual marriage and that was in need of strong male leaders.

To rescue the province's boys from the effeminizing grip of these church-run schools and their "divirilizing" curriculum, Harvey called on the state to intervene with a new curriculum that recognized the importance of those skills required in a rapidly modernizing economy and that limited nationalist indoctrination in the classroom. A new and more practical curriculum, to be mandatory for everyone under the age of fourteen, Harvey claimed, would transform boys into true individuals and also prepare them to exercise their freedom as men.[100] He pointed to the military training schools that appeared during the Second World War as possible models because he admired their apparent success in transforming weak, sickly, small-minded French Canadian boys, such as the ones he had seen at the Saint-Jean-Baptiste Parade, into strong, independent, and virile men.[101] So he called upon the province to assume its duty by taking control of education in order to assure that French Canadian boys developed into proper men.[102]

JEAN-CHARLES HARVEY DEVELOPED many of these ideas in his novel *Les demi-civilisés* (1934), which offered a stinging critique of the insularity and corruption of French Canadian society. The novel created a stir when it appeared, and it was placed on the church's index of banned books within weeks of its release. Although the ban cost Harvey his job as editor of *Le Soleil*, it did not suppress its central message or silence its author. In any case, Harvey was just one of many figures stepping up to challenge the established order and to push for a fundamental restructuring of society.

The novel traces Max Hubert's journey toward self-discovery and manhood within the confines of a repressive society. Like many other French Canadian boys of the period, Max was educated by priests and even toyed with the idea of becoming a priest himself. But his experiences at boarding school convinced him that the church would inevitably restrict his personal freedom and stifle his budding creativity. Later in life, he recalled the ways that the priests had attempted to suppress "the whims of the little savage I was then; these would be replaced by the yoke which the school master lays on the neck of a 13 year old."[103] So he turned his back on his education and the church, and he chose to spend the rest of his life defending his liberty against lay and clerical elites who appeared determined to limit his individuality and freedom. He went on to establish a magazine to promote reform and would flout the rigid moral code of his society by falling in love with a woman who, like him, enjoyed the "liberty of belonging to each other without any compulsion or formal agreement."[104]

Throughout the novel, Max is constantly disappointed by his society and frustrated by the apparent deterioration of French Canadian manhood. He laments that he is the "descendant of a people who had become miserably domesticated" and complains that

> once the English had conquered the country and the Indians had fallen victim to the vices of Europe, our vanquished Frenchmen – ignorant, rough and quite unprepared for a quiet and regulated existence – had nothing to do but congregate in little groups of gossips and organize a communal life. They could soon be taken for well-tended animals, penned up in their zoo, well fed and content to be stared at, as objects of curiosity, by other nations.[105]

Max thus transposes the period's prevailing assumptions about women as frivolous and confined to the private domestic sphere onto men. French Canadian men had, in other words, become feminized. Max also believes that French Canadian society is too inward-looking, claiming, "We take cover behind our history like frightened kids behind their mothers' skirts."[106]

Max shudders at what he believes French Canadian men have become because he has idealized the values associated with those men who worked the land, "where the purity, strength and wildness of nature instil a hatred of servitude in the men it supports." "It's not among them that you find the malady of backwardness," he concludes, but "among our elite."[107] A conversation with an old sailor one day reinforces his disappointment and convinces him to take control of his manhood. Relating his desire to join the priesthood to the old sailor, who represents a particular form of rugged and independent manhood, the old man responds, "Come on, my boy, grow up like everyone else, make your own way, be a real man, and then get married."[108] Max thus learns that heterosexuality, economic self-sufficiency, and status derived from one's place at the head of a family are the markers of true manhood. He decides to turn away from the teachings of the church, a moment he will describe later as the one when, "throwing off the yoke of the cloister, stripping myself of the miserable frock which covered my true manhood like an outworn cuirass, dashing to the ground at my feet the shattered fragments of my feigned abasements, my adulterated virtues, my unreasoning obedience," he became a man.[109]

It was not uncommon during these years to hear questions about priests' manhood. Some critics have noted that the church's close ties with successive provincial governments and with the Anglo-Canadian bourgeoisie had confined it to what many interpreted as a "feminine" and inferior position. In her study of French Canadian literature, for example, Sister Sainte-Marie-Éleuthère referred to the church as "the true mother of our people," noting that it represented traditional feminine and maternal values, especially since it demanded that a person's attitude toward the church be similar to children's attitude toward their mother.[110] Robert Schwartzwald, too, has pointed out that the church was seen to perform "all womanly vocations, while at the same time effeminizing its own sons." These "men in skirts," as they were sometimes called, could do little except teach boys about their experiences as the submissive – that is, feminine – half of their unequal relationship with their colonial master.[111] Priests' celibate and cloistered lives, therefore, became serious impediments as they sought to teach boys about "normal" manhood at school.

Despite the fact that such grumbling about priests' manhood was not entirely new, the degree to which it became an issue in the 1930s would have come as something of a surprise to the church because it had actively defended and promoted French Canada's patriarchal character for much of the previous century. It had reliably opposed women's formal entry into the public sphere by resisting female suffrage, for example, and it defended a father's absolute right to control his household. Its position had changed little between 1869, when Bishop Ignace Bourget of Montreal declared that the father could be "the only sovereign of the child,"[112] and 1940, when Cardinal Jean-Marie-Rodrigue Villeneuve spoke out against female suffrage on the grounds that it would be contrary to the "unity and authority of the family."[113] Moreover, it had been instrumental in writing women out of the racial script by describing them as mere producers of children, thus downplaying any influence they might have had over their racial formation. And it led the opposition to the feminist movement, which was also gaining momentum in the early twentieth century, dismissing it as an unnecessarily disruptive movement that sought to redress imagined slights. The church also supported Judge Charles-Édouard Dorion, the former dean of the Faculty of Law at Laval University, when he concluded his investigation into women's status in society in 1930 by writing that women were "created to be the companions of men" and should be seen as, "above all else, wives and mothers."[114] The church had done everything, in other words, to defend the patriarchal character of French Canadian society.

But the Depression in many ways overshadowed what might have been described as the church's good record on defending patriarchy. As men lost their jobs, and with them the ability to fulfil their manly duty by providing for their families, wives sometimes turned to their parish priests for support and for help in raising their children. Some people accused the church of exploiting men's weakness in order to gain a foothold in the home. With his authority diluted by the Depression, the French Canadian father proved unable to resist the pressures of the parish priest who appeared more than willing to exploit the patriarch's diminished status in order to increase his own influence within the household. Priests thus became targets because they were thought to be conspiring with mothers to control the province's boys and men.[115] Their power was real, according to the sociologist Jean-Charles Falardeau, who described priests as "the real leaders of the society," as well as the "surrogate heads of families." The result, Falardeau suggested, was that "the adolescent-man remains the prisoner of the mother-priest coupling."[116] Years of forging alliances with mothers, along with priests' own reputations as "mothers" to the people and the view that they were subservient to their English Canadian "masters," it turned out, had compromised the clergy, leaving its members unable to teach boys about manhood from what was said to be their weak and feminine position. Critics concluded that priests were in no position to serve as male role models, accusing them of promoting a form of nationalism that simply undermined French Canadian manhood.[117]

Jean-Charles Harvey illustrated this dilemma in his short novel *Sébastien Pierre* (1935). The novel traces the improbable life of Sébastien Pierre, who is raised in a religious household primarily by a mother who dreams that he will one day die a martyr's death. This dream is partially fulfilled when, at the age of seven, Sébastien's attempt to re-enact Jean-de-Brébeuf's martyrdom at the stake gets out of hand and he ends up burning himself. Her hopes for her son are ultimately dashed, however, when she sends Sébastien on a cruise so that he can overcome his chronic health problems and the cruise ship sinks. Unbeknownst to his mother, he floats ashore in New York with the help of a woman who will change his life. That woman, Mary Curtis, convinces Sébastien to begin a new life with her and to forget his past, including his mother. She changes his name to Tony Jackson and refashions him into a petty gangster who will use his life of crime to support her own dreams of living an extravagant lifestyle. After he lives for a number of years as Tony Jackson, however, the law finally catches up with him, and he is forced to escape back home to Canada in order to elude arrest. As he makes his way back to his family homestead, he decides that he does not have the heart to reveal to his mother, who assumes he died in the shipwreck, what he has become, preferring to leave her with the memory she has constructed of him. But this is not an issue because before he has the opportunity to reunite with his mother, he runs into his brother, who has grown up and become a police officer. Mary Curtis has transformed Sébastien so successfully that his brother believes that he has found Tony Jackson and shoots him dead.

This improbable series of events serves as a warning against women's excessive influence on men. Sébastien escapes the overwhelming pressures placed upon him by his mother only to fall under the spell of an American woman who pushes him into a life of crime. His mother dreams that he will one day become a martyr, and Mary takes immense pride in fashioning this somewhat unworldly and law-abiding boy into a gangster who can provide her with the money and excitement that she has always craved. Both women attempt to live out their own fantasies through Sébastien, a boy raised in the cloistered confines of Quebec, where he never learned how to make his own decisions in life. Sébastien has spent his entire life, in other words, struggling to uphold expectations that women have placed on him.

This reading is reinforced when Sébastien's father, who has been less than visible throughout the novel, steps forward almost two decades later to confront the circumstances surrounding his son's death. He is stricken not just with the grief of losing his son all over again but also with an unbearable feeling that he has failed in his role as a father. Rushing to his son's grave site, he begs for Sébastien's forgiveness, sobbing, "I am the one who killed you by leaving you alone. I am the one who killed you. Will you suffer damnation? No, no, you are not damned. Why would you be expected to pay for the mistakes of your father?"[118] The father is filled with guilt for having neglected his son. By allowing Sébastien to take the fateful voyage that ultimately led to his death, the father blames himself for not being a proper father and for his failure to protect his son. He is guilty, in other words, because he delegated parental duties to his wife, who appears to have been doing the bidding of the priest by dreaming of her son's martyrdom. As a result, he failed to prepare his son to fend for himself in the real world. In the same way, Harvey appears to suggest, nationalism was failing to prepare French Canadian men for the challenges awaiting them in the real world.

THE NOTION THAT NATIONALISM was stifling full French Canadian manhood comes through most fully in one of the period's most celebrated works of fiction. Roger Lemelin's novel *The Town Below* (1944), the first novel in Quebec set entirely in an urban milieu, brought him instant recognition and fame and earned him the Prix David. The novel transformed French Canadian literature with its glimpse into the gritty working-class district of Saint-Sauveur in Quebec City and with its provocative assault on the province's social and cultural landscape. It also highlighted the ways that the clergy, mothers, and an insular nationalist ideology were thwarting French Canadian manhood. The mother in the novel, according to Jean-Charles Falardeau, is not simply a distant figure or behind-the-scenes presence. Rather, she is "the direct, steadfast, and effective ally of the spiritual head of the family: the parish priest."[119]

The novel revolves around the relationship between Denis Boucher, a restless and ambitious eighteen-year-old boy, his friend Jean Colin, Lise Lévesque, the girl they both love, and Denis' mother, Flora. Denis is not unlike many of the other young men in Saint-Sauveur who were, Lemelin notes, "deprived of a field of action which might have provided their country with a body of strong and capable young men, [and] were obliged to content themselves with the semblance of moral torture, from want of anything better to do."[120] He is also unexceptional in that his mother completely dominates his world and refuses to let him grow up or enter into full manhood. When she discovers that Denis is pursuing Lise, for example, she flies into a jealous rage and becomes obsessed with finding ways to disrupt their courtship. She loathes Lise, describing her as "a veritable serpents' nest of impurity and seduction," and sets out to protect her son from "any feminine contamination." She is so determined to remain the primary woman in her son's world that she fantasizes about "how much she would enjoy giving Lise a phenomenal beating" and about seeing "the creature writhing under her sturdy arm, humiliated in front of Denis."[121] So when she discovers that Denis has kissed Lise, she is so overcome with jealousy and rage that she vows never to permit her son to "abandon her for a mistress."[122]

Denis feels trapped by his mother but remains unsure about how to escape her influence. He recognizes that he is attached to his mother "by bonds which death itself would not be able to sever," but her interference in his life makes him wonder whether he can ever "rid himself of the hold which that woman, whom he looked upon as being so 'parochial minded,' had upon him." Her behaviour angers him, and at one point he lashes out at her, declaring, "I've had enough of this! I don't want any more of your protection."[123] He grows so frustrated with her hold on him, and with her attempts to thwart his budding romance with Lise, that he shouts at his mother, "I loathe you!"[124]

While Denis' mother is busy competing with Lise for his affection, his father, Joseph, does little to interfere. Joseph was something of a free spirit as a young man and even managed to escape the parish for a time to live out west. But when he returned to the parish, this "sentimental and passionate" man fell in love with Flora, courted her with his poetry, and married her. After they were married, Flora seemed to thrive as a wife, whereas Joseph withdrew, becoming an acquiescent husband and ineffectual father. Once he became a father, "There was nothing of the *vers-libriste* about him any longer; he rather resembled a tree that with the coming of autumn had shed its flowers, fruit, and leaves."[125] In one particularly revealing scene, Joseph is "engaged in the circumspect operation of winding the clock and Flora, as she combed out her frizzled hair, was scolding him for setting it twenty minutes fast." As Joseph keeps time, and indeed attempts to accelerate it, he decides, as he usually does, that "it was better to keep still and not get into any argument."[126]

Denis has little respect for his father, interpreting his inability to escape the parish as a mark of his failure as a man. When he discovers some of his father's old love letters to his mother, including one that promised her that "one day we will go far from this place that kills all the most delicate impulses of your soul," he thinks, "So, the old man, too, had been unwilling to accept things as they were." But because his father has been "vanquished" and has failed to escape "this place," Denis deems him a failure and vows that "they were not going to trap *him*."[127] Determined to avoid repeating his father's mistakes, he sets out to overcome the forces that he believes have conspired to turn him into a passive and dominated figure. He has already confronted his mother, but he knows that he has to confront the church – the source of his mother's power – as well.

Everything in Saint-Sauveur revolves around the church, and everyone regards Monsieur le Curé as the "absolute master" of the parish. The priest, we learn, "kept a hold on his little flock by denouncing houses of ill fame and penances redeemed with money. Like the capable leader that he was, he chose his church wardens as a sovereign does his ministers. They were men who loved honours well enough to yield to the slightest whim of the one who bestowed them."[128] Priests were the true leaders of society, Jean-Charles Falardeau pointed out, because "they were said to embody the prevailing social values such as authority, tradition, and morality." But parish priests were also "the surrogate heads of families" because fathers were very often unavailable to effectively head their families since they were either "engaged in important work in the parish" or, as was often the case, "failures or drunkards." Priests were able to easily displace fathers in their role as head of the family because they had been able to forge powerful relationships with the mothers of the parish.[129]

Early in the novel, Denis believes that Lise represents a means of escaping his mother's grip. But as soon as he recognizes that the entire parish is blocking his path toward manhood, Lise becomes just one more impediment to his development. He grows to resent her femininity, her role in distracting him from his ambition to become a man, and the fact that she has come between him and his friend Jean. Like Denis, Jean longs to escape the parish and has also grown up without a strong male role model in the home. Jean's father is an alcoholic who becomes a true father to his son only when Jean is diagnosed with meningitis and faces the prospect of losing a leg. Overcome with guilt because he is worried that his own drinking might have contributed to his son's illness, Jean's father makes a pilgrimage to Sainte-Anne-de-Beaupré and promises to give up drinking. When he returns, he tells his son, "Today – I'm your father again."[130] But by the time he attempts to reconcile with his son, Jean is close to death.

As Jean nears death, Denis abandons his pursuit of Lise, deciding that his friendship with Jean means more to him than any relationship he might have with her. In the meantime, he has developed a deep anger and hatred toward women and become "contemptuous of the weapons they wielded."[131] Denis comes to see Lise as nothing more than "an intruder" and "a minor disturbance," as well as "responsible for the meanness of which he himself had been guilty."[132] He tells Jean that he plans to write a novel both to expose "the weakness of our youth and the sentimental, narrow culture that is crammed down their throats" and to attack the religious figures in the parish because "they stuff us with romantic nonsense out of the last century. And all we are good for is to make a conquest of the first washerwoman that comes along. Do you understand something of my revolt against women? She symbolizes our decadence, the manner in which we cling to our outworn sentimentality."[133] Denis no longer sees Lise as his means of escaping the parish. Instead, he views her as an accomplice in a wider attempt to keep him from becoming a real man and from leaving the parish. So he attempts to repair his relationship with Jean, angry that he ever let a woman come between them.

Arriving at Jean's deathbed, Denis is "carried away by the flood of affection that mounted within him." He "tenderly stroked the dying lad's hands," saying, "I have come to tell you that I am your friend for all eternity. You have shown yourself a man. All is over between Lise and me, and I have come back to you, old man. That's final. You have to admit, don't you, that we have been silly to let ourselves be taken in by that myth called love?" He feels that he has to "sweep away the past with his will power as Jean was doing with his death," and in this act of male friendship, Denis succeeds in purging Lise from his thoughts.[134]

In the end, Denis spends his entire youth searching for ways to escape his fate as a French Canadian man. We follow him as he struggles to overcome the obstacles blocking his path toward personal fulfilment and adulthood, watching as he peels away the various national, religious, and cultural layers that are covering up his manhood. We see him confront his mother and struggle to emerge from her protective embrace in order to avoid becoming the failed and emasculated man he believes his father has become, and we see him reject Lise, who has turned out to be yet another trap sent to emasculate him and to prevent him from escaping his surroundings. Denis becomes a real man, in the end, only when he emerges from the overwhelming pressures and expectations that he and every other French Canadian boy faced during the 1930s.

By the 1930s and 1940s, the idea that a boy could find personal fulfilment, including full manhood, through his national identity was being challenged by a growing number of critics. The Depression, it turned out, had weakened the church's authority and emboldened its critics, who seized upon its vulnerability to accuse it of emasculating the province's boys through its failure to prepare them for the challenges associated with industrial society. When Jean-Charles

Harvey accused church-run schools of producing "effeminate" men, he was in reality attacking a nationalist curriculum that taught cultural pride and national loyalty rather than how to achieve independent manhood. His call on schools to produce men rather than French Canadians, and especially his treatment of these goals as separate, struck at the very heart of national manhood. Saint-Denys Garneau and François Hertel also sought to distinguish manhood from national identity, as did Victor Barbeau, who claimed that renewed manhood would have to *precede* any national and economic revival. And by showing the ways that Denis Boucher was prevented from growing up and becoming a real man because he was being suffocated by his parish, Roger Lemelin challenged the nationalist claim that manhood flowed from a man's sense of national belonging. Each of these critics approached the so-called crisis of French Canadian manhood in his own way, emphasizing his own priorities about the meaning of national identity and manhood. But they all defined the province's challenges in gendered terms and shared a determination to disentangle French Canadian manhood from national identity.

Conclusion

On February 20, 1940, the Liberal government of Adélard Godbout announced in its speech from the throne its intention to introduce legislation that would grant women the right to vote in Quebec elections. After decades of dire warnings from conservative nationalists as well as members of the clergy that any attempt to expand the franchise to include women would imperil the sanctity of the family, the health of women, and civilization itself, the passage of this legislation two months later would take place without much discussion. Until this moment, Quebec stood alone among the provinces in denying women the right to vote, making its position increasingly untenable and difficult to justify. Moreover, two decades of women exercising their vote at the federal level had blunted some of the radicalism associated with the idea of women voting, especially when it turned out, much to the disappointment of some of those women who had fought so hard to win the right to vote, that women did not vote as a bloc and did not in any significant way alter the political landscape by advancing so-called women's issues. So by 1940 the proposal to extend the franchise to women was made more out of a desire to eliminate an increasingly awkward state of affairs than out of any desire to advance the rights of women. Few observers expected that women's formal entry into the electoral process would fundamentally alter the political character of the province. Nonetheless, the moment that women turned out to vote for the first time in 1944 marked the end of close to a century of men's exclusive control over the political world.

For much of the previous century, beginning in the 1830s when political leaders in Lower Canada moved to formally deny women the right to vote, men had been consolidating their control of the public sphere. This development was hardly unique to Quebec. In fact, it placed Quebec firmly in line with a larger process of modernization taking place during that time that witnessed the emergence of the institutions of the state. All of this was occurring at the same time that industrialism was hardening the lines separating the public and increasingly male political world from the private and increasingly female domestic world. Nor was the Quebec experience fundamentally different from what the rest of Canada experienced simply because of the prominent place that the Catholic Church was said to play in the province. In fact,

French-speaking Canadians in Quebec were expressing many of the same reservations about industrialization, urbanization, and all of the other challenges associated with modernization that other Canadians were having. As did people in English Canada, many French Canadians expressed concern about the manner in which industrial capitalism appeared to be sweeping away the values associated with traditional rural life in favour of an individualistic and materialistic ethos that appeared to have little room for older traditions or religious belief.

Many English Canadians responded to the changes associated with modernity by turning to an imagined simpler past, one steeped in agrarian rituals. For some men, the surest means of arresting the supposed feminizing effects of industrial modernity was to experience the more primal emotions that were said to have prevailed in the premodern period. For these men, the wilderness was venerated as the site where men could test their bodies and minds as well as a place where they could find physical and masculine rejuvenation by escaping the enervating comforts of the domestic sphere as well as the monotony of the industrial workplace. For a number of English Canadian men by the end of the nineteenth century, one means of arresting the presumed decline arising from modernity was to pursue a more vigorous type of manhood through a form of military adventurism that would accompany greater imperial integration. The peculiarity of Quebec's response to industrialization arose less from its reaction to the threats associated with modernity and more from some of the proposed solutions emanating from the province to the problems said to have been caused by this modernity. French Canadian leaders found themselves in the position of having to respond both to the challenges associated with modernity as well as to English Canadian responses to that modernity.

Approaching these matters through the period's gendered discourses permits us to modify our assumptions about French Canadians' reactions to industrial and social change during the late nineteenth and early twentieth centuries. Much has been made of the province's supposed backwardness during the first half of the twentieth century, including French Canadians' supposed attachment to the land, family, and the church. In the 1930s and 1940s scholars like Horace Miner could still characterize French Canada as a folk society, and Everett Hughes could argue that French Canadians had "not aggressively sought new solutions for their economic problems."[1] And in 1956 Pierre Elliott Trudeau produced one of the most influential interpretations of the period when he wrote that French Canadians "sometimes overvalued all those things that set them apart from others, and showed hostility to all change (even progress) coming from without." Claiming that "our social thinking was so idealistic, so a priori, so divorced from reality, in sum so futile," he argued that "it was hardly ever able to find expression in living and dynamic institutions," and he lamented that "the industrial workers of Quebec were suffocating in a society burdened with inadequate ideologies and oppressive institutions."[2] This view persists to this day, even in light of considerable effort on the part of historians to correct this assumption. Michel Sarra-Bournet, for example, has identified the 1960s as the moment when French Canadians finally abandoned their conservatism and "reunited the marriage between nationalism and liberalism in Quebec."[3] And the general public, as Jocelyn Létourneau has reminded us, continues to regard the Quiet Revolution as the moment when the province finally entered the modern world.[4]

Although it is true that many people remained attached to a rapidly disappearing agrarian world during the first half of the century, it is also true that many people appeared eager to embrace modern industrial life. French Canadian men were willing to embrace modernity but remained anxious about the supposed effeminizing effects of industrialization and urbanization. To avoid becoming overwhelmed by these effeminizing influences, a number of French Canadians turned to nationalism as an instrument to promote a new version of manhood, one that would be suitable for the new century. By making their national identity central to their sense of manhood, these French Canadian men retreated from the notion that manhood should be defined by the land and promoted, instead, an ideal whereby manhood would be measured according to the degree to which they embraced their nationality. This coupling of national and masculine identities released French Canadian men from the supposed effeminizing grip of modernity as well as from the confines of biological racial identity, and it permitted them to regain some of the power that they claimed they had lost over their fates by making male identity dependent upon their commitment to national identity. A crucial part of regaining this ability to control their identities as men was to remove those constraints that served to limit their sense of power. This involved turning away from those forces, including the church, that were said to exert too much control over their lives.

Over time, these men turned increasingly to the state as the vehicle for the promotion of their national identity as well as of their identity as men. In the years after the Second World War, the state assumed a larger role in the defence of French Canadian nationality. Taking on greater responsibilities in the areas of education as well as the delivery of social services, and taking the lead in defending the province's rights against the incursions of an increasingly interventionist federal government, the Quebec state was in the process of assuming a much larger role in the lives of French Canadians. As the role of the state grew during these years, more men turned to it as the primary defender of their interests. It was through the exercise of state power that men would be freed from the emasculating and feminizing grip of the church and of industrial capitalism, which had come to be regarded by many as having kept them in a figurative state of femininity. Once the state became the centre of power in the province, it came to be seen as the primary vehicle for the emancipation of men. In the process, the expansion of state power became a central feature of the nationalist movement. Manhood would come to be tied ever more closely to the state in the postwar years, in the same way that it had been tied to national identity prior to the war. The expansion of state power came to be seen as an expression of masculine power as well as the primary vehicle for the emancipation of French Canadian men in the province.

THE GROWING IMPORTANCE of the state in the postwar years represented a significant shift in the values associated with national manhood. National manhood had been marked by confidence and optimism and had taken shape as a means of allowing men to reclaim their sense of manhood in an industrial world that appeared to be passing them by. Men had found that their identities as men could be upheld and nurtured most effectively if they were freed from the constraints of the workplace, the home, the family, and the church, as well as permitted to negotiate a relationship with their nationality as individuals. It was a moment of emancipation for men, who would be freed from the mundane and material constraints of society and permitted to form independent identities as men that depended on their own sense of national identity.

This confidence and optimism would dissipate in the years following the Second World War and be replaced by a more pessimistic and even melancholy form of nationalism. In 1962 the writer Hubert Aquin announced that French Canadian culture "shows all the symptoms of extreme fatigue, wanting both rest and strength at the same time, desiring both existential intensity and suicide, seeking both independence and dependency." Aquin, who would commit suicide in 1977, argued, "French Canadian culture has long been dying; it makes frequent recoveries, followed by new relapses, and thus leads a precarious existence of fits, starts, and collapses."[5]

By the second half of the twentieth century, the province's nationalist leaders appeared to have abandoned the optimism that had marked their early-twentieth-century discourse, and they began peddling a discourse of failure that was reminiscent of nineteenth-century clerical nationalism. According to the political philosopher Jocelyn Maclure, "there exists in Quebec a whole discourse about the fragility, the precariousness, the tragic existence, the fatigue, the modesty, the philistinism, the mediocrity, the immaturity, and the indecision of the Québécois people."[6] Jocelyn Létourneau, too, has noted that these "melancholy scholars," who "tend to remember the mistakes they have made, the pain caused them, what they did not do, or what they could have done," have created a "narrative of lack," whereby French Canadians once again "carry their past like a cross."[7]

This melancholy, it turned out, became more intense as French Canadians increased their power and influence within the province's political institutions. This apparently paradoxical state of affairs is one legacy of early-twentieth-century efforts to conflate manhood and nationality. This melancholy grew out of the work being produced by historians at the University of Montreal beginning in the 1930s and 1940s. This group of historians was attempting to reinvigorate the historical narrative by portraying French Canadians as virile and aggressive nation builders. But at the same time, and somewhat paradoxically, they were also portraying French Canadians as helpless victims in the face of historical circumstances. They were beginning to challenge Lionel Groulx's more optimistic version of the past and to question whether he had overstated French Canadians' historical agency. Guy Frégault, for example, warned that "the French Canadians style themselves stronger than they are," and he reminded his readers that "any historical explanation of the present situation of French Canada in regard to English Canada must begin with a consideration of the fundamental fact in the history of this country: the British Conquest."[8] Maurice Séguin, too, characterized the Conquest as "a catastrophe that tore this young colony out of its protective, nurturing environment, impairing its organization as a society and a budding nation, condemning it to annexation, to political and economic subordination."[9] These historians, then, recentred the Battle of the Plains of Abraham as the key moment in French Canada's collective imagination. As the Conquest emerged once again as a calamity, Confederation, which Groulx had lauded for creating a "fraternity of two races,"[10] also came under attack because, according to Aquin, it had "institutionalized this inequality and, even if we go along with the system, we shall wear ourselves out in defence of our status as a conquered people." He warned, "if we remain in Confederation, our history is written in advance and allows no possibility of starting afresh."[11]

The French Canadian man who had been told that he could find fulfilment and liberation by embracing his national identity increasingly found in the middle decades of the twentieth century a nationalist movement that informed him that emancipation and full manhood could be achieved only once the nation was moored to a strong state. Complete manhood, then, could be fulfilled only once complete political independence for Quebec was achieved. French Canadians' apparent reluctance to take that final step toward independence/

manhood has come to weigh heavily on the collective consciousness, whereby, according to Létourneau, "this country [Quebec] always refuses to consummate its utopian re-foundation through the ultimate fulfillment of its quest for affirmation – political independence."[12] As long as French Canadians fail to achieve full political sovereignty, then, nationalists will continue to insist that French Canadians are humiliated and subservient to English Canadians. As a result, according to Létourneau, French-speaking Quebecers remain "stuck in an inconsolable sadness resulting from their supposed situation as 'failed rebels.'"[13] And since manhood has come to rely so heavily upon a political resolution to the national question, the continued failure to achieve independence condemns French Canadian men to a perpetual state of unmanliness.[14]

THE LATE NINETEENTH and early twentieth centuries thus stand apart as a period of uncommon optimism when a group of French Canadian leaders redefined manhood in an attempt to compete with English Canadians and to embrace the modern industrial world. These leaders rejected the pessimism exhibited by figures such as François-Xavier Garneau, who had written,

> May the French Canadians remain faithful to themselves; may they be wise and persevering; and may they not let themselves be seduced in any way by the glitter of social and political innovation! They are not strong enough to give themselves free rein in this field. It is up to the great peoples of the world to put new theories to the test.[15]

They proclaimed, instead, their intention to compete with anyone in the world and their willingness to participate in modern industrial life. But this optimism was replaced by the pessimism or melancholy of the 1950s and 1960s, whereby any masculine fulfilment would have to await the day that Quebec achieved its political independence. What had been an attempt to liberate men by encouraging them to define their manhood through their sense of national belonging became a movement that made full manhood contingent upon the province's accession to political independence.

Notes

Introduction

Some of the historiographical material in the Introduction appeared in "Liberal Nationalism and the Challenge of Masculinity Studies in Quebec," *Left History* 11, 2 (2006): 96–117; and in "Writing the History of Sexuality and 'National' History in Quebec," *Journal of Canadian Studies* 39, 2 (2005): 31–55.

1 I use the term "French Canadian" to refer to French-speaking Canadians living in Quebec and the term "English Canadian" to refer to English-speaking Canadians living in the rest of Canada. I also use the terms "Quebec" and "French Canada" interchangeably since my use of both terms is meant to refer to the French-speaking inhabitants of the province. Similarly, I use the term "English Canada" to mean English-speaking Canadians outside Quebec. When greater precision is necessary, such as when I discuss English-speaking Canadians living in Quebec or when I refer to English-speaking Canadians both inside and outside Quebec, I use the term "English-speaking Canadians."

2 For the classic expression of this interpretation, see Guy Frégault, *Canada: The War of the Conquest,* trans. Margaret M. Cameron (Toronto: Oxford University Press, 1969), originally published as *La Guerre de la Conquête* (Montreal: Fides, 1955).

3 See Fernand Ouellet, *Histoire économique et sociale du Québec, 1760–1850* (Montreal: Fides, 1966).

4 Michel Brunet, "Trois dominantes de la pensée canadienne-française: L'agriculturisme, l'anti-étatisme et le messianisme," in *La présence anglaise et les Canadiens,* 113–66 (Montreal: Beauchemin, 1958). See also Pierre Elliott Trudeau, "La province de Québec au moment de la grève," in *La Grève de l'amiante: Une étape de la révolution industrielle au Québec,* ed. Pierre Elliott Trudeau (Montreal: Les Éditions Cité Libre, 1956), reprinted as "The Province of Quebec at the Time of the Strike" in *The Asbestos Strike,* trans. James Boake (Toronto: James Lewis and Samuel, 1974), 6, 66. For an overview of the historical writing, see Ronald Rudin, *Making History in Twentieth-Century Quebec* (Toronto: University of Toronto Press, 1997).

5 The classic example of this approach is Paul-André Linteau, René Durocher, and Jean-Claude Robert, *Quebec: A History, 1867–1929,* trans. Robert Chodos (1982; reprint, Toronto: James Lorimer and Company, 1983). The authors, with François Ricard, produced a second volume, *Quebec since 1930,* trans. Robert Chodos and Ellen Germaise (1986; reprint, Toronto: James Lorimer and Company, 1991). See also Brian Young and John A. Dickinson, *A Short History of Quebec,* 4th ed. (Montreal and Kingston: McGill-Queen's University Press, 2008).

6 Intellectual and cultural historians have also contributed to this reinterpretation of Quebec's past by emphasizing that liberal ideologies flourished from the late nineteenth century up to the end of the Duplessis era. See Fernande Roy, *Progrès, harmonie, liberté: Le libéralisme des milieux d'affaires francophones à Montréal au tournant du siècle* (Montreal: Boréal, 1988); Gilles Bourque, Jules Duchastel, and Jacques Beauchemin, *La société libérale duplessiste, 1944–1960* (Montreal: Les Presses de l'Université de Montréal, 1994); Paul-André Linteau, *Maisonneuve ou comment des promoteurs fabriquent une ville,*

1883–1918 (Montreal: Boréal Express, 1981); Yvan Lamonde, *La modernité au Québec,* vol. 1, *La Crise de l'homme et de l'esprit, 1929–1939* (Montreal: Fides, 2011); Yvan Lamonde, *Histoire sociale des idées au Québec,* vol. 1, *1760–1896* (Montreal: Fides, 2000); and Yvan Lamonde, *Histoire sociale des idées au Québec,* vol. 2, *1896–1929* (Montreal: Fides, 2004).

7 Quoted in Ronald Rudin, "Bargaining from Strength: Historical Writing and Political Autonomy in Late-Twentieth-Century Quebec," in *Secession, History and the Social Sciences,* ed. Bruno Coppieters and Michael Huyssene (Brussels: VUB Brussels University Press, 2002), 167.

8 On this trend, see Rudin, *Making History,* 190. There are exceptions, including Brian Young, *In Its Corporate Capacity: The Seminary of Montreal as a Business Institution, 1816–1876* (Toronto: University of Toronto Press, 1986).

9 See, for example, E.-Martin Meunier and Jean-Philippe Warren, *Sortir de la 'Grande noirceur': L'Horizon 'personnaliste' de la Révolution tranquille* (Sillery, QC: Septentrion, 2002); Michael Gauvreau, *The Catholic Origins of Quebec's Quiet Revolution, 1931–1970* (Montreal and Kingston: McGill-Queen's University Press, 2005).

10 Francis Parkman, *France and England in North America,* ed. David Levin (New York: Library of America), vol. 2, 869. It should be noted that not all historians have interpreted the autocratic and religious nature of the colony as necessarily negative. W.J. Eccles, one of the leading English Canadian historians of New France, pointed out that much of the success that the colony did enjoy was precisely because of its autocratic nature. In addition, Eccles notes that the influence of the church, which had been regarded by so many historians as evidence that New France was less progressive and less enlightened than the English colonies, was instrumental in fostering a strong sense of community in the colony and served as a vital link to the religious and intellectual legacy of Europe. See W.J. Eccles, *The French in North America, 1500–1783,* 3rd ed. (1972; reprint, Markham, ON: Fitzhenry and Whiteside, 1998), 63–65.

11 On the Loyalists and attitudes toward Canada and the Constitutional Act of 1791, see Alan Taylor, *The Civil War of 1812: American Citizens, British Subjects, Irish Rebels, and Indian Allies* (New York: Alfred A. Knopf, 2010), 15–43; and Maya Jasanoff, *Liberty's Exiles: American Loyalists in the Revolutionary World* (New York: Alfred A. Knopf, 2011), 177–209.

12 Most historians would agree that those colonists who did not hold positions of power or who were not connected to larger commercial interests were affected in only limited ways. The question becomes contentious, however, when the psychological and social impact of the Conquest is considered. For historians like Guy Frégault, the Conquest is an important moment because it traumatized the French Canadian population in a manner that prevented it from believing that it could compete with the English-speaking colonists. Others like Fernand Ouellet dismiss such an interpretation, sticking to quantifiable data that he uses to demonstrate more continuity than rupture. Although psychological approaches to the past in the Frégault tradition have fallen out of fashion, the advent of postcolonial studies has permitted us to see that even if there were no immediate or material disadvantages arising from the Conquest, the colonizer's view of the colonized as the "other" would have been internalized by the colonized. Such a reading does not mean that French Canadians must forever be viewed as colonized in the traditional sense or that Quebec remains a colony, as some observers have suggested. Rather, it means that those actors who are operating as members of the majority community will necessarily play a decisive role in determining the narrative and discourse of a particular era, and this narrative can certainly have an impact on how the minority is treated. The rise of gender history in the 1980s has also permitted us to view the Conquest as well as the English-French dynamic in Canada in this light. The historian

Joan Wallach Scott's notion that discourse is key to understanding relationships of power is relevant here because even if no discernable impact from the Conquest can be felt, and even if all actors within a particular political space enjoy the same rights and privileges, discourse will play a role in perpetuating power differences. See Joan Wallach Scott, "Gender: A Useful Category of Historical Analysis," *American Historical Review* 91, 5 (1986): 1053–75. Canada's own self-conscious relationships, first with Britain and then with the United States, have produced what some might call an inferiority complex. This development serves as a reminder that the attainment of political independence for a particular national group does not necessarily end these feelings or fully emancipate a group's consciousness from feelings of colonial inferiority. On the continuing relevance of the Conquest in the public imagination, see Phillip Buckner and John G. Reid, eds., *Remembering 1759: The Conquest of Canada in Historical Memory* (Toronto: University of Toronto Press, 2012); and Phillip Buckner and John G. Reid, eds., *Revisiting 1759: The Conquest of Canada in Historical Perspective* (Toronto: University of Toronto Press, 2012).

13 An influential interpretation of this era comes from Fernand Ouellet, who has argued that the politically ambitious middle classes in the colony capitalized on this perception to stir nationalist sentiment that could be used to increase their own power. See Fernand Ouellet, *Lower Canada, 1791–1840: Social Change and Nationalism*, trans. Patricia Claxton (Toronto: McClelland and Stewart, 1980).

14 Arthur Laurendeau, "A la recherche d'une mystique nationale," *L'Action nationale* 8, 4 (1936): 227, quoted in Michael Oliver, *The Passionate Debate: The Social and Political Ideas of Quebec Nationalism, 1920–1945* (Montreal: Véhicule, 1991), 92.

15 Pierre Elliott Trudeau, "Some Obstacles to Democracy in Quebec," in *Federalism and the French Canadians*, ed. John T. Saywell (Toronto: Macmillan, 1968), 103. This article was originally published in *Canadian Journal of Economics and Political Science* 24, 3 (1958): 297–311.

16 On the resistance to social reform and the timidity of various governments in Canada, see Alvin Finkel, *Social Policy and Practice in Canada: A History* (Waterloo, ON: Wilfrid Laurier University Press, 2006).

17 Mariana Valverde, *The Age of Light, Soap, and Water: Moral Reform in English Canada, 1885–1925* (Toronto: McClelland and Stewart, 1991); Carolyn Strange and Tina Loo, *Making Good: Law and Moral Regulation in Canada, 1867–1939* (Toronto: University of Toronto Press, 1997); Angus McLaren, *Our Own Master Race: Eugenics in Canada, 1885–1945* (Toronto: McClelland and Stewart, 1990); Steven Maynard, "'Horrible Temptations': Sex, Men, and Working-Class Male Youth in Urban Ontario, 1890–1935," *Canadian Historical Review* 78, 2 (1997): 191–235; Franca Iacovetta, "The Sexual Politics of Moral Citizenship and Containing 'Dangerous' Foreign Men in Cold War Canada, 1950s–1960s," *Histoire sociale/Social History* 33, 66 (2000): 361–89.

18 See Étienne Parent's talk in 1846 to the Institut canadien, "Industry as a Means of Survival for the French Canadian Nationality," reprinted in *French Canadian Nationalism: An Anthology*, ed. Ramsay Cook, 82–91 (Toronto: Macmillan, 1969). On Henri Bourassa's reformist ideas, see Joseph Levitt, "Henri Bourassa and Modern Industrial Society, 1900–1914," *Canadian Historical Review* 50, 1 (1969): 37–50.

19 See Dominique Marshall, "The Language of Children's Rights, the Formation of the Welfare State, and the Democratic Experience of Poor Families in Quebec, 1940–55," *Canadian Historical Review* 78, 3 (1997): 410.

20 René Hardy, "Regards sur la construction de la culture catholique québécoise au XIXe siècle," *Canadian Historical Review* 88, 1 (2007): 9–11.

21 Lionel Groulx, *Orientations* (Montreal: Les Éditions du Zodiaque, 1935), 115.

22 A number of scholars have noted this preoccupation. See, for example, Gérard Bouchard, *Les deux chanoines: Contradiction et ambivalence dans la pensée de Lionel Groulx* (Montreal: Boréal, 2003), 41; Fernand Dumont, "Les années 30: La première révolution tranquille," in *Idéologies au Canada Français, 1930–1939*, ed. Fernand Dumont, Jean Hamelin, and Jean-Paul Montminy (Quebec: Les Presses de l'Université Laval, 1978), 13.

23 André Marois [Lionel Groulx, pseud.], "Pour vivre," *L'Action nationale* 7, 4 (1936): 233.

24 Lionel Groulx, *Faites-nous des hommes: Préparations des jeunes à leurs tâches prochaines* (Montreal: Éditions de la J.I.C., 1938).

25 Louis Lalande, *La fierté* (Montreal: Bibliothèque de l'Action française, 1918), 23.

26 Georges Courchesne, "La famille et le choix d'une carrière," in *La Famille: 4e Session des Semaines Sociales du Canada* (Montreal: Bibliothèque de l'Action française, 1923), 255–56.

27 Henri Bourassa, *Femmes-hommes ou hommes et femmes? Études à bâtons rompus sur le féminisme* (Montreal: Imprimerie du Devoir, 1925), 60.

28 *Le Jour*, May 14, 1938.

29 André Laurendeau, "Manifeste des jeunes," *L'Action nationale* 1, 2 (1933): 120. See also André Laurendeau, *Qui sauvera Québec?* (Montreal: Imprimerie populaire, 1936), 52.

30 Pierre Dansereau, "Jeune-Canada," *L'Action nationale* 1, 5 (1933): 272, quoted in Oliver, *Passionate Debate*, 107–8.

31 Important early works include E. Anthony Rotundo, *American Manhood: Transformations in Masculinity from the Revolution to the Modern Era* (New York: Basic Books, 1993); R.W. Connell, *Masculinities* (Berkeley: University of California Press, 1995); and Michael Kimmel, *Manhood in America: A Cultural History* (New York: Free Press, 1996). For a sense of the field in English Canada, see Cecilia Morgan, *Public Men and Virtuous Women: The Gendered Languages of Religion and Politics in Upper Canada, 1791–1850* (Toronto: University of Toronto Press, 1995); Ross D. Cameron, "Tom Thomson, Antimodernism and the Ideal of Manhood," *Journal of the Canadian Historical Association* 10, 1 (1999): 185–208; Tina Loo, "Of Moose and Men: Hunting for Masculinities in British Columbia, 1880–1939," *Western Historical Quarterly* 32, 3 (2001): 296–319; Karen Dubinsky and Adam Givertz, "'It Was Only a Matter of Passion': Masculinity and Sexual Danger," in *Gendered Pasts: Historical Essays in Femininity and Masculinity*, ed. Kathryn McPherson, Cecilia Morgan, and Nancy M. Forestell, 65–79 (Don Mills, ON: Oxford University Press, 1999); Franca Iacovetta, "Defending Honour, Demanding Respect: Manly Discourse and Gendered Practice in Two Construction Strikes, Toronto, 1960–61," in *Gendered Pasts: Historical Essays in Femininity and Masculinity*, ed. Kathryn McPherson, Cecilia Morgan, and Nancy M. Forestell, 199–222 (Don Mills, ON: Oxford University Press, 1999); Craig Heron, "The Boys and Their Booze: Masculinities and Public Drinking in Hamilton, 1890–1946," *Canadian Historical Review* 86, 3 (2005): 411–52; Craig Heron, "Boys Will Be Boys: Working-Class Masculinities in the Age of Mass Production," *International Labor and Working-Class History* 69, 1 (2006): 6–34; Christopher Dummitt, *The Manly Modern: Masculinity in Postwar Canada* (Vancouver: UBC Press, 2007); and Christopher J. Greig and Wayne J. Martino, eds., *Men and Masculinities: Historical and Contemporary Perspectives* (Toronto: Canadian Scholars' Press, 2012).

32 The founding text of the male-liberation movement is generally said to be Jack Sawyer, "On Male Liberation," *Liberation* 15, 6–8 (1970): 32–33. Warren Farrell became a leading member of this movement, writing *The Liberated Man* (New York: Random House, 1974). Before long, however, Farrell developed second thoughts, and he began to talk less about the common oppression that men and women faced and more about how men were more severely circumscribed than women by societal pressures to conform to gender norms. By the 1980s, a growing number of observers would come to see men as

being in a state of crisis, which they suggested was largely precipitated by the women's movement. See Warren Farrell, *The Myth of Male Power: Why Men Are the Disposable Sex* (New York: Simon and Schuster, 1993); and Robert Bly, *Iron John: A Book about Men* (Reading, MA: Addison-Wesley, 1990). On the men's movement see Barbara Ehrenreich, *The Hearts of Men: American Dreams and the Flight from Commitment* (Garden City, NY: Anchor Books, 1983); and Andrew Kimbrell, *The Masculine Mystique: The Politics of Masculinity* (New York: Ballantine Books, 2005).

33 The "father of the men's movement" in Quebec, according to Anouk Bélanger, is the psychoanalyst Guy Corneau. In his bestselling book *Absent Fathers, Lost Sons: The Search for Masculine Identity,* trans. Larry Shouldice (Boston: Shambhala, 1991), Corneau argued that there existed a "fragility of masculine identity" (3) because fathers had failed to teach their sons what it meant to be a man, leaving them vulnerable to the influence of their mothers, who were unable to teach them about manhood. Corneau suggested that men could reverse their slide into effeminacy by becoming reacquainted with their aggressive natures and rediscovering that "primitive man who slumbers in the unconscious" (128–29). He worried that "too many men live cut off and isolated from the male community" (172). The social worker and writer Michel Dorais also suggested that men should work to cultivate friendships with other men in order to counteract the effects of an increasingly feminized world reshaped by reproductive technology, increased rates of divorce, and the disruption of traditional gender roles. See Michel Dorais, *L'homme désemparé: Les crises masculines: Les comprendre pour s'en dépendre* (Montreal: VLB éditeur, 1988), 14. The sociologist Germain Dulac has traced the beginning of a men's movement in the province to the 1970s, when a number of support groups for divorced men purported to offer help for those men who were feeling increasingly besieged in a world supposedly transformed by a feminist agenda. Dulac argued that men had been hit hard in those years because they did not have the necessary tools to deal with these changes. See Germain Dulac, *Penser le masculin: Essai sur la trajectoire des militants de la condition masculine et paternelle* (Quebec: Institut québécois de recherche sur la culture, 1994), 12, 25; Germain Dulac, "De la métamorphose au genre masculin," *Recherches sociographiques* 32, 3 (1991): 419–22; and Germain Dulac, "Masculinité et intimité," *Sociologie et société* 35, 2 (2003): 14–15, 28. See also Renée-B. Dandurand, *Le mariage en question, essai sociographique* (Quebec: Institut québécois de recherche sur la culture, 1988); Germain Dulac, *Aider les hommes ... aussi* (Montreal: VLB éditeur, 2001), 140–42; and Marc Chabot, *Des hommes et de l'intimité* (Montreal: Éditions Saint-Martin, 1987). Anouk Bélanger described Corneau as the "father of the men's movement" in "The Last Game? Hockey and the Experience of Masculinity in Quebec," in *Sport and Gender in Canada,* ed. Philip White and Kevin Young (Don Mills, ON: Oxford University Press, 1999), 299.

34 Over time, what might have been described as an attempt on the part of men to liberate themselves from the same gendered burdens that were said to harm women turned into a backlash against women and came to focus on the ways that men were particularly affected by gender expectations and even harmed by feminism. For an overview of this phenomenon, see Susan Faludi, *Stiffed: The Betrayal of the American Man* (New York: William Morrow and Company, 1999); and Susan Faludi, *Backlash: The Undeclared War against American Women* (New York: Anchor Books, 1992). Expressions of this backlash against women in Quebec include Reggie Chartrand, *La dernière bataille* (Montreal: Éditions Parti pris, 1972), 160–61; Reggie Chartrand, *Dieu est un homme parce qu'il est bon et fort: La révolte d'un homme contre le féminisme* (Montreal: Stanké, 1984), 20, 107, 158–59; Jacques Grand'Maison, *La révolution affective et l'homme d'ici* (Montreal: Leméac, 1982); Rock Côté, *Manifeste d'un salaud* (Montreal: Éditions du Portique, 1990);

Mathieu-Robert Sauvé, *Échecs et mâles: Les modèles masculins au Québec, de Marquis de Montcalm à Jacques Parizeau* (Montreal: Éditions des Intouchables, 2005); Jean-Philippe Trottier, *Le grand mensonge du féminisme, ou, le silence sur la triple castration de l'homme québécois* (Montreal: Michel Brûlé, 2007); and Yvon Dallaire, *Homme et fier de l'être* (Quebec: Option Santé, 2001). Critiques of these attitudes can be found in Mélissa Blais, *J'haïs les feministes! Le 6 décembre 1989 et ses suites* (Montreal: Les Éditions du remue-ménage, 2009); Mélissa Blais, Francis Dupuis-Déri, Lyne Kurtzman, and Dominique Payette, eds., *Retour sur un attentat antiféministe: École Polytechnique de Montréal, 6 décembre 1989* (Montreal: Les Éditions du remue-ménage, 2010); and Mélissa Blais and Francis Dupuis-Déri, *Le movement masculiniste au Québec: L'antiféminisme démasqué* (Montreal: Les Éditions du remue-ménage, 2015).

35 See, for example, Mark C. Carnes, *Secret Ritual and Manhood in Victorian America* (New Haven, CT: Yale University Press, 1989).

36 Linda Kerber, "Separate Spheres, Female Worlds, Woman's Place: The Rhetoric of Women's History," *Journal of American History* 75, 1 (1988): 9–39.

37 For the view that such work is "rather more about men than about gender," see Nancy Cott, "On Men's History and Women's History," in *Meanings for Manhood: Constructions of Masculinity in Victorian America*, ed. Mark C. Carnes and Clyde Griffen (Chicago: University of Chicago Press, 1990), 208. See also Joy Parr, "Gender History and Historical Practice," *Canadian Historical Review* 76, 3 (1995): 369.

38 Scott, "Gender," 1067.

39 Franca Iacovetta and Linda Kealey, "Women's History, Gender History and Debating Dichotomies," *Left History* 3, 2 (1995), and 4, 1 (1996): 227.

40 Parr, "Gender History," 366; Bryce Traister, "Academic Viagra: the Rise of American Masculinity Studies," *American Quarterly* 52, 2 (2000): 292.

41 Joan Sangster, "Beyond Dichotomies: Re-assessing Gender History and Women's History in Canada," *Left History* 3, 1 (1995): 117–18.

42 Traister, "Academic Viagra," 297.

43 Historians who insisted on depicting French Canadian history as different were often criticized for reinforcing old stereotypes about the province's backwardness and sometimes accused of professional mischief for supposedly politicizing their work, which was a significant rebuke within a profession that had come to define itself by its scientific approach to the past. See Serge Gagnon, *Quebec and Its Historians: The Twentieth Century*, trans. Jane Bierley (Montreal: Harvest House, 1985), 119, 161; Rudin, "Bargaining from Strength," 170–71. On the retreat from this scientific approach, see Ronald Rudin, "From the Nation to the Citizen: Quebec Historical Writing and the Shaping of Identity," in *Contesting Canadian Citizenship: Historical Readings*, ed. Robert Adamoski, Dorothy E. Chunn, and Robert Menzies (Peterborough ON: Broadview, 2002), 106–8.

44 This threat has been a particular challenge for historians of women in Quebec. See Micheline Dumont, "Un champ bien clos: L'histoire des femmes au Québec," *Atlantis* 25, 1 (2000): 102, 113–14; Micheline Dumont, "Can National History Include a Feminist Reflection on History?" *Journal of Canadian Studies* 35, 2 (2000): 102–18; Rudin, *Making History*, 195–98; Andrée Lévesque, "Réflexions sur l'histoire de femmes dans l'histoire du Québec," *Revue d'histoire de l'Amérique française* 51, 2 (1997): 279, 283; and Diane Lamoureux, *L'amère patrie: Féminisme et nationalisme dans le Québec contemporain* (Montreal: Éditions du remue-ménage, 2001), 179–81. This challenge has not prevented the growth of women's history in the province. See Collectif Clio, *L'histoire des femmes au Québec depuis quatre siècles* (Montreal: Quinze, 1982); Andrée Lévesque, *Making and Breaking the Rules: Women in Quebec, 1919–1939*, trans. Yvonne M. Klein (Toronto: McClelland and Stewart, 1994); Marta Danylewycz, *Taking the Veil: An Alternative to*

Marriage, Motherhood, and Spinsterhood in Quebec, 1840–1920 (Toronto: McClelland and Stewart, 1987); Bettina Bradbury, *Working Families: Age, Gender, and Daily Survival in Industrializing Montreal* (Toronto: McClelland and Stewart, 1993); Bettina Bradbury, *Wife to Widow: Lives, Laws, and Politics in Nineteenth-Century Montreal* (Vancouver: UBC Press, 2011); Denyse Baillargeon, *Making Do: Women, Family, and Home in Montreal during the Great Depression*, trans. Yvonne Klein (Waterloo, ON: Wilfrid Laurier University Press, 1999); and Chantal Maillé, *Les Québécoises et la conquête du pouvoir politique: Enquête sur l'émergence d'une élite politique féminine au Québec* (Montreal: Éditions Saint-Martin, 1990).

45 Lamoureux, *L'amère patrie*, 111–12.

46 Robert Schwartzwald, "Fear of Federasty: Québec's Inverted Fictions," in *Comparative American Identities: Race, Sex and Nationalism in the Modern Text*, ed. Hortense J. Spillers (New York: Routledge, 1991), 179, 185.

47 On the connections between Quebec nationalism and sexuality, see Robert Schwartzwald, "'Symbolic' Homosexuality, 'False Feminine,' and the Problematics of Identity in Québec," in *Fear of a Queer Planet: Queer Politics and Social Theory*, ed. Michael Warner, 264–99 (Minneapolis: University of Minnesota Press, 1993); Elspeth Probyn, "Bloody Metaphors and Other Allegories of the Ordinary," in *Between Woman and Nation: Nationalism, Transnational Feminism, and the State*, ed. Caren Kaplan, Norma Alarcón, and Minoo Moallem, 47–62 (Durham, NC: Duke University Press, 1999); Elspeth Probyn, *"Love in a Cold Climate": Queer Belongings in Quebec* (Montreal: Research Group on Cultural Citizenship, 1994); Elaine Pigeon, "Hosanna! Michel Tremblay's Queering of National Identity," in *In a Queer Country: Gay and Lesbian Studies in the Canadian Context*, ed. Terry Goldie (Vancouver: Arsenal Pulp, 2002), 27–40; Peter Dickinson, *Here Is Queer: Nationalisms, Sexualities, and the Literatures of Canada* (Toronto: University of Toronto Press, 1999), 101–30.

48 Katherine A. Roberts, "Making Women Pay: Revolution, Violence, Decolonizing Quebec in Hubert Aquin's *Trou de mémoire*," *Québec Studies* 30 (2000): 26.

49 Ibid., 20.

50 See Mary Jean Green, "Jacques Godbout and the Québec Writer: Engendering the National Text," *Québec Studies* 30 (2000): 8. See also Francine Bordeleau, "L'écrit du masculin," *Lettres québécoises* 100 (2000): 14–18; Richard Duchaine, "De quelques occasions de bonheur sur le Plateau Mont-Royal," *Voix et Images* 18, 1 (1992): 39–51; and Jean-Pierre Lapointe, "Narcisse travesti: L'altérité des sexes chez trois romanciers québécois contemporains," *Voix et Images* 18, 1 (1992): 11–25.

51 Patricia Smart, *Writing in the Father's House: The Emergence of the Feminine in the Quebec Literary Tradition* (Toronto: University of Toronto Press, 1991), 190. See also Michael Klementowicz, "Jacques Godbout's *Salut Galarneau!* Identity and Violence Towards Women," *Québec Studies* 14 (1992): 83–91; Gordon Sheppard, "Violence and the French Canadian Male," in *Canada: A Guide to the Peaceable Kingdom*, ed. William Kilbourn (Toronto: Macmillan, 1970), 193; Katherine A. Roberts, "'Mère, je vous hais!': Quebec Nationalism and the Legacy of the Family Paradigm in Pierre Vallières' *Nègres blanc d'Amérique*," *British Journal of Canadian Studies* 20, 2 (2007): 289–304; and Lori Saint-Martin, "The Body Politic and the Erotic Body: The (Male) Novel and the Quiet Revolution in Quebec," *British Journal of Canadian Studies* 21, 2 (2008): 195–217. The novelist and translator Daniel Poliquin has also illustrated the degree to which nationalism is bound up with manhood: "The entire nationalist discourse is that of a father who prolongs the minority status of his son, enslaving him to his dream of territorial integrity." See Daniel Poliquin, *In the Name of the Father: An Essay on Quebec Nationalism*, trans. Don Winkler (Vancouver: Douglas and McIntyre, 2001), 46–47.

52 Some works that consider the gendered dimension of manhood in Quebec include Michael Gauvreau, "Forging a New Space for Lay Male Piety: St. Vincent de Paul Societies in Urban Quebec and Ontario, 1846–1890," *Histoire sociale/Social History* 42, 83 (2009): 35–67; Thierry Nootens, "'What a Misfortune that Poor Child Should Have Married Such a Being as Joe': Les fils prodigues de la bourgeoisie montréalaise, 1850–1900," *Canadian Historical Review* 86, 2 (2005): 225–56; Thierry Nootens, "'Je crains fort que mon pauvre Henri ne fasse pas grande chose ...': Les héritiers 'manqués' et les querelles de la succession Masson, 1850–1930," *Revue d'histoire de l'Amérique française* 59, 3 (2006): 223–57; Bélanger, "Last Game?"; Jarrett Rudy, *The Freedom to Smoke: Tobacco Consumption and Identity* (Montreal and Kingston: McGill-Queen's University Press, 2005); Jarrett Rudy, "Unmaking Manly Smokes: Church, State, Governance, and the First Anti-smoking Campaigns in Montreal, 1892–1914," *Journal of the Canadian Historical Association* 12, 1 (2001): 95–114; Suzanne Morton, "A Man's City: Montreal, Gambling and Male Space in the 1940s," in *Power, Place and Identity: Historical Studies of Social and Legal Regulation in Quebec*, ed. Tamara Myers, Kate Boyer, Mary Anne Poutanen, and Steven Watt, 169–82 (Montreal: Montreal History Group, 1998); and Suzanne Morton, *At Odds: Gambling and Canadians, 1919–1969* (Toronto: University of Toronto Press, 2003).

53 Louise Bienvenue and Christine Hudon, "'Pour devenir homme, tu transgresseras ...': Quelques enjeux de la socialisation masculine dans les collèges classiques québécois (1880–1939)," *Canadian Historical Review* 86, 3 (2005): 485–511; Louise Bienvenue and Christine Hudon, "Une affaire d'hommes: Adolescence masculine et projections sociales dans quelques romans d'apprentissage de l'entre-deux-guerres," in *Nouvelles masculinités dans la littérature québécoise*, ed. Isabelle Boisclair, 23–47 (Montreal: Nota bene, 2008); Christine Hudon and Louise Bienvenue, "Entre franche camaraderie et amours socratiques: L'espace trouble et ténu des amitiés masculines dans les collèges classiques (1870–1960)," *Revue d'histoire de l'Amérique française* 57, 4 (2004): 481–507; Christine Hudon and Louise Bienvenue, "Des collégiens et leur maîtres au tournant du XXe siècle," *Globe: Revue internationale d'études québécoises* 8, 2 (2005): 41–71; Christine Hudon, "'Le Muscle et le Vouloir': Les sports dans les collèges classiques masculins au Québec, 1870–1940," *Historical Studies in Education* 17, 2 (2005): 243–63; Christine Hudon, "L'éducation sentimentale et sexuelle dans les collèges pour garçons, du milieu du XIXe siècle à la Révolution tranquille," in *Une histoire des sexualités au Québec au XXe siècle*, ed. Jean-Philippe Warren, 32–53 (Montreal: VLB éditeur, 2012); Louise Bienvenue, Ollivier Hubert, and Christine Hudon, *Le collège classique pour garçons: Études historiques sur une institution québécoise disparue* (Montreal: Fides, 2014).

54 Peter Gossage, "*Au nom du père?* Rethinking the History of Fatherhood in Quebec," *American Review of Canadian Studies* 44, 1 (2014): 49–67; Cynthia Fish, "La puissance paternelle et les cas de garde d'enfants au Québec, 1866–1928," *Revue d'histoire de l'Amérique française* 57, 4 (2004): 509–33; Vincent Duhaime, "'Les pères ont ici leur devoir': Le discours du mouvement familial québécois et la construction de la paternité dans l'après-guerre, 1945–1960," *Revue d'histoire de l'Amérique française* 57, 4 (2004): 535–65. On fatherhood and the family in Montreal during the 1940s, see Magda Fahrni, *Household Politics: Montreal Families and Postwar Reconstruction* (Toronto: University of Toronto Press, 2005).

55 Forty years later, during the 1980 referendum on sovereignty-association, women were less likely than men to support the yes side. Some nationalist men blamed women for the defeat of the referendum that year, pointing to the Parti Québécois' supposed courting of feminist support and Lise Payette's famous gaffe during the campaign. The journalist Lysiane Gagnon noted that in the days after the referendum, some people made Payette the "scapegoat" for the loss. See Lysiane Gagnon, *Vivre avec les hommes: Un nouveau*

partage (Montreal: Québec/Amérique, 1983), 178. Payette acknowledged that some people within the party blamed her remarks for the loss. See Lise Payette, *Des femmes d'honneur,* vol. 3, *Une vie engagée, 1976–2000* (Montreal: Éditions Libre Expression, 1999), 89–90. It is true that women were less likely than men to support sovereignty in the referendum, and fewer female than male members of the Parti Québécois cite sovereignty as the reason for their work on behalf of their party. See Évelyne Tardy, with Rébecca Beauvais and André Bernard, *Égalité hommes-femmes? Le militantisme au Québec: Le PQ et le PLQ* (Montreal: Hurtubise HMH, 2003), 108, 113. If some observers attribute the referendum's defeat to this reluctance on the part of women to support the sovereignty option, others suggest that women were unwilling to join a movement that was so obviously masculinist in orientation. See Diane Lamoureux, "Nationalism and Feminism in Quebec: An Impossible Attraction," in *Feminism and Political Economy: Women's Work, Women's Struggles,* ed. Heather Jon Maroney and Meg Luxton (Toronto: Methuen, 1987), 51; and Roberta Hamilton, "Pro-Natalism, Feminism, and Nationalism," in *Gender and Politics in Contemporary Canada,* ed. François-Pierre Gingras (Toronto: Oxford University Press, 1995), 143–44, 146.

Chapter 1: The Roots of National Manhood

Parts of the discussion of nineteenth-century manhood in Chapter 1 appeared in "Quebec Manhood in Historical Perspective," in *Canadian Men and Masculinities: Historical and Contemporary Perspectives,* ed. Christopher J. Greig and Wayne J. Martino, 22–41 (Toronto: Canadian Scholars' Press, 2012).

1 See Jean-Pierre Wallot "Religion and French Canadian Mores in the Early Nineteenth Century," *Canadian Historical Review* 52, 1 (1971): 56–91. On the tradition of libertinism in French-speaking Canada, see Robert L. Séguin, *La vie libertine en Nouvelle-France au XXVIIe siècle,* 2 vols. (Montreal: Leméac, 1972); and Serge Gagnon, *Plaisir d'amour et crainte de Dieu: Sexualité et confession au Bas-Canada* (Sainte-Foy, QC: Les Presses de l'Université Laval, 1990), 61. On the tension between these two types of manhood, see Louise Bienvenue and Christine Hudon, "'Pour devenir homme, tu transgresseras ...': Quelques enjeux de la socialisation masculine dans les collèges classiques québécois (1880–1939)," *Canadian Historical Review* 86, 3 (2005): 485–511.

2 On the mythical allure of the fur trade, see Carolyn Podruchny, "Baptizing Novices: Ritual Moments among French Canadian Voyageurs in the Montreal Fur Trade, 1780–1821," *Canadian Historical Review* 83, 2 (2002): 165–95; and Carolyn Podruchny, "Festivities, Fortitude, and Fraternalism: Fur Trade Masculinity and the Beaver Club, 1785–1827," in *New Faces of the Fur Trade: Selected Papers of the Seventh North American Fur Trade Conference, Halifax, Nova Scotia, 1995,* ed. Jo-Anne Fiske, Susan Sleeper-Smith, and William Wicken, 31–52 (East Lansing: Michigan State University Press, 1998). On popular disturbances and protests in seventeenth- and eighteenth-century French Canada, see Terence Crowley, "'Thunder Gusts': Popular Disturbances in Early French Canada," *Historical Papers/Communications historiques* 14, 1 (1979): 11–32. On the persistent allure of the independent man who resists constituted authority, see Darcy Ingram, "'Au temps et dans les quantités qui lui plaisent': Poaching and Rural Banditry in Quebec," *Histoire sociale/Social History* 42, 83 (2009): 1–34.

3 The conventional view has been that state and institution building, which were thought to be necessary to produce a bourgeois and capitalist class in French Canada, took place in the 1840s following the Rebellions. See, for example, Brian Young, "Positive Law, Positive State: Class Realignment and the Transformation of Lower Canada, 1815–1866," in *Colonial Leviathan: State Formation in Mid-Nineteenth-Century Canada,* ed. Allan Greer and Ian Radforth, 50–63 (Toronto: University of Toronto Press, 1992). Recently,

scholars have begun to demonstrate the manner in which state formation was evident prior to the 1840s. On the development of the criminal justice system in Lower Canada, see Donald Fyson, *Magistrates, Police, and People: Everyday Criminal Justice in Quebec and Lower Canada, 1764–1837* (Toronto: University of Toronto Press, 2006).

4 Gagnon, *Plaisir d'amour,* 61.

5 Ollivier Hubert, "Ritual Performance and Parish Sociability: French Canadian Catholic Families at Mass from the Seventeenth to the Nineteenth Century," in *Households of Faith: Family, Gender, and Community in Canada, 1760–1969,* ed. Nancy Christie (Montreal and Kinston: McGill-Queen's University Press, 2002), 60–63.

6 On the Catholic elite's embrace of a larger bourgeois sensibility that emphasized the desirability of a restrained form of manhood as a means of maintaining public order and also marginalizing women in the public sphere, see Dan Horner, "'Shame upon you as men!': Contesting Authority in the Aftermath of Montreal's Gavazzi Riot," *Histoire sociale/Social History* 44, 87 (2011): 29–52.

7 Recent work on the Rebellions has placed them in the context of Atlantic revolutions and has pointed to the rhetoric of liberty that defined this era. See Michel Ducharme, *The Idea of Liberty in Canada during the Age of Atlantic Revolutions, 1776–1838,* trans. Peter Feldstein (Montreal and Kingston: McGill-Queen's University Press, 2014). Others works have suggested that the Rebellions were a popular expression of discontent among the masses, who had a history of organizing collectively and in a manner that exhibited an independence of spirit that was not always welcomed by church authorities. See Allan Greer, *The Patriots and the People: The Rebellion of 1837 in Rural Lower Canada* (Toronto: University of Toronto Press, 1993). This view challenged an earlier interpretation that suggested that the Rebellions were precipitated by a frustrated French-speaking middle class that had turned to the language of nationalism to mobilize the masses against the established power structure in the colony as a means of propelling them into positions of greater power. The most influential statement of this interpretation can be found in Fernand Ouellet, *Lower Canada, 1791–1840: Social Change and Nationalism,* trans. Patricia Claxton (Toronto: McClelland and Stewart, 1980).

8 Ducharme, *Idea of Liberty,* 107–17.

9 Gerald M. Craig, ed., *Lord Durham's Report: An Abridgement of Report on the Affairs of British North America* (Montreal and Kingston: McGill-Queen's University Press, 2007), 13.

10 Ibid., 56.

11 Ibid., 149.

12 Durham believed that the colonists had become ungovernable in large part because of the government's failure to establish a strong system of education. See ibid., 23.

13 G.-A. Nantel, *La colonisation du Nord-Ouest de la province de Québec: Conférence de l'Honorable G.-A. Nantel, le 7 mai 1895* (Montreal: E. Senécal, 1895), 11.

14 On this new domesticated manhood as an expression of modernity, see Ollivier Hubert, "The Invention of the Margin as an Invention of the Family: The Case of Rural Quebec in the Eighteenth and Nineteenth Centuries," in *Mapping the Margins: The Family and Social Discipline in Canada, 1700–1975,* ed. Nancy Christie and Michael Gauvreau (Montreal and Kingston: McGill-Queen's University Press, 2004), 193–94.

15 To note that the province was beginning to urbanize is not to suggest that there were no efforts to reverse this trend. On the colonization movement, a drive by some church and political leaders to encourage French Canadians to settle outside urban areas as a means of reconquering the land and ensuring cultural survival, see Gabriel Dussault, *Le Curé Labelle: Messianisme, utopie et colonisation au Québec, 1850–1900* (Montreal: Hurtubise

HMH, 1983); Serge Courville, *Immigration, colonisation et propagande: Du rêve américain au rêve colonial* (Sainte-Foy, QC: Éditions MultiMondes, 2002); and Serge Courville, *Quebec: A Historical Geography*, trans. Richard Howard (Vancouver: UBC Press, 2008), esp. ch. 8.

16 Paul-André Linteau, René Durocher, and Jean-Claude Robert, *Quebec: A History, 1867–1929*, trans. Robert Chodos (Toronto: James Lorimer and Company, 1983), 28.

17 Étienne Parent, "Industry as a Means of Survival for the French Canadian Nationality," in *French Canadian Nationalism: An Anthology*, ed. Ramsay Cook (Toronto: Macmillan, 1969): 82–91.

18 Victor Barbeau, *Pour nous grandir: Essai d'explication des misères de notre temps* (Montreal: Imprimé au Devoir, 1937), 51, 153; Victor Barbeau, *Mesure de notre taille* (Montreal: Imprimé au Devoir, 1936), 16.

19 Theodore Roosevelt, "The Law of Civilization and Decay," *Forum* 22 (1897): 579, quoted in Gail Bederman, *Manliness and Civilization: A Cultural History of Gender and Race in the United States, 1880–1917* (Chicago: University of Chicago Press, 1995), 185.

20 George Beard, *American Nervousness: Its Causes and Consequences* (New York: Putnam, 1881).

21 Kristin L. Hoganson, *Fighting for American Manhood: How Gender Politics Provoked the Spanish-American and Philippine-American Wars* (New Haven, CT: Yale University Press, 1998).

22 See Donald A. Wright, "W.D. Lighthall and David Ross McCord: Antimodernism and English-Canadian Imperialism, 1880s–1918," *Journal of Canadian Studies* 32, 2 (1997): 142–45.

23 Carl Berger, *The Sense of Power: Studies in the Ideas of Canadian Imperialism, 1867-1914* (Toronto: University of Toronto Press, 1970), 259.

24 See Greer, *Patriots and the People*, esp. ch. 7. On the masculinization of public life in the rest of Canada, see Lykke de la Cour, Cecilia Morgan, and Mariana Valverde, "Gender Regulation and State Formation in Nineteenth-Century Canada," in *Colonial Leviathan: State Formation in Mid-Nineteenth-Century Canada*, ed. Allan Greer and Ian Radforth, 163–91 (Toronto: University of Toronto Press, 1992); and Cecilia Morgan, *Public Men and Virtuous Women: The Gendered Languages of Religion and Politics in Upper Canada, 1791–1850* (Toronto: University of Toronto Press, 1996).

25 See Bettina Bradbury, "Women at the Hustings: Gender, Citizenship, and the Montreal By-Elections of 1832," in *Rethinking Canada: The Promise of Women's History*, 6th ed., ed. Mona Gleason, Tamara Myers, and Adele Perry, 117–34 (Toronto: Oxford University Press, 2011).

26 On the feminization of religion, see Christine Hudon, "Des dames chrétiennes: La spiritualité des catholiques québécoises au XIXe siècle," *Revue d'histoire de l'Amérique française* 49, 2 (1995): 169–94. For an important corrective to this feminization thesis, see Michael Gauvreau, "Forging a New Space for Lay Male Piety: St. Vincent de Paul Societies in Urban Quebec and Ontario, 1846–1890," *Histoire sociale/Social History* 42, 83 (2009): 35–67.

27 Henri Bourassa, *Guerre Sud-Africaine: Discours de M. Henri Bourassa, M.P., Ottawa, mardi, 13 mars, 1900* (Ottawa: n.p., 1900), 13; Henri Bourassa, *The French Canadian in the British Empire* (London: J. Murray, 1902), 34.

28 Lionel Groulx, *Orientations* (Montreal: Les Éditions du Zodiaque, 1935), 115.

29 In the original French-language version, Groulx used notably gendered language: "Le grand mal des Canadiens français, il faut oser le dire: c'est qu'il n'y a pas de Canadiens français." Groulx, *Orientations*, 224, 231.

Chapter 2: Reinforcing Heterosexual Manhood

Some of the historiographical material in Chapter 2 appeared in "Liberal Nationalism and the Challenge of Masculinity Studies in Quebec," *Left History* 11, 2 (2006): 96–117; and in "Writing the History of Sexuality and 'National' History in Quebec," *Journal of Canadian Studies* 39, 2 (2005): 31–55.

1 On the growing attention paid to adolescent behaviour and sexuality, see Tamara Myers, "Embodying Delinquency: Boys' Bodies, Sexuality, and Juvenile Justice History in Early-Twentieth-Century Quebec," *Journal of the History of Sexuality* 14, 4 (2005): 383–414; and Tamara Myers, *Caught: Montreal's Modern Girls and the Law, 1869–1945* (Toronto: University of Toronto Press, 2006). For a look at how this growing interest in children and adolescence had the effect of limiting women's freedom, see Andrée Lévesque, *Making and Breaking the Rules: Women in Quebec, 1919–1939*, trans. Yvonne M. Klein (Toronto: McClelland and Stewart, 1994); and Denyse Baillargeon, *Babies for the Nation: The Medicalization of Motherhood in Quebec, 1910–1970*, trans. W. Donald Wilson (Waterloo, ON: Wilfrid Laurier University Press, 2009). For an overview of these developments in English Canada, see Mary Louise Adams, *The Trouble with Normal: Postwar Youth and the Making of Heterosexuality* (Toronto: University of Toronto Press, 1997); Mona Gleason, *Normalizing the Ideal: Psychology, Schooling, and the Family in Postwar Canada* (Toronto: University of Toronto Press, 1999); Cynthia Comacchio, *"Nations Are Built of Babies": Saving Ontario's Mother's and Children, 1900–1940* (Montreal and Kingston: McGill-Queen's University Press, 1993); Cynthia Comacchio, *The Dominion of Youth: Adolescence and the Making of Modern Canada, 1920–1950* (Waterloo, ON: Wilfrid Laurier University Press, 2006); Christopher J. Greig, *Ontario Boys: Masculinity and the Idea of Boyhood in Postwar Ontario, 1945–1960* (Waterloo, ON: Wilfrid Laurier University Press, 2014); Wendy Mitchinson, *Giving Birth in Canada, 1900–1950* (Toronto: University of Toronto Press, 2002); and Wendy Mitchinson, *The Nature of Their Bodies: Women and Their Doctors in Victorian Canada* (Toronto: University of Toronto Press, 1991).

2 By the 1920s more than half of Quebecers lived in the province's cities. See John Dickinson and Brian Young, *A Short History of Quebec*, 3rd ed. (Montreal and Kingston: McGill-Queen's University Press, 2003), 203.

3 Herbert Brown Ames, *"The City Below the Hill": A Sociological Study of a Portion of the City of Montreal, Canada* (Montreal: Bishop Engraving Company, 1897), 31. See also Bettina Bradbury, *Working Families: Age, Gender, and Daily Survival in Industrializing Montreal* (Toronto: McClelland and Stewart, 1993); and Terry Copp, *The Anatomy of Poverty: The Condition of the Working Class in Montreal, 1897–1929* (Toronto: McClelland and Stewart, 1974).

4 Ames, *"City Below the Hill,"* 56.

5 Ibid., 4–5.

6 Stanley Weir, "Introduction," in Henri Taschereau, *The Social Evil: Toleration Condemned* (Montreal: n.p., 1909), 5. On the connecting of personal hygiene to public health and national survival, see James G. Snell, "'The White Life for Two': The Defence of Marriage and Sexual Morality in Canada, 1890–1914," *Histoire sociale/Social History* 16, 31 (1983): 112; Pierre Hurteau, "Homosexualité, religion et droit au Québec" (PhD diss., Concordia University, 1991), 105–6; and A. Feret, "La beauté physique de l'enfant: Son hygiène à l'école, à l'atelier, et dans l'habitation," *Journal d'hygiène populaire* 10, 4 (1893): 114.

7 L.P. Mercier, *Quoi dire, comment dire, et quoi faire: Éducation sexuelle* (Montreal: Éditions Bernard Valiquette, 1930), 38. See also Jean D'Acier, "Les bienfaits de la gymnastique," *Journal d'hygiène populaire* 9, 1 (1892): 3. For a larger discussion of this phenomenon, see Cynthia Comacchio, "Mechanomorphosis: Science, Management, and 'Human Machinery' in Industrial Canada, 1900–45," *Labour/Le Travail* 41 (1998): 35–67.

8 Raymond Villecourt, "Chronique," *Le Journal pour tous* 1, 1 (1906): 3.

9 D.E. LeCavelier, "La syphilis à Montréal: Quelques moyens prophylactiques," *Montréal-Médical* 1, 10 (1901): 339.

10 J.-I. Desroches, *Traité élémentaire d'hygiène privée,* 2nd ed. (1888; reprint, Montreal: Bureau du Journal d'hygiène populaire, 1890).

11 Villecourt, "Chronique," 3.

12 See E.I. Hart, *Wake Up! Montreal! Commercialized Vice and Its Contributors* (Montreal: Witness, 1919), 55–59. For a discussion of this issue, see Lévesque, *Making and Breaking,* 53–60; Cynthia Comacchio, "Dancing to Perdition: Adolescence and Leisure in Interwar English Canada," *Journal of Canadian Studies* 32, 3 (1997): 5–35.

13 Georges Panneton, *Le garçonnisme* (Montreal: Semaine religieuse de Québec, 1932), 3.

14 See Mary Louise Roberts, *Civilization without Sexes: Reconstructing Gender in Postwar France, 1917–1927* (Chicago: University of Chicago Press, 1994), 19, 46–47.

15 Henri Bourassa, "La famille canadienne, ses périls, son salut," in *La Famille: 4e Session des Semaines Sociales du Canada* (Montreal: Bibliothèque de l'Action française, 1923), 282.

16 Henri Bourassa, *Femmes-hommes ou hommes et femmes? Études à bâtons rompus sur le féminisme* (Montreal: Imprimerie du Devoir, 1925), 6.

17 Ibid., 60.

18 Georges Courchesne, "La famille et le choix d'une carrière," in *La Famille: 4e Session des Semaines Sociales du Canada* (Montreal: Bibliothèque de l'Action française, 1923), 255–56.

19 Peter DeLottinville, "Joe Beef of Montreal: Working-Class Culture and the Tavern, 1869–1889," *Labour/Le Travail* 8–9 (1981–82): 9–40. On the rise of a commercial culture in Montreal, see Yvan Lamonde and Raymond Montpetit, *Le parc Sohmer de Montréal, 1889–1919: Un lieu populaire de culture urbaine* (Quebec: Institut québécois de recherche sur la culture, 1986), 197–98, 209.

20 Gary Kinsman, *The Regulation of Desire: Homo and Hetero Sexualities* (Montreal: Black Rose Books, 1996), 40; Steven Maynard, "Through a Hole in the Lavatory Wall: Homosexual Subcultures, Police Surveillance, and the Dialectics of Discovery, Toronto, 1890–1930," *Journal of the History of Sexuality* 5, 2 (1994): 207–42.

21 On the gay world in Montreal, see Maurice Leznoff, "The Homosexual in Urban Society" (MA thesis, McGill University, 1954); Maurice Leznoff and William A. Westley, "The Homosexual Community," *Social Problems* 3, 4 (1956): 257–63; Line Chamberland, *Mémoires lesbiennes: Le lesbianisme à Montréal entre 1950 et 1972* (Montreal: Éditions du remue-ménage, 1995); Irène Demczuk and Frank W. Remiggi, eds., *Sortir de l'ombre: Histoires des communautés lesbienne et gaie de Montréal* (Montreal: VLB éditeur, 1998); Ross Higgins, *De la clandestinité à l'affirmation: Pour une histoire de la communauté gaie montréalaise* (Montreal: Comeau et Nadeau, 1999); Ross Higgins, "A Sense of Belonging: Pre-liberation Space, Symbolics, and Leadership in Gay Montreal" (PhD diss., McGill University, 1997); Ross Higgins, "Baths, Bushes and Belonging: Public Sex and Gay Community in Pre-Stonewall Montreal," in *Public Sex/Gay Space,* ed. William L. Leap, 187–202 (New York: Columbia University Press, 1999); Ross Higgins and Line Chamberland, "Mixed Messages: Lesbians, Gay Men, and the Yellow Press in Quebec and Ontario during the 1950s–1960s," in *The Challenge of Modernity: A Reader on Post-Confederation Canada,* ed. Ian McKay, 422–38 (Toronto: McGraw-Hill Ryerson, 1992); and Gregory Pablo Rodriguez-Arbolay Jr., "Connecting Fragments: Solidarity and Fragmentation in Montreal's Gay and Lesbian Communities, 1960–1977" (MA thesis, Sarah Lawrence College, 2009).

22 This concern about sex in public spaces persisted well into the twentieth century. One of the first things that Jean Drapeau did when he was elected mayor of Montreal in 1954

was to order city workers to clear away the bushes on the slopes of Mount Royal in the hope that this would cut down on the number of people having sex on the mountain. Although it is unclear just how many men Drapeau prevented from having sex with other men with his so-called "morality cuts," this measure did cause permanent damage to the mountain by accelerating erosion. See Luther A. Allen, "L'aventure sexuelle clandestine: Le cas du mont Royal," in *Sortir de l'ombre: Histoires des communautés lesbienne et gaie de Montréal,* ed. Irène Demczuk and Frank W. Remiggi (Montreal: VLB éditeur, 1998), 90.

23 *La Presse,* June 30, 1886, quoted in Cyrille Felteau, *Histoire de* La Presse, vol. 1, *Le livre du peuple, 1884–1916* (Montreal: La Presse, 1983), 170.

24 For a portrait of New France as a tolerant society, see André Lachance, *Crimes et criminels en Nouvelle-France* (Montreal: Boréal Express, 1984), 53–54. On the notion that the absence of prosecutions might be more indicative of the limited resources of the colony than of tolerance, see Patrice Corriveau, *Judging Homosexuals: A History of Gay Persecution in Quebec and France,* trans. Käthe Roth (Vancouver: UBC Press, 2011), 40.

25 Some observers have interpreted the near absence of evidence of court cases as evidence that sodomy did not occur. Robert L. Séguin, for example, finding only "three or four" cases of sodomy in the judicial record, concluded that sex between men was not all that common in New France. He suggested, moreover, that the harsh realities of New France made it unlikely that men would be interested in having sex with other men. See Robert L. Séguin, *La vie libertine en Nouvelle-France au XXVIIe siècle* (Montreal: Leméac, 1972), vol. 2, 505. Far more likely was that sexual activities between men went unnoticed and unpunished in all but the most public cases. Of course, those very same frontier conditions, along with the nomadic lifestyles of fur traders, as well as the shortage of women in the colony, could be said to have produced ideal conditions for the emergence of homosexual activity. See Paul-François Sylvestre, *Bougrerie en Nouvelle-France* (Hull, QC: Éditions Asticou, 1983). On homosexuality in Lower Canada, see Serge Gagnon, *Plaisir d'amour et crainte de Dieu: Sexualité et confession au Bas-Canada* (Sainte-Foy, QC: Les Presses de l'Université Laval, 1990), 150.

26 On these cases, see Quebec, *Jugements et Délibérations du Conseil souverain de la Nouvelle-France* (Quebec: Imprimerie A. Côté, 1887), vol. 3, 557–58, 574–85, 587–88. See also Corriveau, *Judging Homosexuals,* 40–43; Raymond Boyer, *Les crimes et châtiments au Canada français du XVIIe au XXe siècle* (Montreal: Cercle du livre de France, 1966), 227; Séguin, *La vie libertine,* vol. 1, 343–44; and Sylvestre, *Bougrerie en Nouvelle-France,* 31.

27 Peter Moogk, "The Liturgy of Humiliation, Pain, and Death: The Execution of Criminals in New France," *Canadian Historical Review* 88, 1 (2007): 107.

28 Robert Burns, "'Queer Doings': Attitudes toward Homosexuality in 19th Century Canada," *Body Politic* 6 (1976–77): 7.

29 The seeming lack of interest in Quebec contrasted with the growing interest in boys in the rest of North America and England, where it was seen to be imperative to monitor boys more closely in order to prepare them to be leaders in the military and political worlds. Girls, in contrast, were thought to be destined for the relatively less important domestic role that awaited them as mothers. See Angus McLaren, *The Trials of Masculinity: Policing Sexual Boundaries, 1870–1930* (Chicago: University of Chicago Press, 1997), 30–31.

30 It has been suggested that sex with older men was, for some working-class boys, part of a larger survival strategy in an urban and industrial landscape. See Steven Maynard, "'Horrible Temptations': Sex, Men, and Working-Class Male Youth in Urban Ontario, 1890–1935," *Canadian Historical Review* 78, 2 (1997): 232.

31 Myers, "Embodying Delinquency," 396–97.

32 Ibid., 400.

33 Gaston Desjardins, *L'Amour en patience: La sexualité adolescente au Québec, 1940–1960* (Sainte-Foy, QC: Presses de l'Université du Québec, 1995), 144–45.

34 Ibid., 203–5.

35 Hurteau, "Homosexualité, religion," 120.

36 Victor Germain, *Le point d'interrogation: Exposé sommaire du mystère de la génération humaine et des questions connexes: Rédigé à l'intention des mères de familles perplexes et de leurs filles questionneuses* (Quebec: n.p., 1937), 131–34; Panneton, *Le garçonnisme,* 20. See also Gagnon, *Plaisir d'amour,* 71.

37 Hector Palardy, *Hygiène sexuelle: L'Homme et la génération, la femme et la génération, les maladies vénériennes* (Chicoutimi, QC: Syndicat des imprimateurs du Saguenay, 1922), 4.

38 Terry Chapman, "Sexual Deviation in Western Canada, 1890-1920," paper presented at the Northern Great Plains Conference, Winnipeg, Manitoba, 1979, 15–16, quoted in Kinsman, *Regulation of Desire,* 101. See also Steven Maynard, "Rough Work and Rugged Men: The Social Construction of Masculinity in Working-Class History," *Labour/Le Travail* 23 (1989): 167–68; and Steven Maynard, "Queer Musings on Masculinity and History," *Labour/Le Travail* 42 (1998): 191–92.

39 Hurteau, "Homosexualité, religion," 100–1.

40 Ibid., 60–64; Pierre Hurteau, "L'Homosexualité masculine et les discours sur le sexe en contexte montréalais de la fin du XIXe siècle à la Révolution tranquille," *Histoire sociale/Social History* 26, 51 (1993): 41–66. For a discussion of these changes in the American context, see George Chauncey, *Gay New York: Gender, Urban Culture, and the Making of the Gay Male World, 1890–1940* (New York: Basic Books, 1994), 65–97.

41 Jonathan Ned Katz, "The Invention of Heterosexuality," *Socialist Review* 20, 1 (1990): 14–15.

42 Michel Foucault, *The History of Sexuality,* vol. 1, *An Introduction* (New York: Vintage, 1990), 43; Kinsman, *Regulation of Desire,* 129.

43 Some scholars have pointed to the emergence of these categories as key to the formation of homosexual identity. See, for example, Hurteau, "Homosexualité, religion," 108. A number of scholars, however, have challenged this Foucauldian claim, preferring to see such categories as simply acts of relabelling existing identities. See George Chauncey, "Christian Brotherhood or Sexual Perversion? Homosexual Identities and the Construction of Sexual Boundaries in the World War I Era," *Journal of Social History* 19, 2 (1985): 203.

44 Canada, *Debates of the House of Commons*, Ottawa, April 10, 1890, 3161–62.

45 Myers, "Embodying Delinquency," 402–6. On the declining tolerance for intimate relationships between boys in Quebec's classical colleges during the interwar years, see Louise Bienvenue, Ollivier Hubert, and Christine Hudon, *Le collège classique pour garçons: Études historiques sur une institution québécoise disparue* (Montreal: Fides, 2014), 373. On the homosocial world of Quebec's classical colleges, see Louise Bienvenue and Christine Hudon, "'Pour devenir homme, tu transgresseras ...': Quelques enjeux de la socialisation masculine dans les collèges classiques québécois (1880–1939)," *Canadian Historical Review* 86, 3 (2005): 485–511; Louise Bienvenue and Christine Hudon, "Une affaire d'hommes: Adolescence masculine et projections sociales dans quelques romans d'apprentissage de l'entre-deux-guerres," in *Nouvelles masculinités dans la littérature québécoise,* ed. Isabelle Boisclair, 23–47 (Montreal: Nota bene, 2008); Christine Hudon and Louise Bienvenue, "Entre franche camaraderie et amours socratiques: L'espace trouble et ténu des amitiés masculines dans les collèges classiques (1870–1960)," *Revue d'histoire de l'Amérique française* 57, 4 (2004): 481–507; Christine Hudon and Louise Bienvenue, "Des collégiens et leur maîtres au tournant du XXe siècle," *Globe: Revue internationale*

d'études québécoises 8, 2 (2005): 41–71; Christine Hudon, "'Le Muscle et le Vouloir': Les sports dans les collèges classiques masculins au Québec, 1870–1940," *Historical Studies in Education* 17, 2 (2005): 243–63; Christine Hudon, "L'éducation sentimentale et sexuelle dans les collèges pour garçons, du milieu du XIXe siècle à la Révolution tranquille," in *Une histoire des sexualités au Québec au XXe siècle,* ed. Jean-Philippe Warren, 32–53 (Montreal: VLB éditeur, 2012); and Louise Bienvenue, Ollivier Hubert, and Christine Hudon, *Le collège classique pour garçons: Études historiques sur une institution québécoise disparue* (Montreal: Fides, 2014).

46 André Vachon, "Jean Talon," *Dictionary of Canadian Biography* (Toronto: University of Toronto Press, 1966), vol. 1, 618.

47 Sylvestre, *Bougrerie en Nouvelle-France,* 11, 51.

48 See Louis Lalande, "La revanche des berceaux," *L'Action française* 2, 3 (1918): 98–108; Bourassa, "La famille canadienne," 279–88; Olivier Maurault, "Veillée religieuse," in *La Famille: 4e Session des Semaines Sociales du Canada* (Montreal: Bibliothèque de l'Action française, 1923), 310; Lionel Groulx, "La famille canadienne-française, ses traditions, son rôle," in *La Famille: 4e Session des Semaines Sociales du Canada* (Montreal: Bibliothèque de l'Action française, 1923), 343; and Germain, *Le point d'interrogation,* 49.

49 Hurteau, "Homosexualité, religion," 119. On the homosocial world of Quebec's classical colleges, see Hudon and Bienvenue, "Entre franche camaraderie."

50 Palardy, *Hygiène sexuelle,* 4; Mercier, *Quoi dire, comment dire,* 11–12, 16, 17, 19; Isabelle Perrault, "Morale Catholique et genre feminin: La sexualité dissertée dans les manuels de sexualité maritale au Québec, 1930–1960," *Revue d'histoire de l'Amérique française* 57, 4 (2004): 567–90.

51 Mercier, *Quoi dire, comment dire,* 24, 34; Lucien Royer, *Autour de l'être masculin* (Montreal: Les Éditions de l'Étoile, 1945), 17.

52 Royer, *Autour de l'être masculin,* 36–39, 60.

53 Many observers have tended to interpret the growing acceptance of sex education as evidence of a new enlightened and progressive attitude taking shape in the province rather than as an attempt to reinforce heterosexuality. See, for example, Desjardins, *L'Amour en patience.*

54 Quoted in Rodrigues Normandin, "Nos maîtres catholiques et l'éducation sexuelle," *Revue de l'Université d'Ottawa* 18, 2 (1948): 138–40, 142.

55 Hurteau, "L'homosexualité masculine," 42. On the ties between secular and clerical leaders in English-speaking Canada, see Mariana Valverde, *The Age of Light Soap and Water: Moral Reform in English Canada, 1885–1925* (Toronto: McClelland and Stewart, 1991), 47.

56 On the rise of companionate marriages, see Lucie Piché, *Femmes et changement social au Québec: L'apport de la Jeunesse ouvrière catholique féminine, 1931–1966* (Sainte-Foy, QC: Presses de l'Université Laval, 2003); and Louise Bienvenue, *Quand la jeunesse entre en scène: L'Action catholique avant la Révolution tranquille* (Montreal: Les Éditions du Boréal, 2003). Although historians have tended to point to the possibility that the companionate marriage model might offer women greater freedom, they have also noted that the rise of the nuclear family has, according to Michael Gauvreau, "rendered them [women] more dependent psychologically upon their husbands for satisfying personal relationships." See Michael Gauvreau, "The Emergence of Personalist Feminism: Catholicism and the Marriage-Preparation Movement in Quebec, 1940–1966," in *Households of Faith: Family, Gender, and Community in Canada, 1760–1969,* ed. Nancy Christie (Montreal and Kingston: McGill-Queen's University Press, 2002), 329–30; and Michael Gauvreau, *The Catholic Origins of Quebec's Quiet Revolution, 1931–1970* (Montreal and Kingston: McGill-Queen's University Press, 2005), 96–105. For a general discussion of the ways that the introduction of labour-saving devices, which had been expected to

reduce women's domestic workload but ended up increasing it because new technology had simply raised the standards of domestic cleanliness and thus tied women ever more closely to her role as homemaker, see Ruth Schwartz Cowen, *More Work for Mother: The Ironies of Household Technology from the Open Hearth to the Microwave* (New York: Basic Books, 1983).

57 Quoted in Eric Hutton, "The Happy Sequel to Quebec's Great Ball-Park Wedding," *Maclean's Magazine*, December 6, 1958, 35.

58 See Lévesque, *Making and Breaking*, 46.

59 *La Patrie*, July 24, 1939.

60 *Montreal Gazette*, July 24, 1939; *La Presse*, July 24, 1939.

61 *La Presse*, July 24, 1939.

62 *Montreal Daily Star*, July 24, 1939.

63 *Montreal Daily Herald*, July 24, 1939.

64 Quoted in Hutton, "Happy Sequel," 36.

65 Raymond Villecourt, "La faute des mères," *Le Journal pour tous* 1, 6–7 (1906): 69.

66 Henri Martin, "La dépopulation," in *La Famille: 4e Session des Semaines Sociales du Canada* (Montreal: Bibliothèque de l'Action française, 1923), 150.

67 Léon-Mercier Gouin, "Le divorce," in *La Famille: 4e Session des Semaines Sociales du Canada* (Montreal: Bibliothèque de l'Action française, 1923), 183.

68 On prostitution in Montreal, see, Andrée Lévesque, "Éteindre le Red Light: Les réformateurs et la prostitution à Montréal entre 1865 et 1925," *Urban History Review* 17, 3 (1989): 191–201; Andrée Lévesque, "Le Bordel: Milieu de Travail Contrôlé," *Labour/Le Travail* 20 (1987): 13–32; Danielle Lacasse, *La prostitution féminine à Montréal, 1945–1970* (Montreal: Boréal, 1994): Mary Anne Poutanen, *Beyond Brutal Passions: Prostitution in Early Nineteenth-Century Montreal* (Montreal and Kingston: McGill-Queen's University Press, 2015); and Daniel Proulx, *Le Red Light de Montréal* (Montreal: VLB éditeur, 1997).

69 The classic account of the prostitute in the Victorian mind is Judith R. Walkowitz, *City of Dreadful Delight: Narratives of Sexual Danger in Late-Victorian London* (Chicago: University of Chicago Press, 1992).

70 *Le Devoir*, October 9, 1924; Jean-Paul Brodeur, "La philosophie devant le contrôle social: Vénus doctrinale," in *Objets pour la philosophie: Nationalisme, prostitution, syndicalisme, etc. ...*, ed. Marc Chabot and André Vidricaire (Montreal: Pantoute, 1983), 6–7. Critics of the city's perceived moral laxity often referred to Montreal as "wide-open." See *Enquête judiciaire sur la police de Montréal, 1924–1925*, *Témoignages*, vol. 1, 428, 434, 443, box 054-02-07-02, Fonds Enquête judiciaire sur l'administration de la police de Montréal, 1924–1925, P045 (hereafter Coderre Commission), Archives de la Ville de Montréal.

71 Louis Coderre, "Rapport complet de l'Honorable Juge Louis Coderre," box 054-01-10-05, Coderre Commission.

72 Hart, *Wake Up! Montreal!* 2, 29.

73 *Montreal Star*, April 9, 1923.

74 Lévesque, "Éteindre le Red Light," 196.

75 Amédée Geoffrion, *Témoignages*, vol. 8, 7556, box 054-02-08-04, Coderre Commission.

76 Anonymous, *Montreal by Gaslight* (Montreal: n.p., 1889), 81.

77 F.-X. Dupuis, *Pro Domo Sua: Dissertation sur la prostitution: Prononcée en audience publique le 25 février 1909* (Montreal: n.p., 1909), 1, 5–7; Lévesque, "Éteindre le Red Light," 191–92.

78 Quoted in *Montreal Star*, April 9, 1923.

79 Henri Taschereau, *The Crime of Prostitution: A Timely Message on the Crime of Prostitution and the Duty of the Police to Suppress It* (Toronto: Board of Moral and Social Reform, Presbyterian Church in Canada, n.d.), 8.

80 Lévesque, "Éteindre le Red Light," 193.
81 Brodeur, "La philosophie," 10.
82 Lacasse, *La prostitution féminine*, 24.
83 Lévesque, *Making and Breaking*, 67–68.
84 Coderre, "Rapport complet."
85 Pierre Bélanger, *Témoignages*, vol. 4, 5573, box 054-02-07-05, Coderre Commission.
86 Owen Dawson, *Témoignages*, vol. 1, 459, box 054-02-07-02, Coderre Commission.
87 Bélanger, *Témoignages*, vol. 1, 868–80.
88 Valverde, *Age of Light*, 77–79.
89 Henri Taschereau, *Report of Hon. Justice Taschereau on the Police Investigation and Its Results, Supplement to the Municipal Gazette of Montreal* (Montreal: n.p., 1905), 15.
90 Quoted in Taschereau, *Social Evil*, 3.
91 Dawson, *Témoignages*, vol. 1, 425.
92 Ibid., vol. 1, 435–36.
93 See Renisa Mawani, "Regulating the 'Respectable' Classes: Venereal Disease, Gender, and Public Health Initiatives in Canada, 1914–35," in *Regulating Lives: Historical Essays on the State, Society, the Individual, and the Law*, ed. John McLaren, Robert Menzies, and Dorothy E. Chunn, 170–95 (Vancouver: UBC Press, 2002).
94 See Judith R. Walkowitz, *Prostitution and Victorian Society: Women, Class and the State* (Cambridge, UK: Cambridge University Press, 1980).
95 Geoffrion, *Témoignages*, vol. 8, 7618.
96 Ibid., vol. 8, 7621.
97 Abbé Philippe Perrier, *Témoignages*, vol. 8, 8326, box 054-02-08-04, Coderre Commission.
98 Alfred K. Haywood, *Témoignages*, vol. 2, 1173–74, box 054-02-07-03, Coderre Commission.
99 Tamara Myers, "The Voluntary Delinquent: Parents, Daughters, and the Montreal Juvenile Delinquents' Court in 1918," *Canadian Historical Review* 80, 2 (1999): 248–49; Carolyn Strange, *Toronto's Girl Problem: The Perils and Pleasures of the City, 1880–1930* (Toronto: University of Toronto Press, 1995), 89–91.
100 C.S. Clark, *Of Toronto the Good: The Queen City as It Is* (1898; reprint, Toronto: Coles, 1970), 89. See also Edmond Brossard, *Témoignages*, vol. 6, 6233, box 054-02-08-02, P45, D11, Coderre Commission.
101 Geoffrion, *Témoignages*, vol. 8, 7644.
102 John Swaill, *Témoignages*, vol. 3, 2332–34, box 054-02-07-04, Coderre Commission.
103 Valverde, *Age of Light*, 77–78.
104 Committee of Sixteen, *Some Facts Regarding Toleration, Regulation, Segregation and Repression of Commercialized Vice* (Montreal: Committee of Sixteen, 1919), 14.
105 Taschereau, *Report of Hon. Justice Taschereau*, 14.
106 This view is adopted by Brodeur, "La philosophie," 10. It was not uncommon for those reformers who supported regulation to resort to stereotypes of Anglo-Montrealers in order to discredit suppression. Amédée Geoffrion, for example, frequently associated those figures that opposed regulation with the stereotype of "Ézéchiel de Westmount." See Geoffrion, *Témoignages*, vol. 8, 7554.
107 Alan Gordon, *Making Public Pasts: The Contested Terrain of Montreal's Public Memories, 1891–1930* (Montreal and Kingston: McGill-Queen's University Press, 2001), 40.
108 Primo Morley, "The Political Career of Mederic Martin, 1906–1928," *Register* 3, 1 (1982): 63, 71.
109 See Paul-André Linteau, *Histoire de Montréal depuis la Confédération* (Montreal: Boréal, 1992), 262, 405–7; Harold Kaplan, *Reform, Planning and City Politics: Montreal, Winnipeg,*

Toronto (Toronto: University of Toronto Press, 1982), 313, 327–28; Michel Gauvin, "The Reformer and the Machine: Montreal Civic Politics from Raymond Préfontaine to Médéric Martin," *Journal of Canadian Studies* 13, 2 (1978): 16–26; and Robert-Maurice Migner, "Le bossisme à Montréal: Camillien Houde remplace Médéric Martin (1923–1929)," *Urban History Review* 3, 1 (1974): 2–8.

110 Lévesque, "Éteindre le Red Light," 197.

111 Quoted in ibid., 194. Historians have recently discovered that Julien Saint-Michel was one of the many pseudonyms used by the journalist and poet Éva Circé-Côté. See Andrée Lévesque, *Éva Circé-Côté: Libre-penseuse, 1871–1940* (Montreal: Les Éditions du remue-ménage, 2010), 11–13.

112 Charles Langelier, *La prostitution: Ses dangers – son remède: Deuxième lettre ouverte à son Honneur le maire et à MM. les échevins de la cité de Québec* (Quebec: Imprimerie nationale, 1919), 3.

113 Geoffrion, *Témoignages,* vol. 8, 7460, 7472.

114 Ibid., 7677–78.

115 Ibid., 7619–20.

116 Quoted in *Le Devoir,* December 31, 1924.

117 Gustave Archambault, *Témoignages,* vol. 8, 8023–24, box 054-02-08-04, Coderre Commission.

118 University of Paris economist and professor Charles Gide, a prominent critic of regulation and a supporter of suppression, quoted in Taschereau, *Crime of Prostitution,* 5.

119 Lévesque, *Making and Breaking,* 80.

120 Geoffrion, *Témoignages,* vol. 8, 7742.

121 *Le Devoir,* December 22, 1924.

122 Dupuis, *Pro Domo Sua,* 7.

123 Clark, *Of Toronto the Good,* 86, 87, 89–90.

124 Ibid., 91.

125 Dupuis, *Pro Domo Sua,* 2.

126 Ibid., 7.

127 Geoffrion, *Témoignages,* vol. 8, 7776.

128 *Montreal Star,* April 3, 1923.

129 Ibid.

130 Geoffrion, *Témoignages,* vol. 8, 7475.

131 Hurteau, "Homosexualité, religion," 46.

132 Adélard Dugré, *Témoignages,* vol. 8 (copy), box 054-02-09-01, Coderre Commission.

133 *Le Devoir,* January 7, 1925.

134 Nathan Gordon, *Témoignages,* vol. 8, 7621, box 054-02-08-04, Coderre Commission.

135 Alain Stanké and Jean-Louis Morgan, *Pax: Lutte à finir avec le pègre: Un portrait-robot du célèbre incorruptible Pacifique Plante* (Montreal: La Presse, 1972), 153.

136 Geoffrion, *Témoignages,* vol. 8, 7631–32.

137 Dupuis, *Pro Domo Sua,* 9.

138 Taschereau, *Social Evil.*

139 Coderre, "Rapport complet."

140 See Myers, "Voluntary Delinquent," 249.

141 See William Weintraub, *City Unique: Montreal Days and Nights in the 1940s and '50s* (Toronto: McClelland and Stewart, 1996); and Mathieu Lapointe, *Nettoyer Montréal: Les campagnes de moralité publique, 1940–1954* (Quebec: Septentrion, 2014).

142 Lacasse, *La prostitution féminine,* 86–87.

143 Geoffrion, *Témoignages,* vol. 8, 7478–79, 7545.

144 Brodeur, "La philosophie," 42.

Chapter 3: The Decline of the French Canadian Race

A version of Chapter 3 appeared as "Evolving Racial Identity and the Consolidation of Men's Authority in Early Twentieth-Century Quebec," *Canadian Historical Review* 88, 3 (2007): 413–38. It is reprinted with permission of the University of Toronto Press.

1 Although French Canadians displayed a considerable degree of racial consciousness during the first decades of the twentieth century, few historians have investigated the possibility that English and French Canadians once claimed a distinct racial identity. One reason that historians have not dealt with this prospect is that the question of race in Canada is often approached through the prism of racism. Historians tend to discuss race only to the extent that they seek to establish whether those who used the word "race" were "racist" in the modern sense of the term. See, for example, Séraphin Marion, "L'abbé Groulx, raciste?" *Les cahiers des dix* 43 (1983): 192; René Dionne, "'*L'Appel de la race*' est-il un roman raciste?" *Relations*, November 1978, 317–18; Dominique Garand, "Éléments de réflexion en vue d'une approche non hystérique de Lionel Groulx," *Les cahiers d'histoire du Québec au XXe siècle* 8 (1997): 130–50; and Jean-Éthier Blais, "Le prétendu antisémitisme de Lionel Groulx, un alibi du racisme anti-québécois," *Les cahiers d'histoire du Québec au XXe siècle* 8 (1997): 151–54. Most have avoided the question altogether, however, preferring to treat the word "race" as a synonym of "culture" or "people," something that early-twentieth-century Canadians often appeared to do. The word "race," historians note, "was used at the time as a synonym for nation or people." See Paul-André Linteau, René Durocher, and Jean-Claude Robert, *Quebec: A History, 1867–1929*, trans. Robert Chodos (Toronto: James Lorimer and Company, 1983), 531–32. Another suggests that the word race "was a synonym of people and nation." See Pierre Trépanier, "L'éducation intellectuelle et politique de Lionel Groulx (1906–1909)," in *Lionel Groulx: Correspondance, 1894–1967*, vol. 2, *1906–1909: Un étudiant à l'école de l'Europe*, ed. Giselle Huot, Juliette Lalonde Rémillard, and Pierre Trépanier (Montreal: Fides, 1993), xlviii. See also Esdras Minville, *La vie sociale*, vol. 1, *Le nationalisme canadien-français*, ed. François-Albert Angers (Montreal: Fides and HEC, 1992), 221; Ronald Rudin, *Making History in Twentieth-Century Quebec* (Toronto: University of Toronto Press, 1997), 57; and Jean-Christian Pleau, "Polémique sur un 'mauvais livre': *L'Appel de la race* de Lionel Groulx," *Voix et Images* 28, 2 (2003): 155–56. Jean-Pierre Gaboury does more to highlight the tensions evident in Groulx's ideas about race, suggesting that Groulx believed that French Canadians were both the guardians of a "pure" race and part of a new French Canadian race. See Jean-Pierre Gaboury, *Le Nationalisme de Lionel Groulx: Aspects idéologiques* (Ottawa: Éditions de l'Université d'Ottawa, 1970), 31–36. For the claim that Groulx did not have physical differences in mind when he used the word "race," although the priest-historian sometimes "slipped into biological definitions," see Patrice Groulx, *Pièges de la mémoire: Dollard des Ormeaux, les Amérindiens et nous* (Hull, QC: Vents d'Ouest, 1998), 217–18. For an account of how Canadian historians have used the word "race," and the suggestion that "even those historians most influenced by racist ideas never supposed that biological factors were the ultimate determinants of history," see Joseph Levitt, "Race and Nation in Canadian Anglophone Historiography," *Canadian Review of Studies in Nationalism* 8, 1 (1981): 3. For a perspective that is more definitive in concluding that Lionel Groulx did, in fact, believe the French Canadian race to be defined, at least partly, through blood, see Gérard Bouchard *Les deux chanoines: Contradiction et ambivalence dans la pensée de Lionel Groulx* (Montreal: Boréal, 2003), 133–48. For an acknowledgment that Edmond de Nevers believed that race was tied to blood, see Jean-Philippe Warren, "Préface," in Edmond de Nevers, *La Question des races: Anthologie*, ed. Jean-Philippe Warren (Montreal: Bibliothèque québécoise, 2003), 25, 35. One reason that historians have conflated the words "race" and "culture" is that early-twentieth-century Canadians were

ambiguous in their use of the word "race." A classic study on Canadian imperialism notes, "it is not clear, for instance, whether they [imperialists] generally believed racial character to be permanently fixed and unchangeable or whether they really thought that habits and aptitudes could be learned and acquired. Sometimes the phrase 'Anglo-Saxon race' was simply a synonym for a total culture which was itself understood to be the product of history and not only racial instincts; sometimes, race was quite explicitly associated with the biological analogies of Darwinian science." See Carl Berger, *The Sense of Power: Studies in the Ideas of Canadian Imperialism, 1867–1914* (Toronto: University of Toronto Press, 1970), 117. On the Victorian attitudes on race, see George Stocking, *Victorian Anthropology* (New York: Free Press, 1987). French Canadians' tendency at the beginning of the twentieth century to emphasize the purity of their blood as well as the degree to which they were physiologically distinct from English Canadians suggests that we are dealing not simply with, to borrow the historian Matthew Frye Jacobson's formulation, "an archaic meaning of the word 'race' but rather [with] an archaic perception of 'difference.'" See Matthew Frye Jacobson, *Whiteness of a Different Color: European Immigrants and the Alchemy of Race* (Cambridge, MA: Harvard University Press, 1998), 6. See also Jean-Philippe Warren, *Edmond de Nevers: Portrait d'un intellectuel, 1862–1906* (Montreal: Boréal, 2005), 172.

2 Lionel Groulx, *La naissance d'une race* (Montreal: Bibliothèque de l'Action française, 1919), 7.

3 Lionel Groulx, *Dix ans d'Action française* (Montreal: Bibliothèque de l'Action française, 1926), 258.

4 Lionel Groulx, *Directives* (Montreal: Les Éditions du Zodiaque, 1937), 143.

5 Léo-Paul Desrosiers, "La nationalisation de notre littérature par l'étude de notre histoire," *L'Action française* 3, 2 (1919): 69.

6 See Susan Mann Trofimenkoff, "Henri Bourassa and the 'Woman Question,'" *Journal of Canadian Studies* 10, 4 (1975): 3–11.

7 L.-F.-R. Laflèche, "The Providential Mission of the French Canadians," translation of *Quelques considérations sur les rapports de la société civile avec la religion et la famille* (Trois Rivières, 1866), in *French Canadian Nationalism: An Anthology*, ed. Ramsay Cook (Toronto: Macmillan, 1969), 95.

8 Louis-Adolphe Pâquet, "A Sermon on the Vocation of the French Race in America," translation of "Sermon sur la vocation de la race française en Amérique," June 23, 1902, in *French Canadian Nationalism: An Anthology*, ed. Ramsay Cook (Toronto: Macmillan, 1969), 153, 154. For the context of the sermon, see Dominique Foisy-Geoffroy, "'La vocation de la race française en Amérique,' de Monseigneur Louis-Adolphe Pâquet," *Mens: Revue d'histoire intellectuelle de l'Amérique française* 3, 1 (2002): 61–95. Lionel Groulx echoed these views in *L'Enseignement français au Canada*, vol. 1, *Dans le Québec* (Montreal: Librairie d'action canadienne-française, 1931), 57. See also Le comité permanent de la survivance française en Amérique, *La vocation de la race française en Amérique du Nord* (Quebec: n.p., 1945), 14–15.

9 French Canadians could quickly turn against such hierarchies if they made them appear inferior. When the Frenchman Edmond Demolins published *A quoi tient la supériorité des Anglo-Saxons?* (Paris: F. Didot et cie, 1898), for example, some French Canadians took exception to the implication made in the title. One reviewer attacked the notion that Anglo-Saxons were superior and claimed that success in business and industry simply reflected a superior social and educational structure. See J.A.M. Brosseau, "Étude critique du livre d'E. Demolins: 'A Quoi tient la supériorité des Anglo-Saxons?'" *Revue canadienne* 40, 3 (1904): 235–36. See also Louis Lalande, *La race supérieure* (Montreal: Bibliothèque de l'Action française, 1919). When it suited them, however, French Canadians hailed their own racial traits as superior.

10 Pâquet, "Sermon on the Vocation," 155.
11 Lionel Groulx, *Notre maître, le passé,* 1st series, 3rd ed. (Montreal: Librairie Granger Frères, 1937), 149.
12 Groulx, *Directives,* 244. According to Groulx, the French, at least prior to the Revolution, were not like the other old races because they were the "chosen" European people who had adopted the best traditions from Greek and Roman civilization. See Groulx, *Dix ans d'Action française,* 128, 269, and *La naissance d'une race,* 39–41. See also Bouchard, *Les deux chanoines,* 63, 74–5, 142.
13 Groulx, *Notre maître, le passé,* 2nd series (Montreal: Librairie Granger Frères, 1936), 258.
14 Edmond Lacroix, "Les généologies," *L'Action française* 2, 9 (1918): 411.
15 Quoted in Gail Bederman, *Manliness and Civilization: A Cultural History of Gender and Race in the United States, 1880–1917* (Chicago: University of Chicago Press, 1995), 84–88. See also Henry Charles Merwin, "On Being Civilized Too Much," *Atlantic Monthly* 79 (1897): 838–47.
16 George Miller Beard, *American Nervousness: Its Causes and Consequences* (New York: G.P. Putnam's Sons, 1881).
17 Bederman, *Manliness and Civilization,* 88–94.
18 On eugenics in Canada, see Angus McLaren, *Our Own Master Race: Eugenics in Canada, 1885–1945* (Toronto: McClelland and Stewart, 1990); and Erika Dyck, *Facing Eugenics: Reproduction, Sterilization, and the Politics of Choice* (Toronto: University of Toronto Press, 2013).
19 For Emily Murphy's views on race, see her *The Black Candle* (Toronto: Thomas Allen, 1922).
20 The Legislative Assembly of Alberta passed the Sexual Sterilization Act in 1928 calling for the sterilization of those members of the community who were said to be mentally disabled. The law was repealed in 1972. See McLaren, *Our Own Master Race,* 99–100.
21 McLaren, *Our Own Master Race,* 44–45.
22 There were exceptions. Some proponents of colonization did envision new and more vigorous manhood being created following men's immersion in the wilderness and their interaction with the Native peoples. See Christian Morissonneau, *La terre promise: Le mythe du nord québécois* (Montreal: Hurtubise HMH, 1978), 109–15.
23 Groulx, *La naissance d'une race,* 157.
24 This point is made by Gérard Bouchard, *Les deux chanoines,* 147–48.
25 Louis-Marie Lalande, *Hérédité: Manuel de génétique* (La Trappe, QC: L'Institut agricole d'Oka, 1936), 425–26, 435–36.
26 See the French study by Edouard Jordan and J. Viollet, *Eugénisme et stérilisation* (Montreal: L'École sociale populaire, 1934). See also F.M. Drouin, *Autour de la famille: Stérilisation et "Birth Control"* (Ottawa: Collège dominicaine, 1936); and Hervé Blais, *Les tendances eugénistes au Canada* (Montreal: Institut Familial, 1942).
27 According to McLaren, *Our Own Master Race,* 25, some French Canadians "could not help but see that Francophones would necessarily do poorly when judged according to eugenic measurements."
28 Massachusetts Department of Labor and Industries, *12th Annual Report of the Bureau of Statistics of Labor* (Boston: Rand Avery, 1881), 469–70, quoted in Pierre Anctil, "'Chinese of the Eastern States, 1881,'" *Recherches sociographiques* 22, 1 (1981): 131.
29 Beard's observations were presented to the meeting of the American Neurological Association in New York in 1878 and recorded by M. Josiah Roberts, "Fourth Annual (Adjourned) Session," *Journal of Nervous and Mental Disease* 5, 3 (1878): 526.
30 Denyse Baillargeon, *Babies for the Nation: The Medicalization of Motherhood in Quebec, 1910–1970,* trans. W. Donald Wilson (Waterloo, ON: Wilfrid Laurier University Press, 2009), 49.

31 Quebec's birthrate remained higher than Ontario's, but it also began to decline in the late nineteenth century. See Danielle Gauvreau, Diane Gervais, and Peter Gossage, *La fécondité des Québécoises, 1870–1970: D'Une exception à l'autre* (Montreal: Boréal, 2007).
32 Raoul Masson, "La mortalité infantile dans la province de Québec," *L'Union médicale du Canada* 54, 1 (1925): 4, quoted in Baillargeon, *Babies for the Nation*, 49–50.
33 This is certainly not to suggest that English-speaking Canadians did not target women during these years. See, for example, Carolyn Strange, *Toronto's Girl Problem: The Perils and Pleasures of the City, 1880–1930* (Toronto: University of Toronto Press, 1995).
34 Fadette [Henriette Dessaulles Saint-Jacques], *La Mission de la mère* (Montreal: Bibliothèque de l'Action française, 1921), 2.
35 Fadette, "La canadienne," *L'Action française* 2, 6 (1918): 242.
36 Cardinal James Gibbons, the archbishop of Baltimore, uttered these words to a group of Catholic women on February 15, 1917, quoted in Joseph Gauvreau, "Plus que l'homme," *L'Action française* 1, 2 (1917): 46.
37 Henri Bourassa, *Femmes-hommes ou hommes et femmes? Études à bâtons rompus sur le féminisme* (Montreal: Imprimerie du Devoir, 1925), 11.
38 Errol Bouchette, *Robert Lozé* (Montreal: A.P. Pigeon, 1903), 25.
39 Sherene Razack, "Schools for Happiness: Instituts familiaux and the Education of Ideal Wives and Mothers," in *Delivering Motherhood: Maternal Ideologies and Practices in the 19th and 20th Centuries*, ed. Katherine Arnup, Andrée Lévesque, and Ruth Roach Pierson (New York: Routledge, 1990), 212.
40 Lambert Closse, *La réponse de la race: Le cathéchisme national des Canadiens français* (Montreal: Thérien Frères, 1936), 265, quoted in Esther Delisle, *The Traitor and the Jew: Anti-Semitism and the Delirium of Extremist Right-Wing Nationalism in French Canada from 1929–1939*, trans. Madeleine Hébert, with Claire Rothman and Käthe Roth (Montreal: Robert Davies, 1993), 45.
41 Gauvreau, "Plus que l'homme," 50.
42 Elspeth Probyn, *"Love in a Cold Climate": Queer Belonging in Québec* (Montreal: Research Group on Cultural Citizenship, 1994), 56–57.
43 Ruth Roach Pierson, "Nations: Gendered, Racialized, Crossed with Empire," in *Gendered Nations: Nationalisms and Gender Order in the Long Nineteenth Century*, ed. Ida Blom, Karen Hagemann, and Catherine Hall (New York: Berg, 2000), 44. See also Susan Mann Trofimenkoff, *Action Française: French Canadian Nationalism in the Twenties* (Toronto: University of Toronto Press, 1975), 82; Danielle Juteau, "From Nation-Church to Nation-State: Evolving Sex-Gender Relations in Québec Society," in *Between Woman and Nation: Nationalisms, Transnational Feminism, and the State*, ed. Caren Kaplan, Norma Alarcón, and Minoo Moallem (Durham, NC: Duke University Press, 1999), 147.
44 *Montreal Herald*, November 22, 1929.
45 Bourassa, *Femmes-hommes ou hommes et femmes?* 17, 44.
46 Ibid., 4. See also Georges Courchesne, "La famille et le choix d'une carrière," in *La Famille: 4e Session des Semaines Sociales du Canada* (Montreal: Bibliothèque de l'Action française, 1923), 255.
47 Bourassa, *Femmes-hommes ou hommes et femmes?* 5.
48 Ibid, 4. See also Ferdinand Roy, "L'Autorité dans la famille," in *L'Autorité: 7e Session des Semaines Sociales du Canada* (Montreal: Bibliothèque de l'Action Canadienne Française, 1927), 56–57, 68.
49 See Louis Lalande, "La revanche des berceaux," *L'Action française* 2, 3 (March 1918): 98–108; and Henri Bourassa, "La famille canadienne, ses périls, son salut," in *La Famille: 4e Session des Semaines Sociales du Canada*, 279–88 (Montreal: Bibliothèque de l'Action française, 1923).

50 On male authority in the household, see Roy, "L'Autorité dans la famille," 49–50. For a critique of the idea that Quebec was ever a matriarchal society, see Lori Saint-Martin, *Le nom de la mère: Mères, filles et écriture dans la littérature québécoise au féminin* (Quebec: Nota Bene, 1999), 25–26. The myth of Quebec as a matriarchal society persisted well into the twentieth century and was used against women who complained about their position. See Lysiane Gagnon, *Vivre avec les hommes: Un nouveau partage* (Montreal: Québec/Amérique, 1983), 33–34.

51 Fadette, "Les mères," *L'Action française* 4, 7 (1920): 289.

52 Patricia Smart, *Writing in the Father's House: The Emergence of the Feminine in the Quebec Literary Tradition* (Toronto: University of Toronto Press, 1991), 169.

53 See Saint-Martin, *Le nom de la mère,* 28–32; Mariana Valverde, *Sex, Power and Pleasure* (Toronto: Women's Press, 1985), 52–53; and Elspeth Probyn, "Bloody Metaphors and Other Allegories of the Ordinary," in *Nationalisms, Transnational Feminism, and the State,* ed. Caren Kaplan, Norma Alarcón, and Minoo Moallem (Durham, NC: Duke University Press, 1999), 52.

54 Harry Bernard, *L'Homme tombé* (Montreal: n.p., 1924), 22.

55 Ibid., 161.

56 Ibid., 173.

57 Ibid., 57.

58 The fear of women's bodies is not new, and efforts to transform women into carriers of the next generation, Mariana Valverde has written, reflected a longstanding male fear of a woman's reproductive capabilities and a desire to control it. "Threatened by a vagina ... whose life-giving powers both scare and mystify them," Valverde writes, "men try to ignore the independent life of the vagina and reduce it to a mere container, box, or receptacle." See Valverde, *Sex, Power and Pleasure,* 52. See also Mariana Valverde, "'When the Mother of the Race Is Free': Race, Reproduction, and Sexuality in First-Wave Feminism," in *Gender Conflicts: New Essays in Women's History,* ed. Franca Iacovetta and Mariana Valverde, 3–26 (Toronto: University of Toronto Press, 1992). For the view that women were "reproducers rather than producers, prized and revered objects of protection, rather than agents in their own right," see Geoff Eley, "Culture, Nation and Gender," in *Gendered Nations: Nationalisms and Gender Order in the Long Nineteenth Century,* ed. Ida Blom, Karen Hagemann, and Catherine Hall (New York: Berg, 2000), 32–33.

59 Quoted in Trépanier, "L'éducation intellectuelle," xlvi. G. Stanley Hall referred to adolescence as the moment when children experienced a "physiological second birth" that would mark their entry into the racial family. See Bederman, *Manliness and Civilization,* 103. On men's desire to give birth to a new country in Quebec, see Lori Saint-Martin, "The Body Politic and the Erotic Body: The (Male) Novel of the Quiet Revolution in Quebec," *British Journal of Canadian Studies* 21, 2 (2008), 212. A similar "discursive coup d'état" was evident in Australia following the Great War, when it was suggested that men had given birth to the nation on the battlefield. See Marilyn Lake, "Mission Impossible: How Men Gave Birth to the Australian Nation – Nationalism, Gender and Other Seminal Acts," *Gender and History* 4, 3 (1992): 307. In France, maternity came to be regarded as something that women could contribute to the nation after men had done so much during the war to defend and forge the nation on the battlefield. See Mary Louise Roberts, *Civilization without Sexes: Reconstructing Gender in Postwar France, 1917–1927* (Chicago: University of Chicago Press, 1994), 90, 120. Although some French Canadians adopted a similar rhetorical formulation when they declared that men were the ones who had given birth to the nation, they did not link this idea to men's military service. In Quebec this male fantasy of giving birth can still be detected at the close of the twentieth century.

See Lori Saint-Martin, "Narrative Cross-Dressing and Men 'Doing' Motherhood: The Case of Marie Auger/Mario G.'s *Le ventre en tête*," *Québec Studies* 30 (2000): 44–56.

60 Groulx, *Directives*, 167.

61 François Hertel, *Pour un ordre personnaliste* (Montreal: Les Éditions de l'Arbre, 1942), 44.

62 Lionel Groulx, *La Canadienne française* (Nicolet, QC: n.p., 1950), 20. This attitude placed a much greater burden on mothers, who were being reminded of their duty to raise children properly. But it also removed from women some of their presumed power since the woman's role in transferring physical attributes to her children was downplayed. Groulx was very much in line with the larger intellectual climate of the 1920s, whereby women were still encouraged to have children but were also reminded that the physical and spiritual health of her children were much more important than the number of children one could produce. On the shifts in this natalist rhetoric, see Gauvreau, Gervais, and Gossage, *La fécondité des Québécoises*, 71–94.

63 See Gérard Bouchard, *La Pensée impuissante: Échecs et mythes nationaux canadiens-français, 1850–1960* (Montreal: Boréal, 2004), 25–57.

64 G.-A. Nantel, *La colonisation du Nord-Ouest de la province de Québec: Conférence de l'Honorable G.-A. Nantel, le 7 mai 1895* (Montreal: E. Senécal, 1895), 11. The colonization movement was not merely an expression of nostalgic and agrarian values. Rather, it was an aggressive movement of conquest, an attempt to reconquer the British conquerors. It thus presented men with the opportunity to reclaim the land by giving birth, it might be said, to a new French Canadian power within Confederation. See Gabriel Dussault, *Le Curé Labelle: Messianisme, utopie et colonisation au Québec, 1850–1900* (Montreal: Hurtubise HMH, 1983).

65 See Morissonneau, *La terre promise*, 26, 93–97, 124. On the appeal of the northern climate in the English Canadian mind, see Robert Grant Haliburton, *The Men of the North and Their Place in History: A Lecture Delivered before the Montreal Literary Club, March 31st, 1869* (Montreal: J. Lovell, 1869); William H. Hingston, *The Climate of Canada and Its Relation to Life and Health* (Montreal: Dawson Brothers, 1884); Carl Berger, "The True North Strong and Free," in *Nationalism in Canada*, ed. Peter Russell, 3–26 (Toronto: McGraw-Hill, 1966); and Jane Nicholas, "Gendering the Jubilee: Gender and Modernity in the Diamond Jubilee of Confederation Celebrations, 1927," *Canadian Historical Review* 90, 2 (2009): 247–74.

66 The prospect of escaping the effeminizing clutches of the traditional domestic sphere found in the city and establishing a homosocial society based on male fraternity turned out to be one of the attractions of establishing new settlements. See Victor-Laurent Tremblay, "La 'Patrie homosociale' de Jules-Paul Tardivel," in *Francophonie plurielle: Actes du congrès mondial du Conseil international d'études francophones tenu à Casablanca (Maroc) du 10 au 17 juillet 1993*, ed. Ginette Adamson and Jean-Marc Gouanvic (Montreal: Hurtubise HMH, 1995), 173–76; and Adele Perry, *On the Edge of Empire: Gender, Race, and the Making of British Columbia, 1849–1871* (Toronto: University of Toronto Press, 2001), 21, 30.

67 See Morissonneau, *La terre promise*, 26, 93–97, 124.

68 Nantel, *La colonisation du Nord-Ouest*, 11.

69 For the view that the novel "was not untypical of what French Canadians were thinking in his time. Indeed the whole program was consistent with the mainstream of French-Quebec thought," see A.I. Silver, "Introduction," in Jules-Paul Tardivel, *For My Country – "Pour la Patrie": An 1895 Religious and Separatist Vision of Quebec in the Mid-Twentieth-Century*, originally published as *Pour la patrie: Roman du XXe siècle* (Montreal: Cadieux et Derome, 1895), trans. Sheila Fischman (Toronto: University of Toronto Press, 1975),

xxxvi. On Tardivel's influence, see Mathieu Girard, "La pensée politique de Jules-Paul Tardivel," *Revue d'histoire de l'Amérique française* 21, 3 (1967): 397–98.

70 Tardivel, *For My Country,* 93–4.

71 Ibid., 190.

72 Joanne Meyerowitz, "'How Common Culture Shapes the Separate Lives': Sexuality, Race, and Mid-Twentieth-Century Social Constructionist Thought," *Journal of American History* 96, 4 (2010): 1057–84.

73 Otto Klineberg, *Race Differences* (New York: Harper and Brothers, 1935), 17–18. See also George W. Stocking Jr., "The Turn-of-the-Century Concept of Race," in *Delimiting Anthropology: Occasional Inquiries and Reflections,* 3–23 (Madison: University of Wisconsin Press, 2001).

74 François Hertel, *Leur inquiétude* (Montreal: Éditions Jeunesse, 1936), 93; Hertel, *Pour un ordre personnaliste,* 99–102.

75 Robert Charbonneau, Robert Élie, Paul Beaulieu, and Claude Hurtubise, "Préliminaire à un manifeste pour la patrie," *La Relève* 3, 1 (1936): 23.

76 Quoted in Ramsay Cook and Michael Behiels, eds., *The Essential Laurendeau* (Toronto: Copp Clark, 1976), 51. On Laurendeau's evolving attitude toward nationalism and race, see Donald J. Horton, *André Laurendeau: French Canadian Nationalist, 1912–1968* (Toronto: Oxford University Press, 1992), esp. ch. 3.

77 Michael Gauvreau, *The Catholic Origins of Quebec's Quiet Revolution, 1931–1970* (Montreal and Kingston: McGill-Queen's University Press, 2005), 195. On the church's changing attitude toward sex, see Isabelle Perrault, "Morale catholique et genre féminin: La sexualité dissertée dans les manuels de sexualité maritale au Québec, 1930–1960," *Revue d'histoire de l'Amérique française* 54, 4 (2004): 567–90; Gaston Desjardins, *L'Amour en patience: La sexualité adolescente au Québec, 1940–1960* (Sainte-Foy, QC: Presses de l'Université du Québec, 1995), 234; and Gérard Bouchard, "La sexualité comme pratique et rapport social chez les couples paysans du Saguenay (1860–1930)," *Revue d'histoire de l'Amérique française* 54, 2 (2000): 212.

78 Gauvreau, *Catholic Origins,* 195, 201.

79 Hector Palardy, *Hygiène sexuelle: L'homme et la génération, la femme et la génération, les maladies vénériennes* (Chicoutimi, QC: Syndicat des imprimeurs du Saguenay, 1922), 5, 17. On evolving attitudes about women's role in reproduction, see Thomas Laqueur, *Making Sex: Body and Gender from the Greeks to Freud* (Cambridge, MA: Harvard University Press, 1990), 99–103.

80 *Le Soleil,* February 24, 1931.

81 See Valverde, *Sex, Power and Pleasure,* 52; Eley, "Culture, Nation and Gender," 32–33; Saint-Martin, *Le nom de la mère,* 28; and Jane Lewis, "'Motherhood Issues' in the Late Nineteenth and Twentieth Centuries," in *Delivering Motherhood: Maternal Ideologies and Practices in the 19th and 20th Centuries,* ed. Katherine Arnup, Andrée Lévesque, and Ruth Roach Pierson (New York: Routledge, 1990), 15.

82 Lionel Groulx, *La naissance d'une race,* 2nd ed. (Montreal: Librairie d'Action Canadienne-française, 1930), 10, quoted in Rudin, *Making History,* 56. On Groulx's views on race, see Frédéric Boily, *La pensée nationaliste de Lionel Groulx* (Sillery, QC: Septentrion, 2003), 32.

83 Groulx published the novel under the pseudonym Alonié de Lestres, although it was widely known at the time that he was the author. See Pierre Hébert, with Marie-Pier Luneau, *Lionel Groulx et* L'Appel de la race (Montreal: Fides, 1996), 96–97. The novel was especially well received by nationalist critics who understood its political importance, including one who described the publication of the novel as "the literary event of the year." See "*L'Appel de la race:* Un nouveau roman appelé à un grand retentissement,"

L'Action catholique, October 7, 1922. For discussions of the critical reception of the novel at the time, see Hébert, with Luneau, *Lionel Groulx*, 8–9, 94, 148–53; and Pierre-Yves Mocquais, "L'Appel de la race: Masques narratifs et contre-masques idéologiques," *Voix et Images* 6, 2 (1981): 245. The reissue of the novel *L'Appel de la race* in 1986 under the new title *The Iron Wedge* sidestepped the issue of race entirely. The editor of the new edition explained that "literal renditions of 'l'appel de la race' are awkward at best, and given some of the modern connotations that the word 'race' has assumed, it was felt wise to stay clear of its use." See Michel Gaulin, "Introduction," in Lionel Groulx, *The Iron Wedge*, trans. J.S. Wood (Ottawa: Carleton University Press, 1986), xxxii, originally published as *L'Appel de la race* (Montreal: Bibliothèque de L'action française, 1922).

84 Pleau, "Polémique sur un 'mauvais livre,'" 145.

85 Groulx, *Iron Wedge*, 17.

86 Ibid., 40–1.

87 Ibid., 83.

88 Ibid., 38.

89 Ibid., 31, 33.

90 Ibid., 17–19.

91 Ibid., 175.

92 Ibid., 173.

93 Ibid., 84.

Chapter 4: War and Manhood

1 Quoted in Donald Creighton, *John A. Macdonald: The Old Chieftain* (Toronto: Macmillan, 1955), 411.

2 On English Canadian imperialism, see Carl Berger, *The Sense of Power: Studies in the Ideas of Canadian Imperialism* (Toronto: University of Toronto Press, 1970).

3 John Beynon, *Masculinities and Culture* (Philadelphia: Open University Press, 2002), 28; Joy Parr, *The Gender of Breadwinners: Women, Men, and Change in Two Industrial Towns, 1880–1950* (Toronto: University of Toronto Press, 1990), 163–64.

4 Gail Bederman, *Manliness and Civilization: A Cultural History of Gender and Race in the United States, 1880–1917* (Chicago: University of Chicago Press, 1995), 99.

5 For a discussion of the ways that nineteenth-century English-speaking Montrealers embraced the outdoors and sports and appropriated Aboriginal and French Canadian cultures in the process of fashioning a new Canadian male identity, see Gillian Poulter, *Becoming Native in a Foreign Land: Sport, Visual Culture, and Identity in Montreal, 1840–85* (Vancouver: UBC Press, 2009).

6 Quoted in David Macleod, "A Live Vaccine: The YMCA and Male Adolescence in the United States and Canada, 1870–1920," *Histoire sociale/Social History* 11, 21 (1978): 15.

7 Ernest Thompson Seton, *Wild Animals I have Known* (London: D. Nutt, 1898); Ernest Thompson Seton, *Two Little Savages* (1903; reprint, New York: Grosset and Dunlap, 1911). See also Donald Wright, "W.D. Lighthall and David Ross McCord: Antimodernism and English-Canadian Imperialism, 1880s–1918," *Journal of Canadian Studies* 32, 2 (1997): 137, 145; Daniel Francis, *The Imaginary Indian: The Image of the Indian in Canadian Culture* (Vancouver: Arsenal Pulp, 1992); and Daniel Francis, *National Dreams: Myth, Memory and Canadian History* (Vancouver: Arsenal Pulp, 1997), 88–110.

8 Carman Miller, "The Montreal Militia as a Social Institution before World War I," *Urban History Review* 19, 1 (1990): 60. For a look at manhood and the militia earlier in the nineteenth century, see Brian Young, "The Volunteer Militia in Lower Canada, 1837–50," in *Power, Place and Identity: Historical Studies of Social and Legal Regulation in Quebec*, ed. Tamara Myers, Kate Boyer, Mary Anne Poutanen, and Steven Watt, 37–53 (Montreal:

Montreal History Group, 1998). See also, Stephen Heathorn, *For Home, Country, and Race: Constructing Gender, Class, and Englishness in the Elementary School, 1880–1914* (Toronto: University of Toronto Press, 2000); and Robert H. MacDonald, *Sons of Empire: The Frontier and the Boy Scout Movement, 1890–1918* (Toronto: University of Toronto Press, 1993), 3.

9 Berger, *Sense of Power*, 257–58.

10 On the close association between militarism, imperialism, and manhood, see Mark Moss, *Manliness and Militarism: Educating Young Boys in Ontario for War* (Toronto: Oxford University Press, 2001), 20; Paul Maroney, "'The Great Adventure': The Context and Ideology of Recruiting in Ontario, 1914–17," *Canadian Historical Review* 77, 1 (1996): 92; Mike O'Brien, "Manhood and the Militia Myth: Masculinity, Class, and Militarism in Ontario, 1902–1914," *Labour/Le Travail* 42 (1998): 115–41; and MacDonald, *Sons of Empire*. For the British context, see Graham Dawson, *Soldier Heroes: British Adventure, Empire and the Imagining of Masculinities* (London: Routledge, 1994); Michael C.C. Adams, *The Great Adventure: Male Desire and the Coming of World War I* (Bloomington: Indiana University Press, 1990); and J.A. Mangan and James Walvin, eds., *Manliness and Morality: Middle-Class Masculinity in Britain and America, 1800–1940* (Manchester, UK: Manchester University Press, 1987).

11 Moss, *Manliness and Militarism*, 56, 143.

12 On the French Canadian Zouaves, see René Hardy, *Les Zouaves: Une stratégie du clergé québécois au XIXe siècle* (Montreal: Boréal Express, 1980); and Lionel Groulx, "Nos Zouaves," in *Notre maître, le passé*, 1st series, 3rd ed. (Montreal: Librairie Granger Frères, 1937), 240–41.

13 Joseph-Charles Taché, *Forestiers et voyageurs* (1863; reprint, Montreal: Fides, 1946); Philippe Aubert de Gaspé, *Le chercheur de trésor, ou l'influence d'un livre: Roman historique* (1837; reprint, Quebec: Imprimerie de L. Brousseau, 1878); Patrice Lacombe, *La terre paternelle* (1846; reprint, Montreal: Librairie Beauchemin, 1912).

14 Adélard Dugré, "Le scoutisme," *L'Action française* 15, 1 (1926): 46.

15 Oscar Douglas Skelton, *Life and Letters of Sir Wilfrid Laurier* (Toronto: Oxford University Press, 1921), vol. 2, 64–65.

16 On Canadian reaction to the South African War, see Carman Miller, *Painting the Map Red: Canada and the South African War, 1899–1902* (Montreal and Kingston: McGill-Queen's University Press, 1993); Carman Miller, *Canada's Little War: Fighting for the British Empire in Southern Africa, 1899–1902* (Toronto: J. Lorimer, 2003); and Brian A. Reid, *Our Little Army in the Field: The Canadians in South Africa, 1899–1902* (St. Catharines, ON: Vanwell, 1996). For French Canadian reactions to the war, see John MacFarlane, "La longue marche de l'Afrique du Sud: En mémoire des Canadiens-français qui ont participé à la première intervention militaire du Canada au XXe siècle," *Mens: Revue d'histoire intellectuelle de l'Amérique française* 7, 2 (2007): 197–240; Mason Wade, *The French Canadians, 1760–1967* (Toronto: Macmillan, 1968), vol. 1, 447–535; James I.W. Corcoran, "Henri Bourassa et la guerre sud-africaine," *Revue d'histoire de l'Amérique française* 18, 3 (1964): 343–56; 19, 1 (1965): 84–105; 19, 2 (1965): 229–37; 19, 3 (1965): 414–42; and Jean-Guy Pelletier, "La presse canadienne-française et la guerre des Boers," *Recherches sociographiques* 4, 3 (1963): 337–49. There were exceptions to this linguistic divide. On the French side, the Liberal Party's organ in Quebec City, *Le Soleil*, for example, supported the war. The *Huntingdon Gleaner*, an English-language newspaper in Quebec's Eastern Townships, meanwhile, opposed it. See Robert Hill, *Voice of the Vanishing Minority: Robert Sellar and the Huntingdon Gleaner, 1863–1919* (Montreal and Kingston: McGill-Queen's University Press, 1998); and Carman Miller, "English Canadian Opposition to the South African War as Seen through the Press," *Canadian Historical Review* 55, 4 (1974): 422–38.

17 *Montreal Gazette,* October 6, 1899.
18 *Montreal Gazette,* October 10, 1899.
19 For the claim that "no Canadian government could have kept the English-speaking people of Canada out of the Boer War," see A.R.M. Lower, *Canada: Nation and Neighbour* (Toronto: Ryerson Press, 1952), 22.
20 See Joseph Schull, *Laurier: The First Canadian* (Toronto: Macmillan, 1965), 385.
21 Canada, *Debates of the House of Commons,* Ottawa, March 13, 1900, 1837.
22 See Miller, *Painting the Map Red,* 18.
23 Canada, *Debates of the House of Commons,* Ottawa, March 13, 1900, 1848.
24 Quoted in Casey Murrow, *Henri Bourassa and French Canadian Nationalism: Opposition to Empire* (Montreal: Harvest House, 1968), 29.
25 Henri Bourassa, *Great Britain and Canada: Topics of the Day: A Lecture Delivered at the "Théâtre National Français," Montreal, on the 20th of October 1901* (Montreal: Beauchemin, 1901), 31.
26 Henri Bourassa, *The French Canadian in the British Empire* (London: J. Murray, 1902), 34.
27 Canada, *Debates of the House of Commons,* Ottawa, March 5, 1901, 1292.
28 Henri Bourassa, *Guerre Sud-Africaine: Discours de M. Henri Bourassa, M.P., Ottawa, mardi, 13 mars, 1900* (Ottawa: n.p., 1900), 13.
29 *Les Débats,* December 29, 1899.
30 *Les Débats,* March 11, 1900.
31 *Les Débats,* March 4, 1900.
32 *La Vérité,* October 14, 1899.
33 *Le monde canadien,* January 25, 1900.
34 *Les Débats,* February 4, 1900.
35 *Les Débats,* December 10, 1899.
36 *La Vérité,* December 2, 1899.
37 *La Vérité,* October 14, 1899.
38 *Les Débats,* December 10, 1899.
39 *Le monde canadien,* January 25, 1900.
40 Canada, *Debates of the House of Commons,* Ottawa, March 1, 1900, 1155–56.
41 Bourassa, *Great Britain and Canada,* 4.
42 *Les Débats,* December 24, 1899.
43 *Les Débats,* January 7, 1900.
44 *La Vérité,* November 10, 1900.
45 *Les Débats,* February 25, 1900.
46 *Les Débats,* December 24, 1899.
47 *Les Débats,* February 18, 1900.
48 *Les Débats,* February 11, 1900.
49 *Les Débats,* December 10, 1899.
50 See Miller, *Painting the Map Red,* 443–44.
51 Canada, *Debates of the House of Commons,* Ottawa, March 5, 1900, 1288.
52 Ibid., 1295.
53 Ibid., 1308.
54 *Le monde canadien,* March 8, 1900.
55 Schull, *Laurier,* 383–84.
56 Robert Baden-Powell, *Scouting for Boys: A Handbook for Instruction in Good Citizenship,* rev. ed. (London: n.p., 1910). See also Moss, *Manliness and Militarism,* 115–17.
57 Pierre Savard, "L'Implantation du scoutisme au Canada français," *Les cahiers des dix* 43 (1983), 210–15.

58 Henri Bourassa, *The Duty of Canada at the Present Hour* (Montreal: Le Devoir, 1915), 7.
59 L.G. Desjardins, *Un appel a la jeunesse Canadienne-française* (Quebec: Association civile de recrutement du district de Québec, 1917), 29.
60 Claudius Corneloup, *L'Épopée du vingt-deuxième* (Montreal: La Presse, 1919).
61 Arthur J. Lapointe, *Soldier of Quebec (1916–1919)*, trans. R.C. Fetherstonhaugh (Montreal: Garand, 1931).
62 Desmond Morton, "A Canadian Soldier in the Great War: The Experience of Frank Maheux," *Canadian Military History* 1, 1–2 (1992): 79–80.
63 Quoted in Wade, *French Canadians*, vol. 2, 687.
64 Henri Bourassa, *Canadian Nationalism and the War* (Montreal: n.p., 1916), 27–30.
65 See Moss, *Manliness and Militarism*, 42; and Reid, *Our Little Army*, 6.
66 Gustavus G. Stuart, letter dated July 24, 1917, reprinted in Ferdinand Roy, *L'Appel aux armes et la réponse canadienne-française: Étude sur le conflit de races* (Quebec: J.P. Garneau, 1917).
67 An important analysis of the body and war can be found in Joanna Bourke, *Dismembering the Male: Male Bodies, Britain and the Great War* (Chicago: University of Chicago Press, 1996). On shifting Canadian attitudes about men's bodies during the war, see *Rejected Warriors: Rejected Volunteers of the Canadian Expeditionary Force* (Vancouver: UBC Press, 2015).
68 On the myth of the fallen soldier, see George L. Mosse, *Fallen Soldiers: Reshaping the Memory of the World Wars* (New York: Oxford University Press, 1990), 6–7, 36–37.
69 Sandra Gwyn, *Tapestry of War: A Private View of Canadians in the Great War* (Toronto: Harper Collins, 1992), 98.
70 Ibid., 327.
71 Quoted in ibid., 319.
72 Quoted in ibid., 321.
73 Quoted in ibid., 321–22.
74 Talbot Papineau, *The War and Its Influence upon Canada* (Montreal: n.p., 1920), 6, 8.
75 Ibid., 11.
76 Gwyn, *Tapestry of War*, 338.
77 Ibid., 386.
78 Bourke, *Dismembering the Male*, 37.
79 Henri Bourassa, *"Win the War" and Lose Canada* (Montreal: Le Devoir, 1917), 3.
80 Henri Bourassa, *La conscription* (Montreal: Le Devoir, 1917), 17.
81 See Jean Provencher, *Québec sous la loi des mesures de guerre, 1918* (Trois Rivières, QC: Boréal Express, 1971), 25.
82 Joseph Charlebois, *La conscription: Tristes dessins et légendes* (Montreal: Le Devoir, 1917), 6.
83 For a critique of this interpretation, see L.G. Desjardins, *England, Canada and the Great War* (Quebec: Chronicle Print, 1918).
84 Henri Bourassa, *Independence or Imperial Partnership* (Montreal: Le Devoir, 1916), 19.
85 Henri Bourassa, *Le Devoir et la guerre* (Montreal: Le Devoir, 1916), 35.
86 Bourassa, *Independence or Imperial Partnership*, 52.
87 Ibid., 61.
88 Quoted in Wade, *French Canadians*, vol. 2, 687.
89 Bourassa, *Duty of Canada*, 34.
90 Bourassa, *"Win the War,"* 6.
91 Bourassa, *La conscription*, 7, 8.
92 Bourassa, *"Win the War,"* 13.

93 Hélène Pelletier-Baillargeon, *Olivar Asselin et son temps: Le militant* (Montreal: Fides, 1996), 682–703; Hélène Pelletier-Baillargeon, *Olivar Asselin et son temps: Le volontaire* (Montreal: Fides, 2001), 13–15.

94 Olivar Asselin, *Les volontaires Canadiens-français* (Paris: Comité France-Amérique, 1917); Olivar Asselin, *Pourquoi je m'enrole* (Quebec: Association civile de recrutement du district de Québec, 1916), 22–23, 30.

95 Bourassa, *La conscription,* 10.

96 Bourassa, *Independence or Imperial Partnership,* 60.

97 Bourassa, "*Win the War,*" 14.

98 See, for example, J.A.H., *Les poilus canadiens: Le roman du Vingt-deuxième Bataillon Canadien-français* (Montreal: J. Hope, 1918); *Le capitaine Jean Brillant, C.V., C.M. par ses amis* (Rimouski: Imprimerie générale S. Vachon, 1920); Canada, Army, 22e Bataillon Canadien-français, *Programme souvenir publié à l'occasion du retour d'outre-mer du 22ème Bataillon (Canadien-français)* (Quebec: Imprimerie commerciale, 1919).

99 Arthur Hawkes, *Canadian Nationalism and the War* (Montreal, 1916), 8, 12. Berger, *Sense of Power,* 9, points out that "imperialists were constantly reminded that there must always come a time when children grow up and leave the parental home, or, more pointedly, when every boy must learn to stop sleeping with his mother."

100 Arthur Hawkes, *The Birthright: A Search for the Canadian Canadian and the Larger Loyalty* (Toronto: J.M. Dent and Sons, 1919), 179–80.

101 Ibid., 184–85.

102 Quoted in *Montreal Gazette,* June 2, 1924.

103 James Eayrs, *In Defence of Canada,* vol. 1, *From the Great War to the Great Depression* (Toronto: University of Toronto Press, 1964), 168.

104 Quoted in R. MacGregor Dawson, *William Lyon Mackenzie King: A Political Biography, 1874–1923* (Toronto: University of Toronto Press, 1958), 413.

105 O.D. Skelton, "Canada and Foreign Policy," in *The Canadian Club Year Book, 1921–1922,* ed. Arthur S. Bourinot (Ottawa: Dadson-Merrill, 1922), 60. For the ways that Skelton's views on Canada's place in the world reflected his ideas about manhood, see Terry Crowley, *Marriage of Minds: Isabel and Oscar Skelton Reinventing Canada* (Toronto: University of Toronto Press, 2003), 7. For a recent biography of Skelton, see Norman Hillmer, *O.D. Skelton: A Portrait of Canadian Ambition* (Toronto: University of Toronto Press, 2015).

106 Quoted in J.L. Granatstein, *The Ottawa Men: The Civil Service Mandarins, 1935–1957* (Toronto: Oxford University Press, 1982), 34.

107 See Barry Ferguson, *Remaking Liberalism: The Intellectual Legacy of Adam Shortt, O.D. Skelton, W.C. Clark, and W.A. Mackintosh, 1890–1925* (Montreal and Kingston: McGill-Queen's University Press, 1993), 86.

108 See John MacFarlane, *Ernest Lapointe and Quebec's Influence on Canadian Foreign Policy* (Toronto: University of Toronto Press, 1999), 47–51; Murrow, *Henri Bourassa,* 109.

109 Quoted in Granatstein, *Ottawa Men,* 36–37.

110 MacFarlane, *Ernest Lapointe,* 3, 6.

111 Quoted in Murrow, *Henri Bourassa,* 109.

112 William Lyon Mackenzie King, *Diary,* September 17, 1926, http://www.bac-lac.gc.ca/eng/discover/politics-government/prime-ministers/william-lyon-mackenzie-king/pages/item.aspx?IdNumber=10090&.

113 Ibid., March 7, 1936, http://www.bac-lac.gc.ca/eng/discover/politics-government/prime-ministers/william-lyon-mackenzie-king/pages/item.aspx?IdNumber=16882&.

114 Ferguson, *Remaking Liberalism,* 88. See also Crowley, *Marriage of Minds,* 8.

115 Desmond Morton, *Fight or Pay: Soldiers' Families in the Great War* (Vancouver: UBC Press, 2004), 240; Desmond Morton, *Understanding Canadian Defence* (Toronto: Penguin, 2003), 111; Jeffrey A. Keshen, *Saints, Sinners, and Soldiers: Canada's Second World War* (Vancouver: UBC Press, 2004), 12.
116 Quoted in J.W. Pickersgill, *The Mackenzie King Record,* vol. 1, *1939–1944* (Toronto: University of Toronto Press, 1960), 20.
117 Lionel Groulx, *Directives* (Montreal: Les Éditions du Zodiaque, 1937), 166.
118 Lionel Groulx, "L'éducation nationale et les écoles normales," *L'Action nationale* 4, 1 (1934): 24.
119 See Michael Behiels, *Prelude to Quebec's Quiet Revolution: Liberalism versus Neo-nationalism, 1945–1960* (Montreal and Kingston: McGill-Queen's University Press, 1985), 5, 20.
120 André Laurendeau, "Manifeste des Jeunes," *L'Action nationale* 1, 2 (1933): 117–20, quoted in Ramsay Cook and Michael Behiels, eds., *The Essential Laurendeau* (Toronto: Copp Clark, 1976), 34, 36.
121 André Laurendeau, *Notre nationalisme,* Les tracts des Jeune-Canada, 5 (Montreal: Le Devoir, 1935), 45–46, 49. It should be noted that Laurendeau moderated his views in later years. As he became more liberal in his thinking, he would distance himself from his youthful flirtation with anti-Semitism and separatism. See Donald J. Horton, *André Laurendeau: French Canadian Nationalist, 1912–1968* (Toronto: Oxford University Press, 1992), 46.
122 See Behiels, *Prelude to Quebec's Quiet Revolution,* 25.
123 Pierre Dansereau, "Jeune-Canada," *L'Action nationale* 1, 5 (1933), 271–72, quoted in Michael Oliver, *The Passionate Debate: The Social and Political Ideas of Quebec Nationalism, 1920–1945* (Montreal: Véhicule, 1991), 107–8.
124 Thuribe Belzile, *Nos déficiences, conséquences, remèdes* (Montreal: Le Devoir, 1935), 6–13.
125 Laurendeau, "Manifeste des Jeunes," 120, quoted in Cook and Behiels, eds., *Essential Laurendeau,* 36.
126 Arthur Laurendeau, "A la recherche d'une mystique nationale," *L'Action nationale* 8, 4 (1936), 227, quoted in Oliver, *Passionate Debate,* 92.
127 See Paul-André Linteau, René-Durocher, Jean-Claude Robert, and François Ricard, *Quebec since 1930,* trans. Robert Chodos (Toronto: James Lorimer and Company, 1991), 81; Oliver, *Passionate Debate,* 107; and Jean-Philippe Warren, "Le corporatisme canadien-français comme 'système total': Quatre concepts pour comprendre la popularité d'une doctrine," *Recherches sociographiques* 45, 2 (2004): 219–38. See also the special issue on corporatism of *L'Action nationale* 12, 3 (1938).
128 Susan Mann Trofimenkoff, *The Dream of Nation: A Social and Intellectual History of Quebec* (Toronto: Macmillan, 1982), 241.
129 Oliver, *Passionate Debate,* 99.
130 André Laurendeau, *Qui sauvera Québec?* (Montreal: Imprimerie populaire, 1935), 52.
131 For a discussion of how *La Nation* was the product of French Canadian intellectual values of the 1930s, see Julien Fabre, "*La Nation:* Les groulxiens devant la tentation fasciste, 1936–1939," *Bulletin d'histoire politique* 9, 2 (2001): 40. On Groulx's influence, see Robert Comeau, "Lionel Groulx, les indépendantistes de *La Nation* et le séparatisme (1936–1938)," *Revue d'histoire de l'Amérique française* 26, 1 (1972): 84. On fascism in Quebec, see Esther Delisle, *Myths, Memory and Lies: Québec's Intelligentsia and the Fascist Temptation, 1939–1960,* trans. Madeleine Hébert (Montreal: Robert Davies, 1998); Esther Delisle, *Essais sur l'imprégnation fasciste au Québec* (Montreal: Varia, 2002).
132 *La Nation,* March 7, 1936.
133 *La Nation,* February 15, 1936.

134 Ibid.
135 See Oliver, *Passionate Debate*, 138–42; and Delisle, *Myth, Memory and Lies*. On the fascist idea of manhood, see George L. Mosse, *The Image of Man: The Creation of Modern Masculinity* (New York: Oxford University Press, 1996), esp. 155–80.
136 Oliver, *Passionate Debate*, 142.
137 *La Nation*, January 7, 1937.
138 Laurendeau, *Qui sauvera Québec?* 64–65.
139 Savard, "L'Implantation du scoutisme," 253–54.
140 Interestingly, *La Nation* remained suspicious of the Boy Scouts and continued to view it as an Anglo-Saxon institution. See *La Nation*, July 23, 1936, and July 30, 1936.
141 Paul Grondin, "Notre scoutisme," *L'Action nationale* 3, 4 (1934): 234.
142 Dugré, "Le Scoutisme," 34.
143 *Le Devoir*, March 6, 1926.
144 Lionel Groulx, *Mes Mémoires* (Montreal: Fides, 1971), vol. 2, 320.
145 Savard, "L'Implantation du scoutisme"; Pierre Savard, "Affrontement de nationalismes aux origines du scoutisme canadien français," *Proceedings and Transactions of the Royal Society of Canada*, series 4, 17 (1979): 41–56.
146 Maurice Séguin, "Art de penser," box 2455, Fonds Maurice Séguin, P221, Archives de l'Université de Montréal. See also Jean Lamarre, *Le devenir de la nation québécoise selon Maurice Séguin, Guy Frégault et Michel Brunet, 1944–1969* (Sillery, QC: Septentrion, 1993), 92–94, 102–3.
147 Maurice Séguin, "Théorie, Doctrine," box 2455, Fonds Maurice Séguin.
148 Maurice Séguin, "Pédagogie," box 2455, Fonds Maurice Séguin.
149 Maurice Séguin, notes, box 2453, Fonds Maurice Séguin.
150 J.L. Granatstein, *Canada's Army: Waging War and Keeping the Peace* (Toronto: University of Toronto Press, 2002), 193.
151 C.P. Stacey, *Six Years of War: The Army in Canada, Britain and the Pacific* (Ottawa: Queen's Printer, 1956), 55–56; Trofimenkoff, *Dream of Nation*, 250.
152 André Laurendeau, *La crise de la conscription 1942* (Montreal: Les Éditions du Jour, 1962), 115.
153 Lita-Rose Betcherman, *Ernest Lapointe: Mackenzie King's Great Quebec Lieutenant* (Toronto: University of Toronto Press, 2002), 325.
154 The fact that French Canadian support for Pétain's "national revolution" did not translate into support for Nazi collaboration is rightly pointed out by Éric Amyot, *Le Québec entre Pétain et DeGaulle: Vichy, la France Libre et les Canadiens français, 1940–1945* (Montreal: Fides, 1999), 38–39, 68, 75. See also Mary Louise Roberts, *Civilization without Sexes: Reconstructing Gender in Postwar France, 1917–1927* (Chicago: University of Chicago Press, 1994), 217. On Nazism in Quebec, see Jean-François Nadeau, *The Canadian Führer: The Life of Adrien Arcand*, trans. Bob Chodos, Eric Hamovitch, and Susan Joanis (Toronto: Lorimer, 2011).
155 Behiels, *Prelude to Quebec's Quiet Revolution*, 28; Trofimenkoff, *Dream of Nation*, 265.

Chapter 5: The Revitalization of National History

1 English Canadian writers were not alone in promoting this view. Many French Canadian writers also celebrated the rural aspect of Quebec society in the *romans du terroir*. See, for example, Patrice Lacombe, *La terre paternelle* (1846; reprint, Montreal: Librairie Beauchemin, 1912); and Ringuet [Philippe Panneton], *Trente arpents* (1938; reprint, Toronto: McClelland and Stewart, 2009). The most well-known of such works was Louis Hémon, *Maria Chapdelaine* (1913; reprint, Montreal: Boréal, 1988).

2 Donald A. Wright, "W.D. Lighthall and David Ross McCord: Antimodernism and English-Canadian Imperialism, 1880s–1918," *Journal of Canadian Studies* 32, 2 (1997): 137–38. On English Canadian efforts to appropriate French Canadian culture, see Gillian Poulter, *Becoming Native in a Foreign Land: Sport, Visual Culture, and Identity in Montreal, 1840–85* (Vancouver: UBC Press, 2009).

3 William Parker Greenough, *Canadian Folk-Life and Folk-Lore* (1897; reprint, Toronto: Coles, 1971), 14.

4 Byron Nicholson, *The French Canadian: A Sketch of His More Prominent Characteristics* (Toronto: Bryant, 1902), 35. See also J. Castell Hopkins, *French Canada and the St. Lawrence: Historic, Picturesque and Descriptive* (Toronto: Bell and Cockburn, 1913), 255.

5 William Henry Drummond, *The Habitant: And Other French Canadian Poems* (New York: G.P. Putnam's Sons, 1897), 1–2, 7.

6 Ibid., v.

7 This belief in many parts of the country that French Canada remained untouched by the effects of modernity persisted well into the 1950s and 1960s. See, for example, Daniel Francis, *National Dreams: Myth, Memory, and Canadian History* (Vancouver: Arsenal Pulp, 1997), 88–110; and Grace Pollock, "William Henry Drummond's True 'Canayen': Dialect Poetry and the Politics of Canadian Imperialism," *Essays on Canadian Writing* 79 (2003): 103–31.

8 Wright, "W.D. Lighthall," 135, 137–39; Carl Berger, *The Sense of Power: Studies in the Ideas of Canadian Imperialism, 1867–1914* (Toronto: University of Toronto Press, 1970), 140.

9 Drummond, *The Habitant: And Other French Canadian Poems*, xi.

10 Horace Miner, *St. Denis: A French Canadian Parish* (Chicago: University of Chicago Press, 1939), vii.

11 Everett Hughes, *French Canada in Transition* (Chicago: University of Chicago Press, 1943), 1.

12 On the ways that sociologists interpreted Quebec society, see Marcel Fournier, "Quebec Sociology and Quebec Society: The Construction of a Collective Identity," *Canadian Journal of Sociology* 26, 3 (2001): 336–37. On sociological approaches to Quebec society during these years, see Marlene Shore, *The Science of Social Redemption: McGill, the Chicago School, and the Origins of Social Research in Canada* (Toronto: University of Toronto Press, 1987); and Jean-Philippe Warren, *L'Engagement sociologique: La tradition sociologique du Québec francophone (1866–1955)* (Montreal: Boréal, 2003).

13 Marius Barbeau, *The Kingdom of the Saguenay* (Toronto: Macmillan, 1936), 95, 97–98; James Murton, "La 'Normandie du Nouveau Monde': La société Canada Steamship Lines, l'antimodernisme et la promotion du Québec ancien," *Revue d'histoire de l'Amérique française* 55, 1 (2001): 3–44.

14 On the marketing of French Canadian folk culture, see Nathalie Hamel, "Coordonner l'artisanat et le tourisme, ou comment mettre en valeur le visage pittoresque du Québec (1915–1960)," *Histoire sociale/Social History* 34, 67 (2001): 97–114; Martine Geronimi, "Québec dans les discours des guides touristiques, 1830–1930," *Canadian Folklore Canadien* 18, 2 (1996): 69–89; and Nicole Neatby, "Meeting of Minds: North American Travel Writers and Government Tourist Publicity in Quebec, 1920–1955," *Histoire sociale/Social History* 36, 72 (2003): 465–95. For the larger Canadian context, see Patricia Jasen, *Wild Things: Nature, Culture, and Tourism in Ontario, 1790–1914* (Toronto: University of Toronto Press, 1995), 56, 68; and Ian McKay, *The Quest of the Folk: Antimodernism and Cultural Selection in Twentieth-Century Nova Scotia* (Montreal and Kingston: McGill-Queen's University Press, 1994). Some prominent English Canadian imperialists, such as W.D. Lighthall and David Ross McCord, transformed French Canada into an idealized "antimodern space" to provide themselves with a much needed "psychological retreat"

from the modern world. This "othering" of French Canadian society contributed to the construction of French Canadians as "premodern" and as somehow unsuited to the challenges of modernity. See Wright, "W.D. Lighthall," 135–37.

15 Quebec, Provincial Tourist Bureau, Department of Roads, *Quebec: The French Canadian Province: A Harmony of Beauty, History and Progress* (Quebec: Provincial Tourist Bureau, 1927), 6, 29.

16 Quebec, Provincial Tourist Bureau, Department of Roads, *Quebec: The Holiday Seekers Playland* (Quebec: Provincial Tourist Bureau, 1933). See also Byron Nicholson, *In Old Quebec and Other Sketches* (Quebec: Commercial Printing Company, 1908), 10.

17 Quebec, Provincial Tourist Bureau, Department of Roads, *Quebec: The Good Roads Province* (Quebec: Provincial Tourist Bureau, 1931). Other such pamphlets include Quebec, Provincial Tourist Bureau, Department of Roads, *Four, Five and Six Days in Quebec, Canada* (Quebec: Provincial Tourist Bureau, 1928); and Quebec, Provincial Tourist Bureau, Department of Roads, *Tours in Quebec, Canada* (Quebec: Provincial Tourist Bureau, 1933).

18 See Maurice Lemire, "L'Ambiguïté garnélienne," in *François-Xavier Garneau, une figure nationale,* ed. Gilles Gallichan, Kenneth Landry, and Denis Saint-Jacques (Quebec: Éditions Nota Bene, 1998), 263.

19 François-Xavier Garneau, *Histoire du Canada depuis sa découverte jusqu'à nos jours,* 4th ed. (Montreal: Beauchemin and Valois, 1882), vol. 3, 394–97.

20 For good overviews of the various editions of Garneau's work, see Pierre Savard and Paul Wyczynski, "François-Xavier Garneau," *Dictionary of Canadian Biography* (Toronto: University of Toronto Press, 1976), vol. 9, 297–306; Pierre Savard, "Les rééditions de l'*Histoire du Canada* de François-Xavier Garneau devant la critique, 1913–1946," *Revue d'histoire de l'Amérique française* 28, 4 (1975): 539–53.

21 See Jean B.A. Ferland, *Cours d'histoire du Canada,* vol. 2, *1663–1759* (1861–65; reprint, New York: Johnson Reprint Corporation, 1969), 600, 610–11.

22 See Benjamin Sulte, *L'Histoire des Canadiens français, 1608–1880: Histoire, religion, guerres, découvertes, colonisation, coutumes, vie domestique, sociale et politique, développement, avenir* (Montreal: Wilson, 1882), vol. 6, 104, vol. 7, 110.

23 See Thomas Chapais, *Cours d'histoire du Canada,* vol. 1, *1760–1791* (Quebec: J.P. Garneau, 1919), 7, 21–25.

24 George William Ross, *The Historical Significance of the Plains of Abraham: Address to Canadian Club of Hamilton, April 27, 1908* (Hamilton: n.p., 1908), 1, 3, 5. See also Nicholson, *French Canadian,* 91.

25 For more on the "fusion" of the races and the reconciliation of English and French pasts, see H.V. Nelles, *The Art of Nation Building: Pageantry and Spectacle at Quebec's Tercentenary* (Toronto: University of Toronto Press, 1999), 74, 78–79; H.V. Nelles, "Historical Pageantry and the 'Fusion of the Races' at the Tercentenary of Quebec, 1908," *Histoire sociale/Social History* 29, 58 (1996): 392–93; and Patrice Groulx, "La commémoration de la bataille de Sainte-Foy: *Du discours de la loyauté à la 'fusion des races,'*" *Revue d'histoire de l'Amérique française* 55, 1 (2001): 45–83. On the spectacle of commemoration, see Ronald Rudin, "Marching and Memory in Early Twentieth-Century Quebec: La Fête-Dieu, la Saint-Jean-Baptiste, and le Monument Laval," *Journal of the Canadian Historical Association* 10, 1 (1999): 209–35; Ronald Rudin, "Contested Terrain: Commemorative Celebration and National Identity in Ireland and Quebec," in *La nation dans tous ces états,* ed. Gérard Bouchard and Yvan Lamonde (Montreal and Paris: Harmattan, 1997), 195; and Ronald Rudin, *Founding Fathers: The Celebration of Champlain and Laval in the Streets of Quebec, 1878–1908* (Toronto: University of Toronto Press, 2003). On the ways that historians reassessed Jacques Cartier in the nineteenth century in a manner that upheld their assumptions about modernity, see Alan Gordon, "Heroes, History, and

Two Nationalisms: Jacques Cartier," *Journal of the Canadian Historical Association* 10, 1 (1999): 81–102; and Alan Gordon, *The Hero and the Historians: Historiography and the Uses of Jacques Cartier* (Vancouver: UBC Press, 2010).

26 See Nelles, *Art of Nation Building*, 78. According to Patrice Groulx, the idea of the dual victory builds upon ideas first put forth by François-Xavier Garneau, who argued that the second battle at the Plains of Abraham restored honour to the Canadiens and proved that they did not in fact lose but were abandoned by France. The myth of partnership gained strength in 1852 when human bones and military equipment from 1759–60 were excavated in Lévis, Quebec. It was unclear whether the bones belonged to English or French soldiers, so Étienne-Paschal Taché decided that they belonged to both sides and proposed a monument be erected to commemorate each side's sacrifices. See Groulx, "La commémoration," 53–54, 65–66, 70.

27 Luc Noppen and Gaston Deschênes, *Québec's Parliament Building: Witness to History*, trans. R. Clive Meredith and Audrey Pratt (Quebec: Les Publications du Québec, 1986), 141, 148.

28 Louis Lalande, *La fierté* (Montreal: Bibliothèque de l'Action française, 1918), 12, 18, 23.

29 Dostaler O'Leary, *"L'inferiority complex"* (Montreal: Imprimé au Devoir, 1935), 5–6.

30 Lionel Groulx, *Mes mémoires* (Montreal: Fides, 1971), vol. 2, 78.

31 Ibid., vol. 2, 79. See also Lionel Groulx, *Directives* (Montreal: Les Éditions du Zodiaque, 1937), 225–26.

32 Lionel Groulx, *La naissance d'une race* (Montreal: Bibliothèque de l'Action française, 1919), 155–57; Francis, *National Dreams*, 88–110.

33 Victor Barbeau, *Mesure de notre taille* (Montreal: Imprimé au Devoir, 1936), 16.

34 Édouard Le Doret, "Nos aïeux n'étaient pas des 'fifis,'" *Le Jour*, April 15, 1939, reprinted in Victor Teboul, *Le Jour: Émergence du libéralisme moderne au Québec* (Montreal: Hurtubise HMH, 1984), 391–93.

35 Geneviève Jain, "Nationalism and Educational Politics in Ontario and Québec, 1867–1914," in *Canadian Schools and Canadian Identity*, ed. Alf Chaiton and Neil McDonald (Toronto: Gage, 1977), 51.

36 Georges Courchesne, "L'Enseignement de l'histoire aux cours moyen et universitaire," in *Semaine d'histoire du Canada* (Montreal: Société historique de Montéal, 1926), 381.

37 Groulx, *Directives*, 226.

38 Quoted in Gérard Bouchard, *Les deux chanoines: Contradiction et ambivalence dans la pensée de Lionel Groulx* (Montreal: Boréal, 2003), 73.

39 "Pédagogie pratique," *L'Enseignement primaire* 38, 3 (1916): 131.

40 F.X. Toussaint, *Abrégé d'histoire du Canada a l'usage des jeunes étudiants de la province de Québec*, 1st ed. (Quebec: C. Darveau, 1874), 92. See also Jain, "Nationalism and Educational Politics," 39.

41 See F.X. Toussaint, *Abrégé d'histoire du Canada a l'usage des jeunes étudiants de la province de Québec*, 2nd ed. (Montreal: J. Langlais, 1900), preface; and Groulx, *Directives*, 35. Other manuals and groups stressed the same theme, including the journal *L'Enseignement primaire*, notably Th.-G. Rouleau, "Formons l'homme," *L'Enseignement primaire* 19, 7 (1897): 100; and Arthur Buies, "Le rôle des canadiens-français en Amérique," *L'Enseignement primaire* 19, 11 (1898): 377. See also Paul de Cazes, *Manuel de l'instituteur catholique de la province de Québec* (Montreal: Librairie Beauchemin, 1905), 102; and C.-J. Magnan, "L'Histoire du Canada à l'école primaire, 1825–1925," in *Semaine d'histoire du Canada* (Montreal: Société historique de Montréal, 1926), 2–3, 365, 367, 370, 373.

42 Quoted in Geneviève Laloux-Jain, *Les manuels d'histoire du Canada au Québec et en Ontario (de 1867 à 1914)* (Quebec: Presses de l'Université Laval, 1974), 151.

43 M. Brunetière, "Comment cultiver le sentiment national à l'école primaire," *L'Enseignement primaire* 23, 1 (1901): 28–29.
44 Groulx, *Directives*, 171–72.
45 Bouchard, *Les deux chanoines*, 74, 76, 200.
46 Groulx, *Mes mémoires*, vol. 1, 13–14.
47 Lionel Groulx, *Dix ans d'Action française* (Montreal: Bibliothèque de l'Action française, 1926), 259–61.
48 Lionel Groulx, *Notre maître, le passé*, 1st series, 3rd ed. (Montreal: Librairie Granger Frère, 1937), 20–21.
49 Of course, the same can be said about the writing of English Canadian history. See Carl Berger, *The Writing of Canadian History: Aspects of Canadian Historical Writing since 1900*, 2nd ed. (Toronto: University of Toronto Press, 1986), ix, 2; and M. Brook Taylor, *Promoters, Patriots, and Partisans: Historiography in Nineteenth-Century English Canada* (Toronto: University of Toronto Press, 1989). See also Lisa M. Gasbarrone, "Narrative, Memory, and Identity in François-Xavier Garneau's *Histoire du Canada*," *Québec Studies* 34 (2002–03): 31–34; and Frédéric Boily, *La pensée nationaliste de Lionel Groulx* (Sillery, QC: Septentrion, 2003), 160–65.
50 Thomas Chapais, "La nationalité canadienne française," in *Discours et Conférences* (Quebec: L.-J. Demers, 1897), 8.
51 Jack Warwick, *The Long Journey: Literary Themes in French Canada* (Toronto: University of Toronto Press, 1968), 31.
52 Guy Frégault, *Canada: The War of the Conquest*, trans. Margaret M. Cameron (Toronto: Oxford University Press, 1969), 344, originally published as *La Guerre de la Conquête* (Montreal: Fides, 1955); Jean Lamarre, *Le devenir de la nation québécoise selon Maurice Séguin, Guy Frégault et Michel Brunet, 1944–1969* (Sillery, QC: Septentrion, 1993), 267; Ramsay Cook, *The Maple Leaf Forever: Essays on Nationalism and Politics in Canada* (Toronto: Macmillan, 1971), 123.
53 Michel Brunet, "French Canadian Interpretations of Canadian History," *Canadian Forum* 44, 519 (1964): 5.
54 Jean-Rémi Brault, "Le *Manuel d'histoire du Canada* (1905–1906) de Lionel Groulx," *Les cahiers d'histoire du Québec au XXe siècle* 8 (1997): 14–15.
55 Lionel Groulx, *Manuel d'histoire du Canada: Rédigé pour la classe de rhétorique au Collège de Valleyfield en 1905–6*, vol. 2, 60, box S26–21, 614, Fonds Lionel Groulx, P1, Archives du Centre de Recherche Lionel-Groulx, Montreal. The Fonds Lionel Groulx has moved and is now housed at the Bibliothèque et Archives nationale du Quebec Vieux-Montréal (CLG1).
56 Lionel Groulx, *Nos luttes constitutionelles* (Montreal: Le Devoir, 1916), 21.
57 Lionel Groulx, *Lendemains de conquête: Cours d'histoire du Canada à l'Université de Montréal (1919–1920)* (Montreal: Bibliothèque de l'Action française, 1920), 182–83.
58 See Bouchard, *Les deux chanoines*, 58.
59 Lionel Groulx, *Orientations* (Montreal: Les Éditions du Zodiaque, 1935), 115.
60 Lionel Groulx, "La survivance canadienne-française et la terre," in *Le Problème de la terre: 12e Session des Semaine sociale du Canada* (Montreal: Secrétariat des Semaines Sociales du Canada, 1933), 327.
61 Lamarre, *Le devenir*, 191.
62 See Michel Brunet, "Trois dominantes de la pensée canadienne-française: L'agriculturisme, l'anti-étatisme et le messianisme," in *La présence anglaise et les Canadiens*, 113–66 (Montreal: Beauchemin, 1958); Cook, *Maple Leaf Forever*, 116; and Ronald Rudin, *Making History in Twentieth-Century Quebec* (Toronto: University of Toronto Press, 1997), 111.

63 François-Xavier Garneau, "Exposé présenté par Garneau à la société de discussion le 20 mai 1844," reprinted in *François-Xavier Garneau, une figure nationale*, ed. Gilles Gallichan, Kenneth Landry, and Denis Saint-Jacques, 259–62 (Quebec: Éditions Nota Bene, 1998). See also Daniel Vaillancourt, "Les têtes à Patriote: Une figure retorse au XIXe siècle," *Voix et images* 26, 3 (2001): 468.

64 Groulx, *La naissance d'une race*, 249.

65 See Lamarre, *Le devenir*, 78, 487–88.

66 For the observation that French Canadian historians incorporated the Laurentian thesis into their understanding of French Canada's past, see Brunet, "French Canadian Interpretations," 6. See also Lamarre, *Le devenir*, 141–42; Cook, *Maple Leaf Forever*, 109–11; and Berger, *Writing of Canadian History*, 185–86. Others have argued that Innis had little or no influence on Quebec historical writing. See, for example, Daniel Salée, "Innis and Quebec: The Paradigm That Would Not Be," in *Harold Innis in the New Century: Reflections and Refractions*, ed. Charles R. Acland and William J. Buxton (Montreal and Kingston: McGill-Queen's University Press, 1999), 198, 203; and Alain-G. Gagnon and Sarah Fortin, "Innis in Quebec: Conjectures and Conjunctures," in *Harold Innis in the New Century: Reflections and Refractions*, ed. Charles R. Acland and William J. Buxton (Montreal and Kingston: McGill-Queen's University Press, 1999), 210–12. These scholars tend to downplay Innis's influence in Quebec because their focus on the social sciences in general leads them to miss the profound influence that the Laurentian thesis in particular had on Quebec historical writing.

67 Groulx, *La naissance d'une race*, 157, 293.

68 Guy Frégault, *La civilisation de la Nouvelle-France, 1713–1744* (1944; reprint, Montreal: Fides, 1969), 213.

69 Lamarre, *Le devenir*, 79.

70 Arthur Maheux, *Ton histoire est une épopée*, vol. 1, *Nos débuts sous le régime anglais* (Quebec: Charrier and Dugal, 1941), 5, 8. See also Arthur Maheux, *Pourquois sommes-nous divisés?* (Montreal: Radio-Canada, 1943), 149. Groulx responded that conflict had always defined relations between the two races in his own pamphlet. See Lionel Groulx, *Pourquois nous sommes divisés* (Montreal: Éditions de l'Action nationale, 1943).

71 Groulx, *Dix ans d'Action française*, 63–64.

72 See Rudin, *Making History*, 26; and Lamarre, *Le devenir*, 66–67.

73 Alan Gordon, *Making Public Pasts: The Contested Terrain of Montreal's Public Memories, 1891–1930* (Montreal and Kingston: McGill-Queen's University Press, 2001), 55.

74 Ibid., 56–57. See also Fernande Roy, "Une mise en scène de l'histoire: La fondation de Montréal à travers les siècles," *Revue d'histoire de l'Amérique française* 46, 1 (1992): 7–36.

75 Robert Rumilly, *Histoire de la Société Saint-Jean-Baptiste de Montréal: Des Patriotes au fleurdelisé, 1834–1948* (Montreal: L'Aurore, 1975), 270.

76 Gordon, *Making Public Pasts*, 32, 118–20.

77 Jacques Mathieu and Jacques Lacoursière, *Les mémoires québécoises* (Sainte-Foy, QC: Les Presses de l'Université Laval, 1991), 318.

78 Étienne-Michel Faillon, *Histoire de la colonie française en Canada* (Paris: Imprimerie Poupart-Davyl et cie, 1865), vol. 2, 397–426. For an overview of early accounts of Dollard's exploits, see Terry Crowley, *Clio's Craft: A Primer of Historical Methods* (Toronto: Copp Clark Pittman, 1988), 255–303.

79 Some English Canadian historians disputed the claim that Dollard knowingly marched to his own death. See E.R. Adair, "Dollard des Ormeaux and the Fight at the Long Sault," *Canadian Historical Review* 13, 2 (1932): 121–46.

80 See Patrice Groulx, *Pièges de la mémoire: Dollard des Ormeaux, les Amérindiens et nous* (Hull, QC: Vents d'Ouest, 1998), 198–210, 376.

81 Lionel Groulx, *Si Dollard revenait* (Montreal: Bibliothèque de l'Action française, 1919), 9, 24. Translated as "If Dollard Were Alive Today," in *French Canadian Nationalism: An Anthology*, ed. Ramsay Cook, (Toronto: Macmillan, 1969), 191, 201.
82 Groulx, *Pièges de la mémoire*, 232; Gordon, *Making Public Pasts*, 109.
83 Colin M. Coates and Cecilia Morgan, *Heroines and History: Representations of Madeleine de Verchères and Laura Secord* (Toronto: University of Toronto Press, 2002), 55.
84 This gender anxiety was compounded by the difficult fact that Verchères' acts of bravery were contrasted with the supposed cowardice of the male soldiers at the fort. The Iroquois had taken the male soldiers captive, and the men in the fort remained passive and were relegated to supposedly feminine roles. Such a narrative conflicted with early-twentieth-century attempts to portray French Canadian men at the centre of an active and brave history. See Diane Gervais and Serge Lusignan, "De Jeanne d'Arc à Madeleine de Verchères la femme guerrière dans la société d'ancien régime," *Revue d'histoire de l'Amérique française* 53, 2 (1999): 189.
85 Groulx felt compelled to make these remarks following a conversation with his niece, who had asked him whether Madeleine de Verchères or Dollard des Ormeaux was more heroic. See Groulx, *Notre maître, le passé*, 1st series, 61, 68–69.
86 Coates and Morgan suggest that gender has always been central to how Verchères has been portrayed. For much of the period leading up to the twentieth century, her supposed violation of strict gender boundaries was downplayed, and her femininity was emphasized. By the twentieth century, her presence in the historical narrative had become problematic for conservative writers, who chipped away at her reputation out of a fear that she might become a feminist icon to a new generation of young girls. See Coates and Morgan, *Heroines and History*, 54, 67, 99. Once heroism became a uniquely male virtue, any heroic deeds by women threatened to undermine the delicate gender balance that had been achieved because her acts were interpreted as a transgression of acceptable gender boundaries. See Gervais and Lusignan, "De Jeanne d'Arc," 187.
87 Groulx, *Orientations*, 120, 151.
88 Groulx, *Pièges de la mémoire*, 214, 231–32.
89 Vaillancourt, "Les têtes à Patriote," describes the evolution of the Patriot from "tribune" to "habitant," or everyman, in the popular imagination and argues that this evolution was influenced by Garneau's interpretation of the Rebellions, as well as by the rise in popularity of the "romans de la terre."
90 Jean-Paul Bernard, *Les rébellions de 1837–1838: Les Patriotes du Bas-Canada dans la mémoire collective et chez les historiens* (Montreal: Boréal Express, 1983), 30.
91 Lemire, "L'Ambiguïté garnélienne," 274.
92 Bernard, *Les rébellions de 1837–1838*, 35.
93 Ibid., 30–31.
94 Lamarre, *Le Devenir*, 62.
95 Jean-Paul Bernard, "Jean-Olivier Chénier," *Dictionary of Canadian Biography* (Toronto: University of Toronto Press, 1988), vol. 7, 173–74.
96 Gordon, *Making Public Pasts*, 102–7.
97 This interpretation is not accepted by most historians, who treat this pastoral letter as a direct rebuke to the rebels. See Allan Greer, *The Patriots and the People: The Rebellion of 1837 in Rural Lower Canada* (Toronto: University of Toronto Press, 1993), 233–34.
98 Lionel Groulx, "Les 'Patriotes' de 1837 et les châtiments de l'église," part 1, *L'Action française* 15, 4 (1926), 218, 226–27.
99 Ibid., part 3, *L'Action française* 15, 6 (1926), 350.
100 Groulx, *Notre maître, le passé*, 1st series, 195–97, 210–11.
101 Groulx, *Directives*, 164.

102 Greer, *Patriots and the People,* 213–14; Allan Greer, "La république des hommes: Les patriotes de 1837 face aux femmes," *Revue d'histoire de l'Amérique française* 44, 4 (1991): 507–28. See also Lykke de la Cour, Cecilia Morgan, and Mariana Valverde, "Gender Regulation and State Formation in Nineteenth-Century Canada," in *Colonial Leviathan: State Formation in Mid-Nineteenth-Century Canada,* ed. Allan Greer and Ian Radforth (Toronto: University of Toronto Press, 1992), 162–63, which points to the "masculinization of public power in the period of the rebellions."

103 The Constitutional Act of 1791 did not specifically refer to sex when determining access to the franchise. Although women did participate in elections before 1834, their right to vote was exercised often at the discretion of electoral officials. See Greer, *Patriots and the People,* 204–6.

104 Ibid., 191.

105 For a discussion of the convergence of these nationalisms, see Gordon, *Making Public Pasts,* 110–15.

106 Bernard, *Les rébellions de 1837–1838,* 43, suggests that this consensus view – that the *patriotes* were nationalists above all else and that "ils n'etait ni des démocrates, ni des réformistes, ni des libéraux: ils étaient avant tout des nationalistes" – persisted into the 1930s and characterized the centennial celebration of 1937.

107 Unambiguous definitions of the *coureurs de bois* and *voyageurs* remain elusive in the literature. There is general agreement among historians that the term *voyageur* became widely used sometime during the late seventeenth and early eighteenth centuries to describe the new professional fur trader. See Louise Dechêne, *Habitants and Merchants in Seventeenth-Century Montreal,* trans. Liana Vardi (Montreal and Kingston: McGill-Queen's University Press, 1992), 94. Dale Miquelon reinforces this view when he writes that the *voyageurs* represented "a new body of legitimate Indian traders" and calls them specialists who relied on "canoe men," or *engagés,* who were "typically illiterate young farm boys." By the 1720s, he writes, with the increase in the number of *engagés,* the term *voyageur* "became synonymous with *engagés.*" See Dale Miquelon, *New France, 1701–1744: "A Supplement to Europe"* (Toronto: McClelland and Stewart, 1987), 155–56. Warwick, *Long Journey,* 23, contends that the adoption of the term *voyageur* was an attempt by officials to incorporate independent traders into the structure of the colony. Carolyn Podruchny incorporates all of these views in her work on the latter part of the eighteenth century to make a clear distinction between the *coureurs de bois* and the *voyageurs* based on "labour status," labelling the former independent traders and the latter servants or workers. See Carolyn Podruchny, "Baptizing Novices: Ritual Moments among French Canadian Voyageurs in the Montreal Fur Trade, 1780–1821," *Canadian Historical Review* 83, 2 (2002): 166.

108 The modern reader's understanding of the *voyageur* has been largely conditioned by popular works such as Peter C. Newman, *Company of Adventurers,* vol. 2, *Caesars of the Wilderness* (Markham, ON: Viking, 1987), 25–49. For the argument that the *coureurs de bois* assimilated into Native cultures in part to escape the structure of their own society, see Philippe Jacquin, *Les Indiens blancs: Français et Indiens en Amérique du Nord (XVIe–XVIIIe siècle)* (Montreal: Libre Expression, 1996), 212–13. On *voyageur* and *coureur de bois* culture and manhood, see Carolyn Podruchny, "Festivities, Fortitude, and Fraternalism: Fur Trade Masculinity and the Beaver Club, 1785–1827," in *New Faces of the Fur Trade: Selected Papers of the Seventh North American Fur Trade Conference, Halifax, Nova Scotia, 1995,* ed. Jo-Anne Fiske, Susan Sleeper-Smith, and William Wicken, 31–52 (East Lansing: Michigan State University Press, 1998).

109 Recent work by historians revises this picture of the *voyageurs* and *coureurs de bois* as carefree adventurers and places them into a larger working-class narrative that emphasizes

their positions within a paternalistic commercial structure. Edith I. Burley, for example, has argued, "one must remember that the *voyageurs* did not paddle their canoes just for the fun of it; they were working, transporting trade goods and furs for their employers"; and she notes that these so-called explorers "were workers who came not in search of adventure but of livelihood." See Edith I. Burley, *Servants of the Honourable Company: Work, Discipline and Conflict in the Hudson's Bay Company, 1770–1879* (Don Mills, ON: Oxford University Press, 1997), 1, 12. See also, Carolyn Podruchny, "Unfair Masters and Rascally Servants? Labour Relations among Bourgeois, Clerks and Voyageurs in the Montreal Fur Trade, 1780–1821," *Labour/Le Travail* 43 (1999): 43–70; and Carolyn Podruchny, *Making the Voyageur World: Travelers and Traders in the North American Fur Trade* (Lincoln: University of Nebraska Press, 2006).

110 See Warwick, *Long Journey*, 22; and Jack Warwick, "Les 'pays d'en haut,' dans l'imagination canadienne-française," *Études françaises* 2, 3 (1966): 278. It is important to note that Parkman viewed New France as a somewhat feminine enterprise and that although he presented the *coureurs de bois* as heroic and brave, he nonetheless considered their effectiveness to be attributable to their ability to follow orders, which effectively rendered them passive and ultimately feminine. See Allan Greer, "National, Transnational, and Hypernational Historiographies: New France Meets Early American History," *Canadian Historical Review* 91, 4 (2010): 703–7.

111 Charles W. Colby, *Canadian Types of the Old Regime, 1608–1698* (New York: H. Holt and Company, 1908), 188, 191–94. See also J. Murray Gibbon, "The Coureur de Bois and His Birthright," *Proceedings and Transactions of the Royal Society of Canada*, series 3, 30, section 2 (1936): 61–78.

112 Warwick, "Les 'pays d'en haut,'" 269.

113 Quoted in Allan Greer, *The People of New France* (Toronto: University of Toronto Press, 1997), 84–85.

114 See Pierre François-Xavier de Charlevoix, *History and General Description of New France* (1744; reprint, Chicago: Loyola University Press, 1962), vol. 3, 194, 310.

115 Garneau, *Histoire du Canada*, 4th ed., vol. 1, 241, vol. 2, 62, 144.

116 Ferland, *Cours d'histoire du Canada*, vol. 2, 312.

117 Since the *coureurs de bois* have left few clues for the historian about their own lives, the official image of them has been largely influenced by the opinions of Frontenac and Talon, who often complained of their disruptive activities. See Gibbon, "Coureur de Bois and His Birthright," 61–63; and Jean Blain, "La frontière en Nouvelle-France: Perspectives historiques nouvelles à partir d'un thème ancien," *Revue d'histoire de l'Amérique française* 25, 3 (1971): 399–400.

118 Joseph-Charles Taché, *Forestiers et voyageurs* (1863; reprint, Montreal: Fides, 1946), 15–16.

119 Warwick, *Long Journey*, 40.

120 Benjamin Sulte, "Voyageurs et hommes de cages," in *Mélanges historiques: Études éparses et inédites de Benjamin Sulte*, ed. Gérard Malchelosse (1879; reprint, Montreal: G. Ducharme, 1919), vol. 3, 85, 89.

121 Ibid., vol. 3, 86, 92.

122 Warwick, *Long Journey*, 106.

123 Compare the treatment of explorers in Garneau, *Histoire du Canada*, 4th ed., vol. 1, 239–64, and François-Xavier Garneau, *Histoire du Canada*, 5th ed., ed. Hector Garneau (Paris: Librairie Félix Alcan, 1920), vol. 1, 282–313, which pays greater attention to individual acts of discovery and explicitly names individual explorers and adventurers. Note the tone of the preface of the fifth edition, as well, which stresses French Canada's history of exploration, energy, and military skill. Gabriel Hanotaux, "Préface," in Garneau, *Histoire du Canada*, 5th ed., vol. 1, iii–xi.

124 Hanotaux, "Préface," in Garneau, *Histoire du Canada,* 5th ed., vol. 1, iii, xv.

125 Guy Frégault, "Coureurs de bois," *L'Encyclopédie Grolier* (Montreal: La Société Grolier, 1947–1960), vol. 3, 555. Many writers referred to the originality of the *coureurs de bois* in order to emphasize French Canada's unique ability to adapt to its harsh environment and to face any challenges thrown at it. Mathieu and Lacoursière, *Les mémoires québécoises,* 53, argue that the "Quebec space" gave rise to the *coureur de bois,* who was an adventurous risk-taker capable of great physical endurance – and who was uniquely French Canadian.

126 Quoted in Lamarre, *Le Devenir,* 251.

127 Lionel Groulx, "Le coureur de bois, type social," *L'Action nationale* 31, 1 (1948): 35.

128 See Martin Fournier, *Pierre-Esprit Radisson: Merchant Adventurer, 1636–1710,* trans. Mary E. Brennan-Ricard (Sillery, QC: Septentrion, 2002), 14.

129 Lionel Groulx, *Histoire du Canada Français depuis la découverte* (Montreal: L'Action nationale, 1951), vol. 2, 204–5.

130 Groulx, *Directives,* 175.

131 Groulx, *Orientations,* 120, 142.

132 Quoted in Édouard Bériault, "L'Épopée legendaire des coureurs de bois aux XVIIe siècle," *Revue de l'université d'Ottawa* 4, 4 (1934): 441.

133 Lionel Groulx, *Notre grande aventure: L'Empire français en Amérique du Nord (1535–1760)* (Montreal: Fides, 1958), 177–79.

134 Groulx, *Dix ans d'Action française,* 268.

135 Groulx, *Notre maître, le passé,* 1st series, 84.

136 Groulx, "Le coureur de bois," 31, 33, concluded that "au moral, le coureur de bois que la course n'a pas trop perverti, nous offre une physionomie plutôt amaible, souriante."

137 A similar transformation in collective identity occurred during the Quiet Revolution. As French Canadians came increasingly to admire entrepreneurial drive and business acumen during the 1960s, and came to believe that Quebec's liberation could be accomplished only once they had mastered these once-exclusive English Canadian fields, the businessperson and banker, such as Alphonse Desjardins, the founder of the Mouvement Desjardins, was celebrated as a hero and transformed into the embodiment of what French Canadians hoped to become in the 1970s and 1980s. French-speaking Quebecers acquired a new sense of confidence and drive to succeed during the 1960s, and figures like Desjardins fulfilled their new conception about themselves as businessmen. See Jocelyn Létourneau, "La nouvelle figure identitaire du Québécois: Essai sur la dimension symbolique d'un consensus social en voie d'émergence," *British Journal of Canadian Studies* 6, 1 (1991): 17, 23.

138 On the evolving interpretations of the coureur de bois, see Christian Morissoneau, *La terre promise: Le mythe du nord québécois* (Montreal: Hurtubise HMH, 1978), esp. ch. 4; and Warwick, "Les 'pays d'en haut.'"

Chapter 6: The Critique of National Manhood

1 Hector de Saint-Denys Garneau, *The Journal of Saint-Denys Garneau,* trans. John Glassco (Toronto: McClelland and Stewart, 1962), 104, 106.

2 Quoted in Jean Lamarre, *Le devenir de la nation québécoise selon Maurice Séguin, Guy Frégault et Michel Brunet, 1944–1969* (Sillery, QC: Septentrion, 1993), 241.

3 Garneau, *Journal,* 27, 104–6.

4 Ibid., 61, 83.

5 Ibid., 79.

6 Michel Biron, *L'Absence du maître: Saint-Denys Garneau, Ferron, Ducharme* (Montreal: Les Presses de l'Université de Montréal, 2000), 49, 56. On Garneau's ideas about art and

the role of the artist, see Karim Larose, "Travers de la modernité: Don, culture, et spéculation chez Saint-Denys Garneau," *Québec Studies* 32 (2001–02): 114.

7 See, for example, Émile Bouvier, *Votre Tâche Jeunesse* (Montreal: Les Édtions de l'Action nationale, 1942), 46; Charles Frédéric, SJ, *Toi, l'homme nouveau!* (Montreal: Imprimerie du Messager, 1941), 44–45; and Camille Roy, *Pour former des hommes nouveaux: Discours aux jeunes gens* (Montreal: B. Valiquette, 1941).

8 Garneau, *Journal*, 17.

9 Quoted in Jean Le Moyne, "Saint-Denys Garneau: Testimony for His Times," in *Convergence: Essays from Quebec*, trans. Philip Stratford (Toronto: Ryerson Press, 1966), 214–15.

10 Garneau, *Journal*, 18.

11 Ibid., 32.

12 Garneau would publish only one collection of poetry during his lifetime, *Regards et jeux dans l'espace* (Montreal: n.p., 1937), which was greeted with indifference. See also, Biron, *L'Absence du maître*, 68.

13 Jean Le Moyne, "De Saint-Denys Garneau," *La Nouvelle Relève* 3, 9 (1944): 518.

14 Le Moyne, "Saint-Denys Garneau: Testimony for His Times," 199, 216–17, 200, 203, 220.

15 "Positions," *La Relève* 1, 1 (1934): 1–3.

16 Robert Charbonneau, "Jeunesse et Révolution," *La Relève* 2, 1 (1935): 3.

17 On *La Relève*, see Jean-Charles Falardeau, "La Génération de *La Relève*," *Recherches sociographiques* 6, 2 (1965): 123–33; and Jacques Pelletier, "*La Relève:* Une idéologie des années 1930," in *Voix et images du pays*, vol. 5, *Littérature québécoise*, ed. Ronald Bérubé, 69–139 (Montreal: Presses de l'Université du Québec, 1972). For an analysis of *La Relève* in the ideological context of the 1930s, see Stéphanie Angers-Fabre, "Le versant Canadien-français de la génération 'non-conformiste' Européenne des années trente: La revue *La Relève*," *Recherches sociographiques* 43, 1 (2002): 133–48; Yvan Lamonde, "*La Relève* (1934–1939), Maritain et la crise spirituelle des années 1930," *Les cahiers des dix* 62 (2008): 153–94; and Yvan Lamonde, *La modernité au Québec*, vol. 1, *La crise de l'homme et de l'esprit, 1929–1939* (Montreal: Fides, 2011), 91–96. See also André-J. Bélanger, *L'Apolitisme des idéologies québécoises: Le grand tournant de 1934–1936* (Quebec: Les Presses de l'Université Laval, 1974); André-J. Bélanger, *Ruptures et constantes: Quatres idéologies du Québec en éclatement: La Relève, La JEC, Cité Libre, Parti-Pris* (Montreal: Hurtubise HMH, 1977); and Michael Oliver, *The Passionate Debate: The Social and Political Ideas of Quebec Nationalism, 1920–1945* (Montreal: Véhicule, 1991), 105–47.

18 "Positions," 1–3.

19 Robert Charbonneau, Robert Élie, Paul Beaulieu, and Claude Hurtubise, "Préliminaires à un manifeste pour la patrie," *La Relève* 3, 1 (1936): 9.

20 Ibid., 24; Oliver, *Passionate Debate*, 120.

21 On Mounier, see Joseph Amato, *Mounier and Maritain: A French Catholic Understanding of the Modern World* (Tuscaloosa: University of Alabama Press, 1975); Michael Kelly, *Pioneer of the Catholic Revival: The Ideas and Influences of Emmanuel Mounier* (London: Sheed and Ward, 1979); and John Hellman, *Emmanuel Mounier and the New Catholic Left, 1930–1950* (Toronto: University of Toronto Press, 1981). On personalism, see Jean-Louis Loubet del Bayle, *Les non-conformistes des années 30: Une tentative de renouvellement de la pensée politique française* (Paris: Éditions du Seuil, 1969).

22 Pelletier, "*La Relève:* Une idéologie," 94, 124–25.

23 Ibid., 94, 102.

24 On the absence of a Catholic left tradition prior to the 1930s, see John Hellman, "The Opening to the Left in French Catholicism: The Role of the Personalists," *Journal of the History of Ideas* 34, 3 (1973): 381–90.

25 Amato, *Mounier and Maritain*, 1.

26 This lack of clarity has confounded historians, who have found it difficult to define "personalism" with any precision. On this problem, see Hellman, *Emmanuel Mounier*, 3–5.

27 This point is made in E.-Martin Meunier and Jean-Philippe Warren, *Sortir de la 'Grande noirceur': L'horizon 'personnaliste' de la Révolution tranquille* (Sillery, QC: Septentrion, 2002), 43.

28 "Positions," 3.

29 A major critic of modernity at this time was Leo Strauss, who warned that extreme relativism and the refusal to acknowledge the existence of natural law or to accept that certain truths are universal had made it difficult for individuals to recognize morally repugnant ideologies or regimes and thus rendered them unfree and subject to authoritarian regimes that were developing during the interwar years. Strauss would become a major influence for the neoconservative movement in the United States. See especially Leo Strauss, *On Tyranny: An Interpretation of Xenophon's Hiero* (Glencoe, IL: Free Press, 1948); and Leo Strauss, *Natural Right and History* (Chicago: University of Chicago Press, 1953).

30 Kelly, *Pioneer of the Catholic Revival*, 17.

31 Because it was a journal seeking to shake up the intellectual landscape of the interwar years, it is difficult to identify a single strain of personalist thought that could be said to have influenced *La Relève* the most. Observers in Quebec have tended to point to Maritain and Mounier as the primary sources of influence on the Montreal personalists. See Oliver, *Passionate Debate*, 115. Others have pointed to the significant role that other figures like Alexandre Marc played in the formation of Quebec personalist thinking. See Christian Roy, "Le personnalisme de *l'Ordre nouveau* et le Québec, 1930–1947: Son role dans la formation de Guy Frégault," *Revue d'histoire de l'Amérique française* 46, 3 (1993): 463–84. On personalism in Quebec more generally, see Meunier and Warren, *Sortir de la 'Grande noirceur'*; and Michael Gauvreau, *The Catholic Origins of Quebec's Quiet Revolution, 1931–1970* (Montreal and Kingston: McGill-Queen's University Press, 2005). For an exploration of personalist ideas in Quebec, one should consult the continuing intellectual biography of Pierre Elliott Trudeau by Max Nemni and Monique Nemni, *Young Trudeau: Son of Quebec, Father of Canada, 1919–1944*, trans. William Johnson (Toronto: McClelland and Stewart, 2006), and *Trudeau Transformed: The Shaping of a Statesman, 1944–1965*, trans. George Tombs (Toronto: McClelland and Stewart, 2011).

32 See John Hellman, *The Communitarian Third Way: Alexandre Marc's Ordre Nouveau, 1930–2000* (Montreal and Kingston: McGill-Queen's University Press, 2002), 22. The idea of creating a new Middle Ages to correct the failures of modernity was proposed by Nicholas Berdyaev, *A New Middle Ages* (1924; reprint, New York: Sheed and Ward, 1933), which turned out to be influential among certain personalists.

33 On Frégault's personalism, see Roy, "Le personnalisme"; and Lamarre, *Le devenir*, 233–73.

34 Michel Brunet, "Trois dominantes de la pensée canadienne-française: L'agriculturisme, l'anti-étatisme et le messianisme," in *La présence anglaise et les Canadiens*, 113–66 (Montreal: Beauchemin, 1958).

35 Frégault's interpretation of New France is most fully articulated in his *La civilisation de la Nouvelle-France (1713–1744)* (Montreal: Société des éditions Pascal, 1944).

36 His ideas influenced a generation of leaders, including his student Pierre Elliott Trudeau, who wrote of Dubé's "offhand way of defying social conventions and saying out loud what other people would only think to themselves" and how he "influenced a whole generation of students outside as well as within Brébeuf." See Pierre Elliott Trudeau, *Memoirs* (Toronto: McClelland and Stewart, 1993), 22. See also Esther Delisle, *Essais sur l'imprégnation fasciste au Québec* (Montreal: Varia, 2002), 19–32; and Jean-Philippe

Warren, "Let the Jesuits and the Dominicans Quarrel: A French Canadian Debate of the Fifties," in *The Hidden Pierre Elliott Trudeau: The Faith behind the Politics,* ed. John English, Richard Gwyn, and P. Whitney Lackenbauer, 65–74 (Toronto: Novalis, 2004).

37 Michael Behiels, *Prelude to Quebec's Quiet Revolution: Liberalism versus Neo-nationalism, 1945–1960* (Montreal and Kingston: McGill-Queen's University Press, 1985), 63.

38 For the claim that some passages in Hertel's novel *Le Beau risque* (Montreal: B. Valiquette, 1939), including one where the cleric "dreams of his students, stripped to the waist in their canoes in the woods, radiating strength, health, and masculinity," are "erotically charged," see Robert Schwartzwald, "Fear of Federasty: Québec's Inverted Fictions," in *Comparative American Identities: Race, Sex and Nationality in the Modern Text,* ed. Hortense J. Spillers (New York: Routledge, 1991), 186. For a discussion of the novel in the context of the 1930s, see Louise Bienvenue, "Crise d'adolescence et projection sociale dans le roman *Le beau risque* de François Hertel," in *La jeunesse au Canada français: Formation, mouvements et identité,* ed. Michel Bock, 245–53 (Ottawa: Les Presses de l'Université d'Ottawa, 2007).

39 François Hertel, *Leur inquiétude* (Montreal: Éditions Jeunesse, 1936), 132, 134–35.

40 Ibid., 222.

41 François Hertel, *Pour un ordre personnaliste* (Montreal: Les Éditions de l'Arbre, 1942), 22–23.

42 Ibid., 129, 219.

43 Ibid., 44.

44 Lionel Groulx, *Directives* (Montreal: Les Éditions du Zodiaque, 1937), 167.

45 Hertel, *Pour un ordre personnaliste,* 44.

46 Ibid., 99.

47 Ibid., 44, 103.

48 Ibid., 32.

49 Hertel, *Leur inquiétude,* 95.

50 Hertel, *Pour un ordre personnaliste,* 41, 43.

51 Stéphanie Angers-Fabre, "Le versant canadien-français de la génération 'non-conformiste' européenne des années trente: La revue *La Relève,*" *Recherches sociographiques* 43, 1 (2002): 45.

52 Hertel, *Leur inquiétude,* 105, 110.

53 Hertel, *Pour un ordre personnaliste,* 41.

54 Hertel, *Leur inquiétude,* 227.

55 Hertel, *Pour un ordre personnaliste,* 23; François Hertel, *Nous ferons l'avenir* (Montreal: Fides, 1945), 80.

56 On the Catholic Action Movement, see Gauvreau, *Catholic Origins.*

57 Pierre Dansereau, "Jeune-Canada," *L'Action nationale* 1, 5 (1933): 271–72, quoted in Oliver, *Passionate Debate,* 107–8.

58 See Dominique Foisy-Geoffroy, "Esdras Minville et le nationalisme économique, 1929–1939," *Mens: Revue d'histoire intellectuelle de l'Amérique française* 1, 1 (2000): 53–55, 60.

59 For the claim that there was an emerging consensus during the 1930s in favour of capitalism and liberalism, see Claude Couture, *Le mythe de modernisation du Québec: Des années 1930 à la Révolution tranquille* (Montreal: Méridien, 1991), 10, 121.

60 Denis Monière, *Ideologies in Quebec: The Historical Development,* trans. Richard Howard (Toronto: University of Toronto Press, 1981), 219.

61 Esdras Minville, *La vie sociale,* vol. 1, *Le nationalisme canadiens-français,* ed. François-Albert Angers (Montreal: Fides and HEC, 1992), 301, 352, 354, 396–97, 485–86.

62 Victor Barbeau, *Pour nous grandir: Essai d'explication des misères de notre temps* (Montreal: Imprimé au Devoir, 1937), 190–91.

63 Ibid., 51, 153; Victor Barbeau, *Mesure de notre taille* (Montreal: Imprimé au Devoir, 1936), 16.
64 Victor Barbeau, *Initiation à l'humain* (Montreal: La "Familliale," 1944), 103.
65 Barbeau, *Mesure de notre taille*, 16.
66 Barbeau, *Pour nous grandir*, 51, 92.
67 Barbeau, *Mesure de notre taille*, 16.
68 Barbeau, *Pour nous grandir*, 40.
69 Barbeau, *Mesure de notre taille*, 16.
70 Barbeau, *Pour nous grandir*, 57.
71 Katherine A. Roberts, "Making Women Pay: Revolution, Violence, Decolonizing Quebec in Hubert Aquin's *Trou de mémoire*," *Québec Studies* 30 (2000): 20.
72 See Christian Morissonneau, *La terre promise: Le mythe du nord québécois* (Montreal: Hurtubise HMH, 1978), 26, 93–97, 127.
73 This new space would be male-dominated and necessarily suppress women's rights, according to Henry Milner and Sheilagh Hodgins Milner, *The Decolonization of Quebec: An Analysis of Left-Wing Nationalism* (Toronto: McClelland and Stewart, 1973), 116–17.
74 Lionel Groulx, *Orientations* (Montreal: Les Éditions du Zodiaque, 1935), 115.
75 Lionel Groulx, *Notre maître, le passé*, 2nd series (Montreal: Librairie Granger Frères, 1936), 150.
76 See Roberts, "Making Women Pay," 20.
77 Mary Jean Green, "Jacques Godbout and the Quebec Writer: Engendering the National Text," *Québec Studies* 30 (2000): 8.
78 Behiels, *Prelude to Quebec's Quiet Revolution*, 104–8.
79 Lionel Groulx, *La naissance d'une race* (Montreal: Bibliothèque de l'Action française, 1919), 157, 293.
80 See Lamarre, *Le devenir*, 91, 100, 194.
81 Guy Frégault, *La civilisation de la nouvelle-France, 1713–1744* (1944; reprint, Montreal: Fides, 1969), 213; Lamarre, *Le devenir*, 215–16, 245.
82 Barbeau, *Pour nous grandir*, 238.
83 On the church's reaction to *La Relève*, see Jane Everett, "*Regards et jeux dans l'espace* et la critique cléricale," in *Saint-Denys Garneau et* La Relève, ed. Benoît Melançon and Pierre Popovic (Montreal: Fides, 1995), 96; and Lionel Groulx, "La Relève," *L'Action nationale* 3, 4 (1934): 226–28.
84 See Marcel-Aimé Gagnon, *Jean-Charles Harvey: Précurseur de la révolution tranquille* (Ottawa: Beauchemin, 1970); Yves Lavertu, *Jean-Charles Harvey: Le combattant* (Montreal: Boréal, 2000).
85 On French Canada's attitude toward France during the Second World War, see Éric Amyot, *Le Québec entre Pétain et DeGaulle: Vichy, la France Libre et les Canadiens français, 1940–1945* (Montreal: Fides, 1999), 181.
86 See Lamonde, "*La Relève* (1934–1939)," 158.
87 *Le Jour*, July 22, 1939.
88 On *Le Jour*, see Victor Teboul, *Le Jour: Émergence du libéralisme moderne au Québec* (Montreal: Hurtubise HMH, 1984); Pascale Guimont, "*Le Jour* 1937–1946," in *Idéologies au Canada français 1930–1939*, ed. Fernand Dumont, Jean-Paul Montiminy, and Jean Hamelin, 131–63 (Quebec: Les Presses de l'Université Laval, 1978).
89 *Le Jour*, September 16, 1937.
90 *Le Jour*, May 14, 1938.
91 *Le Jour*, June 18, 1938.
92 *Le Jour*, June 25, 1938.
93 *Le Jour*, July 6, 1940.

94 Ibid.
95 *Le Jour,* September 25, 1937.
96 Jean-Charles Harvey, *Art et Combat* (Montreal: Éditions de l'A.C.-F., 1937), 139.
97 *Le Jour,* September 16, 1937.
98 *Le Jour,* September 25, 1937.
99 *Le Jour,* October 15, 1938.
100 *Le Jour,* August 5, 1939.
101 *Le Jour,* August 14, 1943. Note that Harvey wrote under the pseudonym Paul Riverin.
102 *Le Jour,* April 25, 1942.
103 Jean-Charles Harvey, *Fear's Folly,* trans. John Glassco, ed. John O'Connor (Ottawa: Carleton University Press, 1982), 37, originally published as *Les demi-civilisés* (Montreal: Les Éditions du Totem, 1934).
104 Ibid., 82.
105 Ibid., 49.
106 Ibid., 143.
107 Ibid., 162–63.
108 Ibid., 29.
109 Ibid., 66.
110 Sister Sainte-Marie-Éleuthère, *La mère dans le roman canadien-français* (Quebec: Les Presses de l'Université Laval, 1964), 201.
111 See Schwartzwald, "Fear of Federasty," 185–86.
112 Brian Young, *The Politics of Codification: The Lower Canadian Civil Code of 1866* (Montreal and Kingston: McGill-Queen's University Press, 1994), 148–50.
113 Quoted in Thérèse F. Casgrain, *A Woman in a Man's World,* trans. Joyce Marshall (Toronto: McClelland and Stewart, 1972), 92.
114 "Premier Rapport de Commission des droits civils de la femme," *La revue du notariat* 32, 8 (1930): 242. See also Jennifer Stoddart, "Quebec's Legal Elite Looks at Women's Rights: The Dorion Commission, 1929–31," in *Essays in the History of Canadian Law,* vol. 1, ed. David H. Flaherty, 323–57 (Toronto: University of Toronto Press, 1981); and Collectif Clio, *L'histoire des femmes au Québec depuis quatre siècles* (Montreal: Quinze, 1982), 333–42.
115 Lori Saint-Martin, *Le nom de la mère: Mères, filles et écriture dans la littérature québécoise au féminin* (Quebec: Éditions Nota Bene, 1999), 24, 48.
116 Jean-Charles Falardeau, *Notre société et son roman* (Montreal: Éditions HMH, 1967), 195, 224–25. The literary critic Patricia Smart has described a similar tendency in earlier novels of the land: "There appears to be a strange alliance between women and nature, and even to some extent between women and the 'foreigners' who threaten the continuity of the national heritage – an alliance whose function in the tradition is to subvert the paternal lineage." See Patricia Smart, *Writing in the Father's House: The Emergence of the feminine in the Quebec Literary Tradition* (Toronto: University of Toronto Press, 1991), 71.
117 See Robert Schwartzwald, "'Symbolic' Homosexuality, 'False Feminine,' and the Problematics of Identity in Québec," in *Fear of a Queer Planet: Queer Politics and Social Theory,* ed. Michael Warner (Minneapolis: University of Minnesota Press, 1993), 273–74; and Schwartzwald, "Fear of Federasty," 188.
118 Jean-Charles Harvey, *Sébastien Pierre* (Lévis, QC: Éditions du Quotidiens, 1935), 125.
119 Falardeau, *Notre société et son roman,* 224.
120 Roger Lemelin, *The Town Below,* trans. Samuel Putnam (Toronto: McClelland and Stewart, 1961), 259–60, originally published as *Au pied de la pente douce* (Montreal: Éditions de l'Arbre, 1944).
121 Ibid., 162, 218.

122 Ibid., 228, 232.
123 Ibid., 165.
124 Ibid., 251.
125 Ibid., 26.
126 Ibid., 230–31.
127 Ibid., 134, emphasis in original.
128 Ibid., 84.
129 Falardeau, *Notre société et son roman,* 195.
130 Lemelin, *The Town Below,* 271.
131 Ibid., 52.
132 Ibid., 278.
133 Ibid., 170.
134 Ibid., 278–79.

Conclusion

1 Horace Miner, *St. Denis: A French Canadian Parish* (Chicago: University of Chicago Press, 1939), vii; Everett C. Hughes, *French Canada in Transition* (Chicago: University of Chicago Press, 1943), 209.
2 Pierre Elliott Trudeau, "La province de Québec au moment de la grève," in *La Grève de l'amiante: Une étape de la révolution industrielle au Québec,* ed. Pierre Elliott Trudeau (Montreal: Les Éditions Cité Libre, 1956), reprinted as "The Province of Quebec at the Time of the Strike," in *The Asbestos Strike,* trans. James Boake (Toronto: James Lewis and Samuel, 1974), 6, 7, 66.
3 Michel Sarra-Bournet, "Nationalisme et question nationale au Québec," in *Les nationalismes au Québec du XIXe au XXIe siècle,* ed. Michel Sarra-Bournet and Jocelyn Saint-Pierre (Quebec: Presses de l'Université Laval, 2001), 336.
4 Jocelyn Létourneau, "The Current Great Narrative of Québécois Identity," *South Atlantic Quarterly* 94, 4 (1995): 1052.
5 Hubert Aquin, "The Cultural Fatigue of French Canada," in *Writing Quebec: Selected Essays,* ed. Anthony Purdy (Edmonton: University of Alberta Press, 1988), 42.
6 Jocelyn Maclure, *Quebec Identity: The Challenge of Pluralism*, trans. Peter Feldstein (Montreal and Kingston: McGill-Queen's University Press, 2003), 19.
7 Jocelyn Létourneau, "'Remembering (from) Where You're Going': Memory as Legacy and Inheritance," in *A History for the Future: Rewriting Memory and Identity in Quebec,* trans. Phyllis Aronoff and Howard Scott (Montreal and Kingston: McGill-Queen's University Press, 2004), 15.
8 Quoted in Ronald Rudin, *Making History in Twentieth-Century Quebec* (Toronto: University of Toronto Press, 1997), 105.
9 Quoted in Maclure, *Quebec Identity,* 24.
10 Lionel Groulx, *Manuel d'histoire du Canada: Rédigé pour la classe de rhétorique au Collège de Valleyfield en 1905–6,* vol. 3, 71, 109, box S26–21, 614, Fonds Lionel Groulx, P1, Archives du Centre de Recherche Lionel-Groulx, Montreal. The Fonds Lionel Groulx has moved and is now housed at the Bibliothèque et Archives nationale du Quebec Vieux-Montréal (CLG1).
11 Hubert Aquin, "The Politics of Existence," in *Writing Quebec: Selected Essays,* ed. Anthony Purdy (Edmonton: University of Alberta Press, 1988), 9.
12 Jocelyn Létourneau, "Going from Heirs to Founders: The Great Collective Narrative of Quebecers as Revisited by Gérard Bouchard," in *A History for the Future: Rewriting Memory and Identity in Quebec,* trans. Phyllis Aronoff and Howard Scott (Montreal and Kingston: McGill-Queen's University Press, 2004), 38.

13 Létourneau, "'Remembering (from) Where You're Going,'" 15.

14 Trudeau criticized the "self-deluding passion of a large segment of our thinking population for throwing themselves headlong – intellectually and spiritually – into purely escapist pursuits." See Pierre Elliott Trudeau, "New Treason of the Intellectuals," in *Federalism and the French Canadians,* trans. Patricia Claxton (Toronto: Macmillan, 1968), 168.

15 François-Xavier Garneau, *Histoire du Canada,* 5th ed., ed. Hector Garneau (Paris: Librairie Félix Alcan, 1920), vol. 2, 717–18, quoted in Trudeau, "Province of Quebec," 9.

Index